Pink Floyd FAQ

Pink Floyd FAQ

Everything Left to Know . . . and More!

Stuart Shea

Backbeat
Books

An Imprint of Hal Leonard Corporation
New York

Published in 2009 by Backbeat Books
An Imprint of Hal Leonard Corporation
7777 West Bluemound Rd.
Milwaukee, WI 53213

Trade Book Division Editorial Offices
19 West 21st Street, New York, NY 10010

Printed in the United States of America

"I Was There—Mark Campbell: The 1972 and 1973 Tours Through a Fan's Eyes" by Mark Campbell. Printed by permission.

"A Pink Floyd Live Top Ten" by Steven Leventhal. Printed by permission.

"I Was There—Ron Geesin: The Story of 'Atom Heart Mother'" by Ron Geesin. Printed by permission.

"I Was There—John Leckie: With the Floyd, Both as a Fan and as a Recording Engineer" by John Leckie. Printed by permission.

Afterword by Ginger Gilmour. Printed by permission.

All images in this book are from the private collection of the author unless otherwise noted.

Every reasonable effort has been made to contact copyright holders and secure permissions. Omissions can be remedied in future editions.

Book design by Snow Creative Services

Library of Congress Cataloging-in-Publication Data
Shea, Stuart.
   Pink Floyd FAQ : everything left to know– and more! / Stuart Shea.
     p. cm.
   Includes bibliographical references.
   ISBN 978-0-87930-950-3 (alk. paper)
   1. Pink Floyd (Musical Group)—Miscellanea. I. Title. II. Title: Pink Floyd frequently asked questions.
   ML421.P6S44 2009
   782.42166092'2–dc22

                                                            2009024674

www.backbeatbooks.com

This book is dedicated to the five members of Pink Floyd—
the late Syd Barrett, David Gilmour, Nick Mason, Roger Waters,
and the late Richard Wright—for their artistry and hard work
and for the gift of music that they have given the world.

Thank you, gentlemen.

Contents

Preface

Tell Me More

One Sunday evening early in 2007, not long before I began this book project, I was listening to the radio while making dinner. (A *real* radio, not a satellite channel or the Internet.) A local rock station was starting a three-hour special on Pink Floyd.

Great! I thought. People still buy Floyd music and are interested in their story. Maybe this special will help me gain some perspective on their career and get some new viewpoints on their music.

This three-hour program began with a *very* brief history of how the band came together at university in London. Forty-five seconds in, the host was already playing the Floyd's second single, 1967's "See Emily Play." After that 2:45 gem, Mr. Silver-Tongued Radio Host blazed through Syd Barrett's departure, and the next five years of Pink Floyd's history, in less than *one minute* before going straight to 1973's *Dark Side of the Moon.*

That's why I needed to write this book.

The host didn't play "Arnold Layne," or a single song from the first album (*The Piper at the Gates of Dawn*), or anything off *A Saucerful of Secrets,* or 1968's "Careful with That Axe, Eugene," or the double album *Ummagumma.*

No mention was made of PF's music from three films (*Zabriskie Point, More,* and *Obscured by Clouds*) or of the band's own film shot in the ruins of Pompeii. This program featured nothing from 1970's *Atom Heart Mother* or the 1971 *Meddle,* which includes the key tracks "Echoes" and "One of These Days," or either of Syd Barrett's solo discs.

Nearly all of a three-hour special, then, was spent on the seven *last* Pink Floyd albums. Their *first* seven albums were papered over entirely, with Pink Floyd presented as nothing more than a purveyor of classic-rock "anthems."

That's why I needed to write this book.

This essay and this book are not meant to denigrate those last seven Pink Floyd albums, although I'll certainly not be mistaken for an overly enthusiastic fan of the last few. Rather, *Pink Floyd FAQ* is meant to examine the story of this most enigmatic of bands by putting its story into appropriate context, closely examining the musicians, their environment, and their time.

Pink Floyd's career started with black-and-white television and ended in the Internet age. A blues-influenced beat group at the start, they changed styles and vehicles many times, experimenting with electronics, recording film soundtracks, incorporating found sound and ethnic music, singing pure pop, creating "concept" albums and art-rock suites, and even including shreds of opera.

Fearless, daring, and sometimes overreaching, Pink Floyd's catalog has both jagged points and perfectly fitting pieces, fusing elements that are easy to love with some that are difficult to understand.

Examining the band's music (that from 1966–72 as well as its more famous period) as well as a nearly incessant touring schedule, intra-band power struggles, and the individual story of each member, sheds light on why Pink Floyd made a "sudden" leap with *Dark Side*, a breakthrough that in actuality was far from sudden.

That's why I needed to write this book.

Pink Floyd were known as *the* Pink Floyd through 1967, and for the early years of their career I will refer to them this way. In addition, I'll call the aggregation "the Floyd" or "PF" throughout the proceedings.

The band was a huge underground attraction in America, and had topped the British charts, years before Roger Waters dreamed up the concept behind *Dark Side of the Moon*. Yet these days, *most* Pink Floyd history seems to begin with 1973 and end in 1980. But not everyone agrees that this is their best or most important period.

A few insist on the 1966–67 Barrett era as the Floyd's be-all and end-all. Some devotees of electronic and chill-out music hold up their ambient, spacey 1969–72 output as their most influential and lasting. Others say Roger Waters' *The Final Cut* (1983) is one of the band's peaks, while a few—very few—claim that post-Waters opuses *A Momentary Lapse of Reason* (1986) and *The Division Bell* (1994) are up to the band's early standard.

Which, if any, of these arguments hold water? Is their 1973–83 music the best because it *sold* the most? If so, why aren't their earlier albums, which also sold well, played more often? Is it simply that a certain rock generation grew up with the four "key" albums (*Dark Side* through *The*

Wall) and won't let go? Did a "perfect storm" create the mid-seventies Pink Floyd media explosion?

What does it mean to be a Pink Floyd fan today, with the band splintered and various members still feuding twenty-five years after a bitter—and very typically Floyd—falling-out, in which nobody came through looking good and everyone involved suffered financial and personal heartache?

What stimuli helped create their music? How did the five members of Pink Floyd find their way? How did these musicians who strove for anonymity become such huge stars? Which artists influenced the Floyd or have been influenced by them? What bit players have added to their story? And which of Pink Floyd's songs and albums have stood the test of time?

These questions should be addressed, but not by the record company flacks, agents, and marketing consultants responsible for the decline of FM radio (and for mediocre specials promoting the same old Pink Floyd albums) attempting to rewrite history for their own ends.

Perhaps by exploring these questions in greater detail, we, the record buyers, can all better understand the breadth and depth of Pink Floyd and why its legend has not only endured, but even grown in the nearly thirty years since the band's last full concert.

And *that's* why I needed to write this book!

Everyone comes from an individual perspective on music. My perspective on Floyd is informed by my interest in pop, punk, R&B, and the avant-garde. I won't pretend that I'm as enamored of *The Final Cut* as of *Meddle*, or that I enjoy *Wish You Were Here* as much as *Piper at the Gates of Dawn*. And I *do* think "Fearless" is a better song than "Run Like Hell."

But I did my best to analyze every curve of their winding road and relate important points even concerning work I don't consider the band's best. Each step of the Pink Floyd's arc is interesting, with every success and mistake part of its very individual journey.

I hope that these essays spark honest responses and interesting discussions. The conversation is what it's all about; all we need to do is make sure we keep talking.

Acknowledgments

I hope my friends and family know how much I love them; they have been instrumental in my journey as a writer. Nephew Marco and nieces Carolina and Ava Marie make me smile just by being there.

My interviewees—Ms. Ginger Gilmour, Mr. John Leckie, Ms. Toni Tennille, Dr. Ron Geesin, Mr. Mark Campbell, and Dr. Dave Bessell—were more than generous with their time and memories. Ms. Becky Greenlaw of NAA was especially helpful.

I appreciate Steve Leventhal contributing a thought-provoking list of his top ten Floyd gigs.

Tom Shea, writer, actor, and singer of no little ability, contributed important research and personal recollections of Pink Floyd. Thank you, bro.

Thank you, Angie Maurello, for providing me a haven in which I could get through some of the most difficult parts of this book.

Friends and colleagues Mark Campbell, Jon Mills, Kim "Howard" Johnson, John Blaney, Gary Gillette, Steve Obuchowski, Paul Cortese, Doug White, James Ricks, and Steve Leventhal shared memories, stories, CDs, etc. I appreciate all of their help.

Of all my friends, Mark Caro and Ted Harris perhaps shared the most, reading chapters, providing feedback, and giving their own insight. These two have been in my life for so long that it's hard to imagine a world without them. Thanks, guys, and peace to you both always.

Thanks also, of course, to Mike Edison and John Cerullo at Hal Leonard as well as my co-conspirator in creating the *FAQ* series, Rob Rodriguez. (Rob, I haven't forgotten that our full-band version of "Lucifer Sam" was pretty good.)

Sarah Gallogly and Jessica Burr at Backbeat Books provided critical proofreading and editorial suggestions.

Paul Keyes helped increase my interest in Pink Floyd many years ago by lending a callow nineteen-year-old a cassette of *A Nice Pair*. Thank you, Paul, wherever you are.

And I wish to thank, for perhaps the millionth time, Cecilia Garibay: manuscript reader, reality check, confidante, partner in crime, love of my life, rock. Shortly after we met, we discovered the magic of *The Piper at the Gates of Dawn.*

Only a Stranger at Home

Who Are the Key Players in the Pink Floyd Story?

The characters in our story are many and diverse . . . but ten of the most important parties in the forty-year-plus pageantry of success and tragedy that is the Pink Floyd Story are listed below.

This list does not include Floyd wives, girlfriends, or children; the band members have always worked hard to protect their private lives, and since their family lives don't seem to have impacted PF's work that much, we will also focus on the music.

The dramatis personae are presented in relative order of their joining (the) Pink Floyd or working with them.

Nick Mason, Drummer

Born in Birmingham, England on January 27, 1944, Nicholas Berkeley Mason grew up around the things that would eventually become his lifetime obsessions: music, film, art, cars, and motor racing.

His father Bill was a documentary filmmaker and, shortly after Nick's birth, moved the family to Hampstead, a well-to-do section of London north of the central area. While the rest of the men who would eventually become members of Pink Floyd were raised middle-class, Mason grew up in an upper-middle-class environment.

Amid failed attempts at learning the violin and piano, Mason began playing drums in the late 1950s. He met his future wife, Lynette (Lindy) Rutter, at prep school in Surrey in 1957.

A gifted illustrator with a sense of humor and a head for the absurd, Mason developed an interest in drafting and architectural illustration. His grasp of mechanics was good, and he would often draw odd machines and contraptions (see the cover of *Relics* for proof).

Mason was impressed when he met the cynical, slightly older, street-smart Waters at London's Regent Street Polytechnic College in 1963.

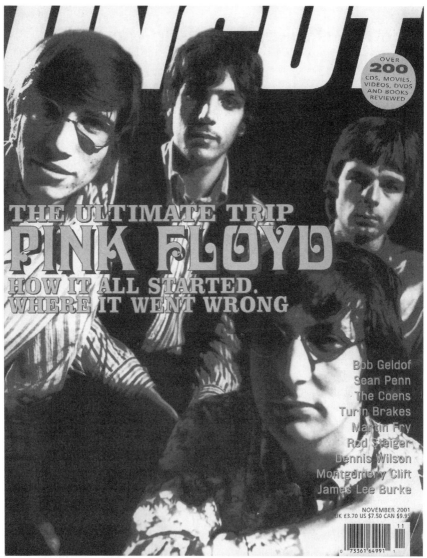

The first four-man lineup, captured in a 1966 photo used on the cover of *Uncut*'s November 2001 edition.

Forty-six years later, the two remain friends in spite of differences and occasional estrangements.

A year after meeting Waters, who at this point was playing guitar, Mason joined him in a fledgling beat group, Sigma 6, along with bassist Clive Metcalfe and guitarist/pianist Rick Wright. Two singers, Juliette Gale and Keith Noble, fronted the six-member combo. Mason was the first member of the band to have a car (an Austin van). As a result, his presence was that much more valued.

From the very beginning, Mason's style owed much to jazz, and he never developed the propulsive Ringo Starr beat group drum style favored by other pop groups. Despite a fairly rudimentary technique, Mason's use of space and tension separated him from other pop and rock drummers of the time.

The group eventually reorganized into the Abdabs in 1965, minus Noble, Gale, and Metcalfe. Guitarist Bob Klose's entry pushed Waters to bass, and Chris Dennis joined for a short time as singer. Soon he left, and Waters' Cambridge acquaintance Roger "Syd" Barrett replaced him, singing and playing twin leads with Klose, who left in 1965.

A name change followed, and the Tea Set began forging their own sound, a mix of jazz, blues, and British rock. Soon, the now four-member group would have a new identity: the Pink Floyd Sound.

Mason is not often credited with playing a significant part in the development of the Floyd's music, but his non-rock-style drumming allowed Waters to veer into a lead bass role, Barrett to create all sorts of rhythmic, percussive guitar runs, and Wright to lay down washes of ambient keyboards without having to worry about hewing to a steady four-four heartbeat.

As the group developed, through the early 1970s, into a singular, fairly progressive act, Pink Floyd's recordings and stage work became more informed by but less dependent on improvisation. Therefore, Mason had to adapt his style. His somewhat sleepy, trademarked slow tempo, present on much of *Dark Side*, became a cliché, and he struggled to come up with new ideas for Roger Waters' increasingly conventional material.

By the early 1980s, Mason had lost much of his confidence as a drummer, and for the next ten years he didn't feel fully comfortable behind the kit. Nonetheless, he remains the *only* member of the Floyd to appear on all of the group's albums.

Like Rick Wright and David Gilmour, Mason found that Roger Waters' late-1970s assumption of near-complete creative control of Pink Floyd left him time, and ideas, enough for solo projects. He produced several acts in the 1970s, including Gong, Robert Wyatt, Steve Hillage, and even the Damned (see "We're Only Ordinary Men").

Working with interesting but more obscure jazz-rock figures Wyatt and Carla Bley, Mason recorded *Nick Mason's Fictitious Sports* in 1981, and duetting with former 10cc member Rick Fenn, he released an album and two soundtracks in the mid-1980s.

In the early part of the decade, Mason and Lindy, who'd given birth to two daughters, divorced with some difficulty. The Floyd's drummer soon married Annette Lynton, with whom he has two sons. Mason's involvement in Pink Floyd, and his various business ventures, most having to do with automobiles (as discussed in "Pile On Many More Layers"), have made him an extremely wealthy man.

Oddly enough for a drummer who rarely troubled himself with songwriting, Mason is the only member of the group to write books. He's released two of them, one (*Into the Red*, 1998) a collection of photos and essays on classic cars, the other (*Inside Out*, 2004) an entertaining and nearly always truthful personal history of the Floyd.

Rick Wright, Keyboardist

Born just north of London, in Middlesex, on July 28, 1943, Richard William Wright grew up listening to classical music and jazz. A multi-instrumentalist, he picked up piano, guitar, saxophone, and even trombone at a fairly early age.

At nineteen, Wright enrolled in Regent Street Polytechnic—future school of Nick Mason and Roger Waters—but did not enjoy being an architectural student. He did, however, enjoy his time with Juliette Gale, a singer he met around this time.

Gale and Wright worked together in Sigma 6, a beat group formed around the Regent Street Poly axis, and even after the group lost several members, the two lovebirds stayed together. They married in 1964, and their marriage lasted through 1982, producing two children.

In 1965, Wright went off to Greece for a short period, with his keyboard role assumed by Patrick Leonard, an instructor at Regent Street Polytechnic.

Wright was, in some ways, Pink Floyd's square peg in a round hole (although all five members found that pop stardom did not agree with their constitutions or their artistic aims). The oldest member of the Floyd, Wright was also said to be the crankiest and certainly was the least comfortable with both R&B and straight rock. A classicist at heart, he showed no little disdain for the trappings of show business and

This fold-out French magazine, *Les Rockers*, dates from 1967. Inside, Syd Barrett admits that his favorite current bands are the Beatles and Cream.

did not enjoy what he saw as a low-intelligence factor in the world of popular music.

As a musician, Wright was happy to move in the direction of free improvisation, which he may have felt was more genuine than the kind of dance music other bands on the circuit played. An improvisational context also gave Wright an opportunity to work out his classical and jazz influences.

Even considering Barrett's singular guitar playing, Wright was viewed as the band's musical force in the early days. His keyboard colorings provided a lot of the magic on *The Piper at the Gates of Dawn*, and his excellent, if delicate, voice worked well in tandem with Barrett (on "Astronomy Domine" and "See Emily Play," among others).

Given the opportunity by Syd Barrett's departure to become a key songwriter for the band, Wright found that writing lyrics was a real problem, and his bandmates gave little encouragement to what he *did* produce. Instead of pushing himself as a possible frontman, Wright folded his musical ideas—many of which were simply sublime—into an uneasy three-man compositional partnership with Roger Waters and David Gilmour.

Wright continued to sing, teaming with Gilmour on classic tracks like "Echoes" and "Breathe," although he rarely took solo vocals, apparently bruising fairly easily from criticism (especially from Roger Waters). The irascible bassist decided, perhaps rashly, around the time of *Wish You Were Here* to sing more of his own material, a decision that crowded Wright out. Gilmour's emergence as the group's sonic architect also may have pushed Wright into a feeling of irrelevance.

It would not be fair, however, to blame Gilmour or Waters for all of Wright's late-seventies artistic drought and personal problems. As a member of a famous and wealthy rock band, Wright had opportunities to work at his own pace that most musicians would have killed for. Instead, like other rockers in his generation, he sank into lethargy, musical solipsism, and cocaine addiction.

His solo album, 1978's *Wet Dream*, is a rather soggy affair, burdened by its lite-jazz pretensions and lack of any musical tension whatsoever. His second solo project, *Broken China*, did not come until 1996 and was seen as an improvement for its fusion of classic Wright keyboard textures and more "modern" production.

Roger Waters kicked Wright out of the group in 1979. The break had been coming for some time, and the final straw was Wright's refusal to give up his vacation time to do keyboard overdubs. Waters wanted *The Wall* finished ahead of schedule in order to collect a hefty bonus from Columbia Records, and saw Wright's refusal as an act of sabotage.

Perversely, though he booted Wright—working into the settlement a clause that the keyboardist could never rejoin—Waters allowed him to *stay in the band* as a work-for-hire session man for the *Wall* concerts. Following this, Wright left the Floyd, even though the general public did not become aware of the break until 1983.

The post-Waters Floyd regrouped in 1986 to record *A Momentary Lapse of Reason*, and Wright unofficially rejoined. For their second album without Waters, 1994's *Division Bell*, Wright was a full-time member again and even took a lead vocal on "Wearing the Inside Out."

He and his second wife, Franka, divorced in 1994 after ten years of marriage. Wright later married Millie, with whom he had a son.

Wright remained an inventive, if somewhat airy, keyboardist, recording and touring with David Gilmour, but a 2006 *Later with Jools Holland* BBC2 appearance singing "Arnold Layne" with Gilmour on guitar showed that his once-lovely voice had lost much of its power.

A further attempt, starring Gilmour, Wright, and Mason, at a memorial for Barrett at London's Barbican Centre, on May 10, 2007, was only slightly more successful. (Roger Waters appeared earlier that evening, but did not take the stage with his former colleagues.) As psychedelic light blobs covered the stage and the players, Wright again struggled to hit Barrett's notes, which were always out of his range. It was all a long way from the Sigma 6 days.

Wright's often turbulent life ended on September 15, 2008, when he died of cancer at his home. Mourned by friends, colleagues, and fans, Wright's passing ended the hopes of many fans that the four 1970s-era Floyds could reunite one last time. Tributes came from all the surviving members, including a particularly touching one from Roger Waters.

To celebrate Wright's memory, David Gilmour on September 23 performed the keyboardist's "Remember a Day" on *Later with Jools Holland.* This was the first time that any member of the group had performed the song anywhere.

Bob Klose, Guitarist

Rado "Bob" Klose, a friend of Syd Barrett's from Cambridge, enrolled at Regent Street Polytechnic in 1964 intending to study architecture. Klose was a solid jazz and blues guitarist, and soon was drafted into the ranks of Sigma 6. His arrival shoved Roger Waters over to rhythm. Soon, Barrett himself joined up, and Waters was moved again, this time to bass.

Although various singers joined and left the band, Klose remained long enough to play on the demonstration recording that the nascent group recorded, according to Nick Mason, around Christmas 1964.

By the 1970s, this demo had achieved legendary status, some of which ebbed when people actually heard the songs. Of the four tracks on the demo, "I'm a King Bee" features a Barrett vocal brimming with nonchalant confidence, but lacks any particularly interesting instrumental backing. It's hard to tell who's playing the somewhat rudimentary "British blues 101" lead guitar, but it's probably Klose, with Barrett on harmonica and Wright on rhythm guitar.

The other three tracks are Barrett originals, which indicate just how quickly the new guitarist had taken over the band's direction. "Lucy Leave" is far more interesting, an aggressive, forward-looking rock tune featuring Wright on organ and Klose's fluid lead guitar. While the beat is fairly conventional, Barrett's lyrics are elliptical, and the way he sings them runs conspicuously against any traditional rhythm. It's very forward-thinking stuff for 1964.

The other two songs have not been widely bootlegged. "Double-O Bo" is said to be a fusion of Bo Diddley and John Barry's "007" theme, while little is known about "Butterfly."

In the summer of 1965, Klose, not a fan of the band's embrace of rock and of the beatnik (read: marijuana-smoking) lifestyle, departed, ostensibly to focus on his studies. His stay with Mason, Waters, & Co. only lasted several months, but his professionalism helped the fledgling band develop. The four-man Floyd lineup was set.

After nearly thirty years of no contact with his old chums, Klose—by this time a successful architect and photographer, although he hadn't given up playing guitar—renewed acquaintances with Mason backstage at a Pink Floyd show at Earls Court, London in 1994.

While Mason was happy to see his old bandmate, he expressed a bit of guilt that the band became so successful only after Klose departed. The guitarist merely laughed off this notion. In 2006, he contributed guitar to Dave Gilmour's solo album *On an Island*.

Roger Waters, Bassist

The younger of two boys, George Roger Waters was born September 6, 1943 in Surrey, south of London. His soldier father, Eric Fletcher Waters, was killed in January 1944 during an ill-fated and probably ill-conceived Allied attempt to capture a bridge at Anzio, Italy.

The remainder of the family moved to Cambridge when Waters was two. Not surprisingly, Waters—someone failed by authority who summarily rejected all forms of it—hated school and took instead to rock and roll and the blues. Although he later wrote the lyric "you bought a guitar to punish your ma," Waters actually *received* a guitar from his mother in 1957 and began to play in earnest.

Despite his longtime anti-violent, anti-imperialist political leanings, Waters has always loved to fish, hunt, and shoot. He tried to make a go of it as a naval cadet, but was eventually kicked out for his truculent and insubordinate manner.

Waters then journeyed to Manchester for college, but left in 1962, first to travel in the Middle East and later to run a CND (Campaign for Nuclear Disarmament) group in Cambridge, where he met Judy Trim, a highly rated potter even farther to the left. The two married in 1969. Waters also met Syd Barrett, a sixteen-year-old beatnik-in-training who already was establishing a reputation around town as a guitarist and presence.

Soon, Waters decided to study architecture and went to London, enrolling at Regent Street Polytechnic. While he didn't like the courses, he did make friends with Nick Mason and helped the latter get through some of his lessons and exams. His anti-authority attitude served Waters no better at Regent Street than it had elsewhere, but by 1964, he no longer cared, having become deeply involved in beat music.

Like many of his contemporaries, he loved early rock and roll, but also dug the Beatles, the Stones, the Kinks, and Bob Dylan, whose no-bullshit lyrics and gravelly voice eventually inspired Waters to tell things exactly as he saw them . . . and Waters had plenty of demons to exorcise through song.

Over time, Waters, like Paul McCartney, was forced from lead to rhythm guitar and finally to bass, and perhaps as revenge he never played his bass as a traditional rhythm instrument, instead running up and down the neck with speed, occasional violence, and a lack of regard for intervals. Described as "tone deaf" early in his career, Waters improved as a vocalist with increased opportunities, but what he gained in pitch, he seemed to lose in tone.

Perhaps the most ambitious member of the Floyd, and the one most interested in questions of wealth and power, the hard-driving, competitive Waters—who, conversely, had to be pushed into practicing his instrument—was no friend to Syd Barrett during the latter's struggles with mental illness. But Waters pushed ahead anyway following the guitarist's departure, seizing the opportunity to become Pink Floyd's dominant force although he was the third-best musician in the band.

Waters' simple determination and work ethic led him to take over concepts, lyrics, and stage presentations, and indicated—to him, anyway—that his thoughts were the stuff of gold. As the Floyd moved through the 1970s, he perhaps began to feel that he alone drove the band, with Gilmour, Mason, and decreasingly Wright, kicked out in 1978, simply the executors of his ideas.

Ironically enough, the key collaborators Waters brought in for 1979's *The Wall* and 1983's *The Final Cut*, Bob Ezrin and Michael Kamen, ended up working with the three-man Floyd years later on *The Division Bell*. One assumes that Ezrin and Kamen could identify with the desire *not* to work with Waters.

Latter-day Pink Floyd lyrics simply weren't as riveting as the best of Waters' work, and the music was, as their onetime bassist pointed out—sometimes with too much relish—often a rehash of Floyd sounds of the past. Music on *Momentary Lapse* and *Division Bell* often floated away with nothing to provide the force of gravity. That the "new" aggregation, however, sold boatloads of albums and far outstripped its departed bassist in chart position as well as in concert attendance, frustrated Waters.

This shouldn't have surprised anyone. For years Waters had been producing increasingly strident music that lacked the melodic and harmonic invention his former collaborators contributed. When Waters' bitterness began to crowd out music in favor of an endlessly harping message, the Floyd's albums became harder to listen to. His solo albums, without the arranging skills or quality voices of the others, were panned by critics and have not sold particularly well.

His personal life had sweet ups and painful downs. Waters' marriage to Judy Trim—during which the two lived in a middle-class section of London and gave away much of their money to the poor—broke up in 1975, and with it apparently went much of Waters' softhearted behavior. The two had no children.

Waters then married Caroline Christie in 1976, and had two children. They divorced in 1992, and Waters hitched up with Priscilla Phillips for eight years. That marriage produced one child.

In recent years, despite having given numerous, withering interviews to various publications denigrating his former mates' contributions to Pink Floyd's success, Waters seems to have mellowed a little. Now the shoe is on the other foot; Dave Gilmour has little interest in reuniting Pink Floyd, and Richard Wright does not appear to have forgiven Waters for his actions of more than a quarter-century ago. At least Waters has been able to rekindle his friendship with Nick Mason.

Roger "Syd" Barrett, Guitarist

Born January 6, 1946 in Cambridge, Roger Barrett grew up in a musical house but also one that featured a history of emotional problems.

His father, who died in 1961, had mental trouble, and Roger was always closer to his mother. She bought him a guitar at age fourteen and encouraged Roger's interest in nature, painting, and poetry. Tabbed "Syd" because an entertainer at a local pub sported the name of "Sid" Barrett, the young man adopted the nickname and kept it with him as a sort of protective shield.

Perhaps as a reaction to his upbringing, and to his father's troubles, Roger Barrett developed an odd, man-child-like way of looking at the world, one that ensured his popularity among friends but left him unable to deal with certain realities and stresses. A good student, but rebellious, even to his beloved mother, he leapt easily and enthusiastically into the early-sixties, beatnik Cambridge lifestyle.

Given the young man's skills at all forms of visual art, most of Barrett's Cambridge friends thought that he would pursue it as a career. He was, however, one of those rare characters who could seemingly do every-thing well. An excellent draftsman, cartoonist, writer, singer, guitarist, conceptual artist, and dope smoker, he was always surrounded by friends and was said to be exceptionally garrulous and enthusiastic.

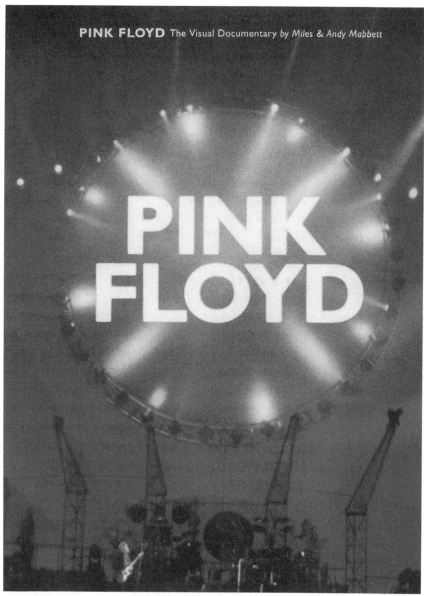

PINK FLOYD The Visual Documentary *by Miles & Andy Mabbett*

Barry Miles, a firsthand observer of the London underground, authored this "visual documentary," *Pink Floyd*, which went through several printings. It gives unparalleled insight into the band and the London scene in 1966.

Both the rise of Bob Dylan and the British beat boom split open Barrett's skull; he was a huge Beatles and Stones fan early on and decided he wanted to combine folk, blues, and rock and become a pop star. He played guitar in Geoff Mott & the Mottoes, then switched to bass when he joined Those Without. He also played bass in a blues band, Hollerin' Blues, in 1964.

At eighteen, Barrett enrolled at Camberwell Arts College in London and hooked up with his old Cambridge associate Roger Waters. Even Waters, competitive and self-focused, realized that Barrett was a huge talent and the youngster joined Sigma 6 late in 1964 when Chris Dennis left the band.

In retrospect, Barrett might have been bound, by the force of his talent, his good looks, and his magnetism, to dominate any situation in which he was involved. He soon became the band's key singer and songwriter—which erased the more jazz-oriented Bob Klose from the picture—and as Sigma 6 became the Abdabs, the Tea Set, and finally the Pink Floyd Sound (from Barrett's combining of blues singers Pink Anderson and Floyd Council, and soon shortened to the Pink Floyd), their magnetic young frontman shaped their direction with his nuanced pop songwriting, his *very* English voice, his fearless guitar technique, and his interest in the avant-garde.

The mid-sixties London underground's restless urge to push farther and harder to break what were seen as unnecessary taboos manifested itself in many ways, some of them extremely harmful. Barrett invested himself heavily in the drug culture of psychedelic London, gobbling LSD the way he'd previously gorged on art, literature, and music. For a while, it seemed to help him.

And almost accidentally, the Pink Floyd became a sensation. Pop history has shown that a hip "underground" movement, usually accompanied by sex, drugs, and even a mystical bent, will soon be co-opted by the masses. Psychedelia was no exception. Soon enough, the psychedelic underground's events and clubs became a hub for those who wanted cheap thrills, rather than those who had something creative to add to the mix.

The Floyd, however, were rarely, if ever, seen as sellouts, even when their first single, "Arnold Layne," went into the Top 20, and the follow-up, "See Emily Play" cracked the Top 10. Barrett was the real deal to the underground: a true artist whose looks and charm left both boys and girls gaping in his wake.

But as soon as he'd become a star, Barrett began to crack under the pressure. His behavior on stage and off became more erratic. He was snappish, irritable, unfocused, and sometimes even violent. Joe Boyd recalls, in *White Bicycles*, running into a disheveled, discombobulated Barrett in spring 1967 and being told by the guitarist's girlfriend that he'd been taking acid every day for a week.

Most observers believe, in retrospect, that the drugs didn't help, but that Barrett really had more serious problems than just his acid intake. David Gilmour told *Rolling Stone* in 1982,

> I wouldn't put it down to drugs or LSD, necessarily. I suspect that it would have happened anyway, and that maybe that stuff acted as a catalyst . . . by the end of 1967, he was in a condition where he couldn't play with the band at all. He would just stand onstage with his amp and guitar turned full up, his left arm hanging down by his side and just sort of smashing the guitar with his right hand, making a fearful racket all night long.

Roger Waters put it more bluntly years later: "Syd is schizophrenic and has been since 1968."

Although he was unraveling, a constant parade of dolly birds, hangers-on, and star-fuckers followed Barrett around, treating him like a holy man rather than a young pop singer.

In addition, little comfort was found at home; some of Barrett's flatmates and "friends" are said to have surreptitiously placed LSD in his tea or drinking water just to see what might happen. Meanwhile, the Floyd and their management were waiting for the next hit song to come from Syd's flowering but addled brain.

There are those who believe that Barrett's dramatic transformation into a psychedelic avatar, with its attendant drug-taking, groupie-snogging, and loss of focus and short-term memory, was a deliberate art project. Few of the people around Barrett at the time, however, hold this view, recalling his utter existential confusion, abuse of girlfriends, and desire to shut himself up in his room whenever possible, and attributing his behavior to a serious emotional imbalance.

Joe Boyd noted that at the June 1967 show a vacant Barrett "hardly sang, standing motionless for long passages, arms by his sides, staring into space."

After a series of British shows ruined by Barrett's atonal guitar slashing and lack of interest in singing, the Floyd postponed several gigs to allow their guitarist to get his head together. A trip to Ibiza, intended as relaxation, seemed to do Barrett no good. The music press, in its sensitivity, reported that Barrett was "going crazy." An American tour was cancelled midway through when Syd found himself unable to contribute, and a long British package tour (an assemblage of acts that played a few minutes each at every show) just prolonged the agony.

By early 1968, Waters, Mason, and Wright had had enough and, in a series of painful meetings, voted to recruit a new guitarist—Barrett's old school friend Dave Gilmour—to augment the quartet. The stated aim was to allow Barrett to compose for and record with the group but not have to turn up for gigs, but that option failed too as Syd brought even more bizarre ideas to the Floyd, such as shape-shifting songs, atonal tuning, and the notion of augmenting the band with a saxophone and banjo player and female backing singers.

The long-expected but still painful break finally came on April 6, 1968, when the original six-man Blackhill partnership—the four Floyds plus Andrew King and Peter Jenner—was dissolved, with the managers taking Barrett and leaving the Floyd on its own.

The ballyhooed Barrett's solo career proved disappointing, however. His first solo album didn't come out for nearly two years after his departure from Pink Floyd. He spent time tooling around Europe in a Mini and tried to write songs. An endless supply of girlfriends and drug dealers kept him occupied, and after having been part of a crowd of creative people for so long, Barrett found it very difficult to keep focused on his own. Nobody in rock and roll knew how to "treat" acid overuse, or schizophrenia for that matter, and his train continued to roll down the track toward disaster.

The two ungainly, incomplete-sounding albums from 1970 (*The Madcap Laughs* and *Barrett*) failed to sell much or generate critical acclaim. They are difficult to listen to but give an accurate picture of a soul in torment, trying to rescue parts of himself from a swirling fog of confusion.

Abortive attempts to bring him back for third album sessions in 1974 produced wholly unusable tracks far less cohesive even than the half-mad work of *Barrett*. After a few gigs—by all accounts shambling, rough events—with ex-Pretty Things drummer Twink and bassist Jack Monck, Barrett gave up stage performance as well.

After years of living in London hotels off his royalties, doing little exercise or work and gaining a lot of weight, Barrett finally headed back to the Cambridge area in the mid-seventies, where he remained for the rest of his life. Regaining some psychic equilibrium simply because he was around extended family rather than the rock-and-roll vultures of the capital city, Barrett settled into a sheltered, childlike half-life of painting, daily walks, and jazz on the stereo.

Totally uninterested in his old days of fame as a guitarist and singer, Barrett poured his creative energy into his canvases, finishing small and large paintings but destroying nearly all of them immediately afterward. His life became a testament to living in the moment, totally for oneself, rather than amassing things or worrying about acceptance from others. He was mad as a hatter, according to family and friends, but at least was well fed, medicated when necessary, financially secure thanks to his royalties, and able to fill most of his days with reasonable, normal activity.

Barrett passed away on July 7, 2006, from cancer. Few of his paintings survive, but the 2007 fortieth-anniversary rerelease of *Piper at the Gates of Dawn* features a small reprinted booklet of Barrett's drawings, jokes, and collages. His music, on the other hand, is easier to hear than ever, and it's more than just a stepping-stone to what Pink Floyd would do later. Barrett's music with the Pink Floyd is the greatest flowering of British progressive music of the 1960s, a capsule of the joys and horrors of the psychedelic experience.

David Gilmour, Guitarist

Born in the Cambridge suburb Grantchester Meadows on March 3, 1946, Gilmour, like Syd Barrett, got a guitar in his early teens and began playing around town shortly thereafter.

Gilmour's parents were teachers and somewhat bohemian, which made such seemingly "odd" notions as folk music and international travel less of a stretch for him in the gray British late 1950s and early 1960s.

In 1962, the sixteen-year-old Gilmour met Syd Barrett, a student at Cambridge Technical College's art department. Both played guitars and they traded licks. Gilmour says that some of the things that Barrett learned to do technically came from their sessions during this period.

The Floyd in aviator jackets and with Roger Waters sporting a rare smile. This publicity photo is probably a composite, given that Mason looks much older than the others. *Photofest*

Since he had flash, technique, and a grounding in both folk and blues on the guitar, Gilmour was in demand as a musician, and played in more advanced bands, such as the Newcomers and Ramblers, than did Barrett. But by 1967, Gilmour was still in Cambridge, playing in Jokers Wild (later rechristened Flowers before their breakup), while everyone else was in London. Asked to join the band in late 1967 by a frustrated Nick Mason, Gilmour readily agreed and made his first appearance with the now five-piece Floyd on January 12, 1968 in Birmingham.

Imagine the difficulty for both Barrett and Gilmour. Two old friends, one having trouble keeping it together, the other taking advantage of a chance to join a "name" band; Barrett feeling as if Gilmour was trying to elbow him out of the band, and Gilmour feeling both exhilarated at the chance to excel and guilty for his part in what must have been a painful situation.

Sooner than later, Barrett essentially gave up, going further inward, and was eased out of the band by a relieved Mason, Waters, and Wright. Gilmour became the only guitarist as well as the singer of much of

Barrett's old material. Stories are told of Barrett showing up at 1968 gigs and, from the audience, staring daggers at Gilmour on stage.

Despite Gilmour's initial reservations about the Floyd's desire to play avant-garde rock, he swallowed hard and went along on *Saucerful of Secrets*, then began developing his own blues-influenced, spacey style. His early tries at solo composition ("The Narrow Way," "Fat Old Sun,") were more promising than successful, but Gilmour quickly proved his worth as a singer, guitar player, and arranger. Capable of playing a wide variety of instruments, he played bass on several Pink Floyd recordings as well as drums on "Fat Old Sun."

While Gilmour used several different guitars in Pink Floyd, his most famous instrument is a tricked-out black Fender Stratocaster featuring the bluesy, treble-heavy tone that colors the band's most famous material. He has, though, used other electrics, most famously a Gibson Les Paul, various Fender Telecasters, and a Bill Lewis model with twenty-four frets (more than the usual guitar), which allows him to play high up the neck, as is his wont.

Gilmour's crystalline acoustic playing defines much of PF's mid-period work. He's used Takamine and Martin guitars, which are among the best acoustics in the world. By *The Wall* he had graduated to using an Ovation, which has a rounded back that provides extra resonance and a crisp, if somewhat thin, tone.

Blessed with great looks, Gilmour spent some time before joining the Floyd as a male model and following Barrett's departure was the only member of the band to carry any conventional "rock star" appeal.

He was also the last of the four to wed, tying the knot with wavy-haired American artist/actress Ginger Hasenbein on June 5, 1975. Their wedding, strangely, took place the day Syd Barrett showed up unexpectedly at Abbey Road; in spite of this freakish omen, the Gilmours remained married fifteen years and had four children together.

Gilmour wed journalist Polly Samson, who wrote much of the lyrical content on Pink Floyd's 1994 *Division Bell*, shortly after the album's release. In addition to raising a son from Samson's first marriage, the two are rearing three children of their own.

As the Floyd became international stars, Gilmour and Roger Waters began to scrape egos. The two were never close friends, and soon had trouble working together. Their fights about songwriting credits are legendary in rock annals, and by the sessions of 1983's *The Final Cut*, the two were sparring in the studio.

It's not surprising, then, that when Roger Waters declared in the mid-1980s that Pink Floyd was "spent" as a creative force, Gilmour was the first to cry foul, choosing to reassemble the band with Mason (and Wright, as a part-timer), record a new album, and hit the road. That the group's two post-Waters solo albums have been patchy seems irrelevant; Pink Floyd's albums and tours have generated huge sums, leaving Waters' solo work in the dust, at least commercially.

Unconfirmed rumors have Gilmour struggling with substance abuse during the 1980s and 1990s. In any case, Gilmour certainly didn't stop working, releasing solo CDs, touring, producing various acts, and playing guest guitar with artists as big as Pete Townshend and Paul McCartney. Following Barrett's death in 2006, he coordinated a tribute concert and single release featuring Rick Wright, Nick Mason, and David Bowie.

The decision, not made lightly, for Pink Floyd to reunite for Live 8 on July 2, 2005—the band's first show as a foursome in more than twenty-four years—largely hinged on the relationship between Waters and Gilmour. Magnanimously, Waters made the call to Gilmour himself to plead organizer Bob Geldof's case, and the somewhat surprised guitarist eventually accepted.

Both men, proud and with strong beliefs in the ideals of the 1960s, wanted to write a triumphant (and quite possibly final) chapter on the band as well as use their platform to do some good. When Pink Floyd album sales spiked dramatically following the successful show, Gilmour pledged to donate all his royalties from the sale of the album toward anti-hunger efforts.

As has been noted over the years, Gilmour has always been the member of the Floyd most vested in making sure that Syd Barrett received all his due royalties from various recording projects. One hopes that by now, Gilmour's numerous good works have helped him get over any guilt he may have had about his "part" in Barrett's condition.

Peter Jenner, Manager

Yet another member of the Cambridge mafia involved in the early days of Pink Floyd, Jenner (born in 1943) had always wanted to be involved with music, even when working as a lecturer at the London School of Economics.

Jenner, a Notting Hill resident, met gadfly/scenester John "Hoppy" Hopkins in 1965. Hopkins was the driving force behind the founding of the Notting Hill Carnival, a Caribbean-themed yearly free party in the streets of the west London neighborhood, and in 1965 convened a meeting to discuss opening a London Free School, which was founded to provide free education to the poor children of the area. Jenner was involved in both of these causes and with the crowd publishing the *International Times* newspaper.

Jenner's first managerial gig involved free-jazz band AMM, perhaps the London underground's first documented musical ensemble. But the ambitious Jenner, who wanted to make both music *and* money, decided he needed an underground, drug-informed, *psychedelic* pop/rock band, and fell in love with the Floyd, whom he saw in early 1966 at the Marquee Club, a mod hangout that was throwing avant-garde events on Sunday afternoons.

Peter Jenner's partner in this band scheme, Andrew King, had been working at British European Airways and had saved enough money to invest in the promising, if raw, Pink Floyd, providing the cash while Jenner worked his underground connections.

Jenner and King quickly signed the band to a management deal and created a six-way partnership, Blackhill Enterprises, to handle the affairs of the Pink Floyd. Eschewing the normal club circuit until the band had improved, Jenner and King instead induced the ambitious young group to play all sorts of underground clubs, charity benefits, and avant-garde happenings.

This strategy did two things for the Floyd: gave them credence with the underground community and allowed them to develop their groundbreaking sound, light shows, and material in a relatively comfortable, friendly environment. A large benefit for the *International Times*, in late 1966, at the Roundhouse helped cement PF's reputation with London's counterculture.

Syd Barrett soon emerged as a star, the light shows blew the local freaks' minds, and even the staid music papers began to take notice of the band late in 1966. Jenner looked around for record deals, first trying Elektra and Island but finding no takers, and eventually hooking up with

EMI, which forced the fledgling band into a very staid and square studio environment for their first album.

By the middle of 1967, Barrett was beginning to show signs of burnout, and despite having a hit record and a well-received album by the end of the year, Blackhill was deeply in debt. An attempt to obtain financing from the country's Arts Council died on the vine, and the management began to bounce checks with regularity. Since PF's booking rate was dropping as word of Barrett's inconsistencies spread, something had to be done.

Bringing in Dave Gilmour was a temporary measure intended to halt the group's spiral, but the wrenching decision to terminate Barrett from the group in early 1968 forced a showdown between the the Floyd and their managers. Who would Jenner and King choose to work with?

Jenner and King, weighing the fact that the other members of the group weren't proven singers or songwriters, went with Barrett, whose confidence they consistently tried to bolster, even, reportedly, to the point of denigrating the contributions of the other band members.

The Floyd had to pay their former managers a sum to acquire rights to the band name, as well as assume Blackhill's debts involving the band's lights, sound system, and van. Nick Mason reckons this figure was around £17,000.

Choosing Barrett was defensible, even in retrospect, but the two got little in return for their faith but heartaches. No matter what they tried, they couldn't keep Barrett stable enough to produce good work, and the talented but troubled singer soon faded into the mist.

Luckily, Jenner and King had diversified by then, putting on free concerts in Hyde Park in the late 1960s (the first of which, on July 29, 1968, the Floyd played) and managing like-minded British wackos such as Kevin Ayers, Roy Harper, the Edgar Broughton Band, and a pre–T. Rex Marc Bolan.

In later years, Jenner would helm the ships of other "outré" acts including the Clash, Billy Bragg, the Disposable Heroes of Hiphoprisy, Robyn Hitchcock, and John Wesley Harding.

Joe Boyd, Record Producer

An American expatriate chasing the developing multicultural popular music of the 1960s, Boyd worked for record companies and promoters with folk and blues artists both in the U.S. and London before settling in the U.K. to set up Elektra's British office in late 1965.

One of the first things Boyd did in London was to become involved, quite accidentally, in London's underground community. Looking for the music, he found it, along with the dope-smokers, scenesters, and political activists of the Notting Hill neighborhood. Soon he met critical underground figures "Hoppy" Hopkins, Andrew King, Caroline Coon, and Barry Miles, becoming involved with the London Free School, the Notting Hill Carnival, and *IT*.

Peter Jenner had already met Boyd through his earlier work with Elektra, and brought him to a Pink Floyd gig in early 1966. Once he saw the Floyd, Boyd was hooked, and recommended them—unsuccessfully—to his boss, Jac Holzman. After another friend, Chris Blackwell, at Island Records, also passed, Boyd decided that this was a sign. So he quit his job and set up his *own* company, Witchseason, to produce Pink Floyd for Polydor Records, the one company that had showed interest in the band.

The band and Boyd decided in late 1966 that "Arnold Layne" was the best bet for a single, and prepared to record it, for release on Polydor, with an option for an album to follow.

Unfortunately for Boyd, the band's success led management to elbow him out of the picture. The Floyd's new booking agent, Bryan Morrison, a more grounded businessman than either Jenner or King, had contacts at EMI and said he could get the band more money up front than Polydor was offering. Since the band needed money for new equipment, they decided to negotiate with EMI.

And signing with the giant recording company meant that the group would have to accept one of the company's staff record producers in place of the young and relatively untried Boyd. This left a frustrated Boyd as, at best, a hired hand in the studio rather than a member of the management team.

Still, Boyd wanted to be involved, so he and the band recorded "Arnold Layne" and "Candy and a Currant Bun" on January 27, 1967, along with an incendiary version of "Interstellar Overdrive" for the film *Tonite Let's All Make Love in London.*

While a neophyte in the recording studio, Boyd had a lot of experience with various types of music. He knew what he thought the band should sound like and had "good ears." Perhaps most important, he had the services of an excellent engineer, John Wood, who would go on to work with Nick Drake on his three spectacular albums.

Regardless of the excellent sound of "Arnold Layne," the Floyd were indeed forced to use Norman Smith (a former engineer of George Martin's) as their producer at EMI for their future work. Smith had designs on stardom himself and had fought to get the Floyd signed.

Boyd continued to work with Pink Floyd as a booking agent. He and Hopkins had, late the previous year, partnered to open UFO, a once-a-week party in London's Tottenham Court Road, in December 1966. The PF played the first four weeks at UFO (pronounced "you-foe") and also appeared once a month in February, March, April, June, July, and September 1967.

Despite the ecstatic reception the burgeoning underground gave the club, storm clouds were gathering. Hopkins was convicted for (unrepentant) hashish possession in early 1967, and was put away for nine months in June.

Trying to make enough money for both himself and Hopkins, Boyd was forced to close UFO in late September after having been evicted by a worried property owner who'd been threatened by the police. Bands were demanding more money to play at the club, local skinheads were causing trouble for the hippies and freaks, and Syd Barrett was behaving erratically.

The end of UFO marked the end of Boyd's work with Pink Floyd, but not with the London underground; he moved on to Fairport Convention, Nick Drake, John and Beverly Martyn, and the Incredible String Band.

Steve O'Rourke, Manager

Peter Jenner and Andrew King's decision to allow Pink Floyd to go free meant that the struggling band had no manager. Bryan Morrison did not think he could handle the task alone, but provided Steve O'Rourke for the job. O'Rourke managed the band from 1968 until his death in 2003.

A tall, apparently mad, but utterly devoted Irishman of lower-middle-class origins (unlike the band's musicians, who were middle- and upper-middle-class), O'Rourke made Pink Floyd his sole project and got the guys off their bums, on the road, and into the studio in order to grow together and find their new direction following the departure of Syd Barrett.

O'Rourke was a tougher businessman than the more idealistic and tripped-out King and Jenner; his sales savvy and firm negotiating hand brought the band higher fees. Touring manager Tony Howard, also one of Bryan Morrison's employees, got the band into universities all over the U.S. and Europe, a brilliant move that helped Pink Floyd find its initial post-Barrett audience: stoned, artistic upper-middle-class intellectuals.

The band also hired its first roadies in 1968, asking Peter Watts and Alan Styles to help lug and fix equipment. In the late sixties and early seventies, O'Rourke, Watts, and Styles became confidants and friends as well as employees of the band. Through years of insane ideas (ballet, Pompeii, inflatable pigs), O'Rourke helped insulate the members of Pink Floyd from the minute details and inevitable screw-ups, allowing them to concentrate on making music and enjoying the fruits of their labors.

During the 1970s, O'Rourke grew closer to Mason and Gilmour as all three of them developed their interest in fast cars. O'Rourke finished

Bespectacled Pink Floyd manager Steve O'Rourke speaks to David Gilmour and Roger Waters (reflected in the mirror) backstage at Birmingham, England, on December 4, 1974 during the band's winter tour.   *Photo by Mick Gold/Redferns*

twelfth at Le Mans in 1979, and he founded his own company, EKMA Racing, in 1981. Even though he had a scary crash in 1991 at La Carrera Panamericana, O'Rourke continued racing until he had to give it up shortly before his death.

What does a band manager do? O'Rourke handled hiring and dismissal of tour employees, negotiated contracts with promoters and record companies, and walked a tightrope when the band was late on a project or wanted to renegotiate a particular point. It's not an easy job.

O'Rourke's passing in 2003 came twenty years after the band's most traumatic time, the rending of the relationship between Roger Waters and the remaining members. O'Rourke was forced to fire Rick Wright during the recording of *The Wall*, had to deal with Waters' conflicts with Alan Parker during the filming of same, and when the break between bassist and band came in 1986, O'Rourke felt it deeply. His falling out with Waters may have been more severe than anyone's.

(Interestingly enough, as the first Pink Floyd album began with the speaking voice of then-manager Peter Jenner, what is probably the last Pink Floyd studio recording ends with the voice of Steve O'Rourke. He is heard at the close of *The Division Bell*'s "High Hopes," speaking into an answering machine before someone hangs up on him.)

Storm Thorgerson, Designer

During the dark days of early 1968 when Syd Barrett and the rest of the Floyd were at odds, band friends Storm Thorgerson and Aubrey "Po" Powell, a pair of young artists with an interest in graphics, "got involved," in their words, "trying in some measure to act as intermediaries."

With the band in desperate straits following the Blackhill partnership's breakup, the two designers, under the name Hipgnosis, volunteered to design the cover for the band's second album, *A Saucerful of Secrets*. Said sleeve was an attractive but not particularly distinctive mishmash of "psychedelic" images.

From this point, however, Hipgnosis—a name garnered from a word scratched into the floor by an unknown guest at Thorgerson's flat—took control of helping shape the public perception of Pink Floyd.

It made sense that Thorgerson, born in 1944 in Herefordshire—located between London and Cambridge—should work with the Floyd. Like the band's music, Thorgerson's art delights in the use of space and the placing of elements in bizarre situations. His design obsessions are the equivalent of Pink Floyd's musical obsessions, giving a disquieting yet appealing feel of a spaceship landing on a deserted beach, of pyramids dissolving into green fields, or of mirrors unfolding in outer space.

As the preeminent rock album designer of the 1970s—only Roger Dean, architect of Yes's covers, was in the same league—Thorgerson was respected as an expert in the genre. His lavish 1977 coffee-table book *The Album Cover Album* ended up in many homes and led to several imitations. He also published *Hipgnosis: Walk Away René*, a nonlinear history of the design firm and their greatest, or at least most interesting, work.

Aside from working with the Floyd, Thorgerson and Powell also lent memorable images to albums by other "progressive" or adult-oriented rock acts such as Led Zeppelin, 10cc, Styx, Dream Theater, Yes, and Genesis.

In 1978, however, Thorgerson was ousted from the inner circle by Roger Waters after, apparently, not having given the bassist enough credit, in some article or other, for the "flying pig" concept on the cover of *Animals*.

But when the Waters-less Floyd reconvened in 1986 to record *A Momentary Lapse of Reason*, the live set *The Delicate Sound of Thunder*, 1994's *Division Bell*, and other live albums, reissues, and compilations in their wake, Thorgerson was once again in the driver's seat concerning the album's visual component.

In recent years, Thorgerson has worked with newer bands, such as the Mars Volta, Younger Brother, and the Catherine Wheel, all of whom can claim some inspiration from the progressive music of the 1970s.

Thorgerson's work with Floyd is best represented, in published form, by *Mind over Matter*, another large-format book now in its fourth edition. He also created the front and back covers for Nick Mason's 2005 autobiography *Inside Out* and did the graphic design for Phil Taylor's (Gilmour's guitar tech) book called *The Black Strat*, a history of Gilmour's guitar.

A few important parties, including Hipgnosis record sleeve designer Aubrey "Po" Powell, onetime manager Bryan Morrison, underground linchpin John "Hoppy" Hopkins, and record producers Norman Smith, Bob Ezrin, and Jeremy Guthrie, are discussed in other chapters.

2

Who Knows Which Is Which

Wasn't Pink Floyd's Career Full of Contradictions?

ink Floyd holds a very unusual place in rock. The band's story, and its members' lives and work, are stuffed with contradictions, dissonant notes, and uncomfortable events that color how the group was regarded in its day and how it is regarded now. Examining these contradictions can help explain why the Floyd is often misunderstood or unfairly dismissed out of hand.

Anonymity

Despite being an internationally known superstar act, the Floyd are nearly anonymous as individuals, which is largely how the band wanted it. While Syd Barrett was a *star*, Wright, Waters, Gilmour, and Mason remained perhaps the most faceless major rock performers around.

Their collective work reeks of raw emotion, especially in the Waters-dominated *Wall* and *Final Cut* albums, yet the members of the band rarely convey their personalities. While their songs and record covers are memorable, their individual faces and personae are not.

And the Floyd have always liked it that way. Their distaste for the press—whom they were able to keep at bay, at least until they *needed* the newspapers to get the word out in the 1980s and beyond—ensured that the public didn't know much about the individual members of the band. "There may have been a time where we wanted more recognition as individual musicians," Gilmour noted in 1978. "But I can't really remember it."

A rather strange photo from the sessions for *Piper at the Gates of Dawn*. Rick Wright is brandishing a guitar (!). Other photos taken concurrently show Syd Barrett seated at an electric organ.   *Photo by Andrew Whittuck/Redferns*

The members of the group have worked hard to keep themselves and their families out of the spotlight for anything other than their music, attempting to retain some sense of privacy in a loony business.

Perhaps Steve O'Rourke and the band felt it was better to allow fans to hold on to a mystique of Pink Floyd as mystical musos rather than the real picture: fairly lazy, wealthy men who watch a lot of television and engage in expensive hobbies like flying, auto racing, and fox-hunting.

Whatever the reason for their tactic, it certainly worked. In a 1976 syndicated article, writer Sean Toolan quoted publicist Suzi Oxley: "Pink Floyd told me that after one concert in the Midwest, the security people would not let the group out of the arena until the crowd had gone. Floyd got tired of waiting and the group just walked out into the crowd. They weren't even recognized."

The Winding Career Path

Following its beginnings as a fairly conventional R&B act in the mid-1960s, the Floyd, with the addition of Syd Barrett, turned around 180 degrees and plunged deep into the London psychedelic underground.

Within eighteen months, after having carved out a reputation as an out-there bunch of blokes, the band moved distinctly aboveground and enjoyed a Top 5 British hit single . . . then within a year, after losing its main composer, chose instead to concentrate on albums and live concerts, constructing a reputation as a wholly singular space-rock entity. And that set of transformations carries us only through 1969.

Pink Floyd's original managers, Andrew King and Peter Jenner, viewed the gifted Syd Barrett as the one to watch after the split. This misapprehension led the rest of the band to work doggedly, rather than folding up their tent, to forge a new path.

After slogging through years of tours and recording in the late 1960s and early 1970s, which made them popular live artists even though their discs were spotty, the band finally became international superstars via 1973's *Dark Side of the Moon*. But with this great success came a terrible price: the emotional unraveling of the act, with tensions finally splintering friendships and the ability to work together by the early 1980s.

Polarized Fandom

Did you ever notice it can be difficult to find anyone who admits to enjoying *all,* or even ninety percent, of Pink Floyd's recorded output?

Beatles, Stones, Radiohead, or Marvin Gaye fans don't necessarily dislike entire periods of their favorite acts' output. But many people who are very passionate about certain parts of Pink Floyd's work are cold, to say the least, to some records in their catalog or entire periods in their career.

Or at least you'd think so. What else could explain the radio industry's lack of interest in the Floyd's pre-1973 output?

Back in the late 1970s, when *Animals* and *The Wall* were the group's big sellers, the group gained a new stateside audience of fans who'd heard Pink Floyd on FM radio and grooved on the clear production and somewhat adolescent, downbeat lyrics. When confronted with earlier albums, these new supporters could only stare blankly . . . which is fair, since it's hard to imagine, at first listen, the same band having done "Julia Dream," "The Gnome," and "Quicksilver" as well as "Time," "Have a Cigar," and "Run Like Hell."

Some fans feel that Pink Floyd's work before *Dark Side of the Moon* is a mere footnote, an embarrassing box of peculiar, blurry baby pictures. Others believe that the group did little, if anything, of value once Barrett departed in 1968.

Rock radio, such as it is, has predictably lined up behind the higher-selling *Dark Side of the Moon / Wish You Were Here / Animals / Wall* section of the band's canon, ignoring the group's early music.

"Instant" Stardom

While most attention these days focuses on the band's 1973–80 work, it is critical to note that by 1970 Pink Floyd was already a *major* underground act in America, France, and England, gaining fame for its pioneering light shows, trippy live performances, and a loose, experimental groove.

America soon took to the group's adventurous, experimental live shows, and the Floyd were filling big halls by the early seventies. Back in England, their 1970 *Atom Heart Mother* LP reached number one in the charts. So much for the "overnight success" of *Dark Side of the Moon.*

The Floyd played at the Fillmores on both American coasts, and had graduated to complicated live performances even before the release of *Meddle.* In fact, the group's nearly endless touring schedule of the early seventies primed the pump for the eventual recording breakthrough that came with *Dark Side.*

Fans of the time were aware of early Floyd standards such as "A Saucerful of Secrets" and "Careful with That Axe, Eugene" from their legendary concert appearances, just as latter-day fans would learn "Breathe" and "Welcome to the Machine" inside out.

Drugs

Though their four members were free of psychedelic substances by the early 1970s, Pink Floyd's music served as a soundtrack to the stoner crowd, creating a soundtrack to all sorts of mind-expanding drug experiences. One would think, given the band's impressionistic, trippy music, that the Floyd were *huge* drug users, but for most of their careers, that just wasn't the case.

The Floyd were understandably circumspect about drugs in 1967; during the early psychedelic era, Britain's famously incendiary press feared that the mere whiff of pot could bring down the Houses of Parliament. While Barrett was bathing his synapses with frequent doses of marijuana and psychedelics, and Wright was holding his own in the toking department (Mason and Waters were more apt to have a drink), band management was busy denying any "psychedelic" intent on the band's part.

Ironically, after Barrett left, talk of drug use in rock became less circumspect. By the late 1960s, even various Beatles and Stones had been arrested and the public and press were outraged by the overly harsh treatment for such relatively small offenses (too late, unfortunately, for Floyd confidant John "Hoppy" Hopkins, thrown in the clink for pot possession in 1967).

In fact, by the 1970s, the musicians were quite openly sanguine about their history. Dave Gilmour told Lynn Van Matre of the *Chicago Tribune* in 1978, "We've done drugs, sure . . . between 1964 and 1969, I took some acid—but it was never a ten-trip-a-week thing or anything like that. Once a month, maybe."

Waters later confessed to smoking a lot of hashish in the early seventies, and Mason readily admitted his taste for alcohol. The band's real drinking education apparently came on their concert excursions; Janis Joplin introduced the rhythm section to the joys of whiskey on their first American tour in 1967.

But in later years, all four members of the band would deny that drugs were heavily involved in the recording process, especially of the more successful albums like *Dark Side*. "I know I couldn't have made that record if I was stoned out on dope," Wright told *Uncut* magazine in 2003. That, of course, says nothing about the apparent cocaine dependency that plagued Wright later in the seventies and helped lead to his ouster from the band.

Prog Floyd?

Though it has been placed firmly in the "progressive rock" firmament by some fans and critics, Pink Floyd really doesn't have much in common with that format, perhaps best epitomized by contemporaries King Crimson, Genesis, Yes, and Emerson, Lake, and Palmer.

With this look, one would imagine the 1970 Pink Floyd as a grungy hard-rock band rather than sonic explorers. *Photofest*

None of the members of the Floyd were instrumental virtuosos, though Gilmour eventually became one of the more *influential* guitarists of his generation, and the Floyd rarely used complicated time signatures, stop/start song structures, or copious amounts of free-form atonality.

Some of their instrumental titles did reference science fiction and mythology. Their lyrics occasionally touched on them, too, but after 1968 did so only obliquely. When Roger Waters assumed full lyric duties by 1972, any talk of gnomes, space exploration, or spelunking was doomed.

What the Floyd *did* have in common with other "progressive rock" bands was the desire to move beyond the three-minute single, and to do so in a purposeful, serious manner that suggested a "concert" more than a "gig." Syndicated rock writer Robb Baker noted after their Fillmore East show in 1970, "I can only describe the music as beauty battling chaos. . . . I had the feeling throughout that they knew exactly what they were doing and where they wanted to go, even when they missed the mark. As new as the space-age sound seemed, they performed it with what was almost the reverence of ritual."

It might be appropriate to suggest that Pink Floyd was a 1970s version of 1980s sensation New Order. At best, both guitar/bass/drums/

keyboards quartets had a knack for assembling sounds into a whole that far outstripped the sum of its parts.

The success of both the Floyd and New Order came down to several qualities having little to do with songwriting or playing: intelligent marketing, excellent record production and the use of negative space in recording, and the conscious creation of a myth centered around drugs, cultural reference points, and a bohemian lifestyle.

Certainly both bands, which had early black music influences, were puzzled by the adoration and attention they received, when what their members really enjoyed doing was going down the pub or watching football.

Asked in 1999, during a fan-submitted-questions interview, which prog-rock groups he "hated," Gilmour remarked, "Probably Yes, E.L.P., Genesis, and King Crimson in that order. . . . Oh, God, what am I *saying?* Funnily enough, I don't really like pop groups very much."

Relevance

Pink Floyd fell into disfavor in the late 1970s amid the rise of more "relevant" punk and new wave bands. Critics derided the suddenly "dinosaur" act for its excess, outlandish and costly live shows, disconnection from the (allegedly) traditional rock-and-roll audience of working-class "street" kids, and aristocratic, downbeat lyrical and musical focus.

In some ways this disdain is totally understandable; the Floyd's live shows *were* over the top, and they *were* completely cut off from the street. But on the other hand, the group, with 1977's angry *Animals*, said a lot more about war, politics, and hunger than most of the unfocused, callow punk bands.

While the Ramones were happy to discuss the joys of sniffing glue and dancing to rock and roll, and the Sex Pistols merely railed against idiots of all stripes, it took the more lyrically focused post-punk acts, like the Gang of Four and Elvis Costello, to wed punk energy and intelligent social commentary.

Roger Waters helped Pink Floyd distinguish itself from its contemporaries with his lyrics, which even in early days drew blood from the military and denizens of the "straight" life. While the Rolling Stones boogied, Genesis' Peter Gabriel dressed up as a salad, and Yes sang about *whatever* they sang about, the dour and overwrought Waters at least tried to make sense of things.

Of course, framing his commentary in increasingly insular and sometimes unlistenable music made Waters and his group easy pickings. The Floyd appeared to have lost the simple joys of playing music, wrapping their work in a package of unfocused fury and misery. Sometimes a spoonful of sugar *does* make the medicine go down.

Lack of Passion and Humanity

A common complaint about the Floyd is that their music seemed cold, mechanized, and devoid of passion. But these qualities appear to be by-products of their approach, not anything the group was aiming for. Rather, the players, from the very beginning, tried to balance their very deep passions with the kind of sounds they felt were their key strength.

Again, Robb Baker: "The whole idea of merging the reasonable with the cosmic is precisely what the Pink Floyd's music is about: pushing the structure and concept of contemporary popular music [as eclectic as that is] to its limits—or beyond—but doing it with a strangely intelligent control."

That penchant for reserve (due to their inherent British calm and reticence to step out as charismatic live performers) led many to dismiss Floyd as a bunch of sourballs—a reputation not helped by Roger Waters' famous crankiness and rock-star whining, which became famously worse from 1975 on.

But to say that Pink Floyd's music is passionless is to fail to read the group's lyrics or hear the obvious fire in Gilmour's lead playing, the chaotic thump of Mason's drumming (especially prior to 1972), Waters' unearthly screams and his primal bass playing; and the obvious ache in Wright's voice.

How could a passionless group have produced material like "Let There Be More Light," "Dogs," "Lucifer Sam," "Money," or "Run Like Hell"?

Sex?

Actually, there is no conundrum here. Despite the presence of former model Dave Gilmour, Pink Floyd are among one of the least overtly sexy groups ever to play rock and roll.

Famous crank John "Sex is two minutes and thirty seconds of squelching noises" Lydon has nothing on the Floyd, whose lyrical attitudes toward lovemaking range from the coolly idealized ("See Emily Play") to cowardly and/or cruel ("Stay," "Summer '68") and terrified, terrifying, and foreboding ("A Pillow of Winds" and most of *The Wall*).

And yet many people find Floyd albums to be among rock's best lovemaking music. The almost Kraftwerk-like sound sculptures of *Wish You Were Here*'s "Welcome to the Machine," for instance, and the swirling "Echoes" have their devotees, while more than one commentator has defined *Dark Side of the Moon*—yes, the one about lunacy, death, and stress—as the ideal sex album due to its smooth sonic sheen, lush instrumental work, and swirling, psychedelically inspired textures.

It is certainly true that the proto-techno "On the Run" and the splashy "Any Colour You Like" are dead sexy in a psychedelic pre–"I Feel Love" fashion. Drawing a line from the Floyd to Donna Summer, though, might cause Roger Waters to lose his lunch.

Mental Health

Each member of the Pink Floyd struggled with emotional problems, and in fact the band even courted such issues in its music. But though they spent much of their career amid the insanity of the rock business and around *real* lunatics, the members of the band tried as hard as possible to live normal lives, perhaps using Syd Barrett's example as a cautionary tale.

The childlike genius of Barrett, and of *The Piper at the Gates of Dawn*, is that much more poignant when one considers that within two years, the mystical young man had fallen into a state of genuine existential confusion from which he never truly emerged. His 1969 all-too-accurately-titled *The Madcap Laughs* shows a man incapable of distinguishing the appropriate from the unspeakable. And he didn't get much help from his "producers."

The rest of the Floyd spent much of the rest of their careers dealing with Barrett's decline from genius to mental case. The guilt over mistreatment of their former composer emerged in many ways: through Waters' compositions and his (and Mason's) attitude toward the rock and roll business; in Wright's misery and gradual recession from the group; and in Gilmour's decision both to produce Syd's solo records

The fragile alliance—Gilmour and Waters—share a mike during a performance of *The Wall* in August 1980 at London's Earls Court. Behind them are members of the Floyd's "shadow band."   *Photo by Peter Still/Redferns*

and to help ensure that his onetime Cambridge colleague's royalties reached his family.

Even before Barrett showed up unexpectedly during the 1975 mixing sessions for the *Wish You Were Here* album, the former Floyd guiding light had inspired Waters' lyrics, all the way back to "If" on *Atom Heart Mother* through *Dark Side* and "Shine On You Crazy Diamond." Barrett would continue to play a part in Waters' process all the way through *The Wall*, notably in the famous hidden message on side two that referenced "Old Pink" at the "Funny Farm, Chalfont."

Waters spent much of his young adult life trying to forget the trauma of losing his father in World War II. But as he developed a fixation on Barrett's condition, Waters found himself unable to repress his pain any longer and became obsessed with questions of sanity, achingly aware by the time of *Wish You Were Here* that his *own* sanity was in question.

Over the last thirty years, Waters' erratic behavior toward his former Floyd mates has caused much pain, and his onetime colleagues have often responded in kind. Waters at times has appeared just one step away from going over the precipice, and all the surviving Pink Floyd members have dealt with their own demons.

The late Wright's personal problems caused him a great deal of anguish, leaving him at half-strength in the late 1970s and early 1980s. Mason and Gilmour retained their sanity only by conquering their fear of flying (through flying lessons) and removing themselves as much as possible from the walking psychodrama that was Roger Waters during the later Floyd period.

The three surviving members of the Pink Floyd have worked their way through various personal traumas—drug addiction, anger management issues, failed marriages—with varying success. But they're all still here, they all have children, and they all seem to have retained most of their humanity.

3

All Aboard for the American Tour

How Did the U.S. Discover Pink Floyd?

Without a hit single or, after 1967, a strong individual personality in the group, the Pink Floyd had to build its American audience brick by brick. Though they were coming off a hit in Europe with "See Emily Play," the Floyd were still unknown in the States when they set off on their first American tour in October 1967.

When early efforts to succeed in the "regular way" of rock acts at the time—by appearing in teen magazines, miming on pop programs, and the like—failed in the U.S., it became necessary for the band to go underground, trying to reach the emerging "counterculture" through any means possible.

By the late 1960s and early 1970s, the means existed to provide new rock music, film, dance, and theater to a ready and willing audience of college students and young intellectuals through a nationwide network of theaters, concert halls, and radio stations.

So despite failing to crack America through Top 40 radio and teen TV programs, the Floyd were able to get radio airplay, television exposure, and concert support from "new" sources that they could not have tapped even a few years before.

Here is a history of the group's attempts to break through in America, first through the "normal" channels of the day, then the more successful path of the "underground."

The 1967 American Concert Tour

Back in 1967, the modern touring mechanisms bands take for granted today did not exist, and it was worse for inexperienced hippie "managers" like Peter Jenner and Andrew King, who were not tied into traditional showbiz. As a result, the Pink Floyd had nothing but trouble on the road, and had to struggle even to get interest from its record company. Syd Barrett was already beginning to lose it by this time, and most of his playing on this tour was below par.

Due to problems obtaining work visas, the band arrived in America more than a week behind schedule and eventually did just a handful of gigs on the West Coast (Los Angeles, San Francisco, and Santa Monica). While the Floyd enjoyed their interaction with other bands on the various bills, they found that their light shows were too small for the huge halls they played and that the equipment they had been promised did not turn up.

As a result, the musicians—especially drummer Mason—spent a lot of time cadging equipment from whatever sympathetic dealers or fellow players they could find. As a result, Mason had to go on stage with mismatched drum parts, Wright was stuck with a Vox organ (he was a Farfisa and Hammond man), and both Waters and Barrett had to use unfamiliar amplifiers. For one of these gigs, Waters played, and later smashed in frustration with Barrett's misbehavior, a Vox bass.

When the Floyd got off in San Francisco from their series of flights, they were greeted by über-promoter Bill Graham screaming at them for being several days late. Even removing drugs and drink from the equation, it's no wonder they felt discombobulated.

1967 American Television: Dick Clark and Pat Boone

The truly groundbreaking music of "Screaming" Jay Hawkins, Little Richard, Elvis Presley, and Jerry Lee Lewis bracketed the 1950s rock and roll movement on one end. On the other end were Dick Clark and Pat Boone.

Boone, a Christian, white-buckskin-shod MOR singer, covered, or more accurately, castrated, songs like "Tutti Frutti" and "Long Tall Sally" for a conservative white audience, becoming one of the biggest stars of the era even though he harbored deep suspicions of rock and roll.

He defended his versions—claiming that the original artists were happy to get royalties—but Boone not only softened up the arrangements, he also changed the lyrics of the songs because he believed the original versions to be dangerous. (He even tried to alter the title of Fats

This poster, advertising a mouth-watering lineup for 60s fans, was created to promote a set of San Francisco gigs on the Floyd's first U.S. tour in 1967. The shows, however, were cancelled, along with most of the tour, due to Syd Barrett's inability to play.

Photo by GAB Archive/Redferns

Domino's "Ain't That a Shame" to "Isn't It a Shame" for *grammatical* reasons.)

Clark, whose *American Bandstand* record-spinning show had run on TV since 1952, first as a local daily program and, from 1962, weekly on ABC, is believed to be as guilty of accepting payola from record companies as ruined fellow DJ Alan Freed, but Clark's squeaky-clean image, charm, and television success made him more acceptable when he testified in 1959, before Congress, concerning payoffs made by record companies to gain radio airplay.

A spot on *Bandstand* didn't guarantee success, but despite its fairly safe format, the show was one of the prime programs for reaching American kids. In the days before cable television, *AB* was among the only ways to get across a visual image.

Through their association with Capitol Records' subsidiary, Tower, the Floyd snagged an appearance on November 4, 1967. Having played a show the previous night in San Francisco (and being booked for two shows back there the same evening) they were a bit disheveled.

None of which excuses the group's painful performance. Barrett, "obligatory Hendrix perm" in full flower, apparently ran through the song just fine during rehearsals, but on the final take barely troubled himself to mouth any of the lyrics to a tape of the as-yet unreleased "Apples and Oranges." The other band members veer between embarrassment, annoyance, and vain attempts to cover their slipping leader's mistakes. A ten-second "interview" found Barrett standoffish.

The next day, the Floyd were back in LA, booked to appear on Boone's syndicated show (his 1966–67 NBC gig had been canceled) and later that night to do a gig in Santa Monica. This time, "See Emily Play" was the choice for miming, and according to observers—the tape is apparently lost to history—Barrett was little more together than the day before, both during the lip-synch and in a mercifully short interview. One would assume that housewives, the intended audience for Boone's chatty little program, found little to enjoy about the Pink Floyd's performance.

A few days later, following alternately good and disastrous shows in San Francisco, in which Barrett would occasionally detune his strings and simply stare at the audience, the group elected to cancel the rest of its U.S. tour and return to Europe. Perhaps because word travels fast in the industry, these were the group's first and last appearances in a commercial American television studio.

The 1968 Concert Tour

Once David Gilmour replaced Syd Barrett in early 1968, PF was able to move forward. One important step was booking a proper American tour that extended beyond the West Coast. The nineteen-date tour took them both west and east, but they played only four non-coastal shows, two each in Illinois and Michigan.

Gilmour had a guitar stolen before the first show on the tour, July 8 at the Kinetic Playground on the north side of Chicago. Four days later, the Floyd took the stage at Detroit's famous Grande Ballroom, where local bands like the MC5, Bob Seger System, and Grand Funk Railroad regularly held court.

From July 15 to 17, the band worked Steve Paul's "The Scene" in New York City, where nearly every big group passing through would visit. Paul's labyrinthine club, which featured tunnels, passageways, and low ceilings, had a great sound system and hosted such various acts as the Doors, the Velvet Underground, and Traffic. Jimi Hendrix was a regular patron and often worked on new material there after hours.

A few days later Pink Floyd returned to Chicago, this time to the Auditorium Theater, probably the first true "concert hall" they played in the United States. (Soon the group would insist on these larger venues whenever possible.) The next day, July 24, they were in Philadelphia for the Summer Music Festival.

The entourage then traveled to Los Angeles for concerts on July 26 and 27, and then had a few days' R&R before three shows at San Francisco's Avalon Ballroom. Two shows in Seattle, two in Sacramento, and two at Torrance, California's "The Bank" closed out a far more successful enterprise than their first American jaunt.

By this time, the Floyd had given up all pretense of being a "pop band," and were playing a more progressive, free-form set that allowed for jamming and experimentation. Some songs from *Piper*, like "Astronomy Domine," "Interstellar Overdrive," and "Pow R. Toc H." fit this bill, but the group was also comfortable playing compositions from the new *Saucerful of Secrets*.

Music in Films

The first exposure that some Americans had to Pink Floyd's music was its presence in counter-cultural films. *More* (1969) featured an all-Floyd soundtrack, while *Zabriskie Point* included a significant amount of their music. The Floyd's love of atmospherics and their cinematically oriented sound palate made them perfect for film.

Sitting in a theater and hearing Floyd's music playing over arresting visual images is a heady experience. It's just a shame that Barbet Schroeder's films weren't better and that the misunderstood and maligned-for-political-reasons *Zabriskie Point* didn't get more positive reviews. One could argue that the group's most *representative* film is 1972's *Live at Pompeii*.

The Floyd, naturally, loved the idea of recording film music, although the reality of those situations—low recording budgets and rushed deadlines for *More* and *Obscured by Clouds* and the nearly impossible demands of Michelangelo Antonioni for *Zabriskie*—soured their view somewhat. Since the early seventies, one could argue, the Floyd have simply made film music without the films.

The 1970 Concert Tours

After spending 1969 recording and touring Europe, Pink Floyd visited the U.S. twice during 1970, once in the spring and once in the fall.

The tour started in New York City, veered to Chicago for one gig (such were itineraries in those days), then back east the next day. According to Nick Mason, at one of two gigs at New York's Fillmore East, Pink Floyd asked that an unkempt bunch of hangers-on be removed, only to find later that said hangers-on were members of the Band, whose *Music from Big Pink* had been a favorite on Floyd turntables.

Their second gig, April 10 in Chicago, was done for some reason without a light show, but impressed anyway. The *Tribune*'s review of the "rock and raga group" (their term) noted that "sibilants die lingering deaths in reverberation's limbo, eradicating their parent words as impossibly precise." Apparently the reviewer was discussing the group's vocal sound.

Unfortunately, on June 16 in New Orleans, the band—in its first jaunt to the American south—lost all its equipment to theft. According to Nick

Mason's *Inside Out*, the disappearance of two drum sets, four guitars, an organ, and various speakers, effects boxes and mikes was no accident.

"There was obviously an imaginative community policing initiative in place whereby officers could offer an all-in, one-stop service of removal and recovery," Mason wrote, noting that as much as they wanted to stiff the police on offering a "reward," they thought they might want to play in New Orleans someday . . . and ensure that other police departments around the country wouldn't mistreat them.

Most of the equipment back in hand, the group called off the last few gigs on the first U.S. swing and headed home before appearing at a well-spaced, apparently leisurely series of European summer festival gigs.

The group returned to America on September 26 for the *Atom Heart Mother* tour. The rise of the album as a viable commercial force in the rock world meant that bands that heretofore had hit the road in the summer (when kids were off school) would now tour to draw attention to (or "support") their new long-player and benefit from the publicity in terms of ticket sales. Once Pink Floyd broke through with *Dark Side*, each subsequent tour would be in service of a particular album.

On this jaunt, the band (and an assembled multitude of brass musicians and backing singers) played just three cities in the east, instead zigzagging for the most part between the northwestern United States and western Canada. They also played a show in Santa Monica, California, by which time huge billboards of the *AHM* cow greeted unsuspecting motorists near Los Angeles' Sunset Strip.

An Hour with Pink Floyd

Pink Floyd's exposure on American television was nearly zilch until 1971, when this one-hour special was broadcast on many public (i.e., government-funded educational) stations.

Produced by KQED in San Francisco, *An Hour with Pink Floyd* is a meditative sixty-minute exploration of sound, a live performance filmed at an empty soundstage on November 30, 1970. Filming a show in front of *no* spectators was a perfectly bizarre group gesture, one that indicates their on-and-off attitudes toward audiences. (They'd repeat the trick with *Live at Pompeii*.)

Rarely had rock music, or musicians, been treated to the kind of sympathetic sound and filming given here, and the result is a trippy and informative slice of group history. To see the four performing uninterrupted for an hour at this point in their career is, for the most part, a joy.

The band isn't even visible until more than six and a half minutes into the first number, the faux-classical "Atom Heart Mother," instead playing for much of the number to films of sea and landscapes. (Given the Floyd's famous lack of stage presence, this isn't a bad idea.) The song's still not much, but this version outclasses that on the album.

The group, resplendent in tie-dye shirts and some of their longest hair ever, also tears through the touring-nightmare diary "Cymbaline," slows down for "Grantchester Meadows" and "Green Is the Colour," then segues into "old favorites" "Careful with That Axe, Eugene" and "Set the Controls for the Heart of the Sun."

During "Grantchester Meadows," Waters' lovely ode to the memories of idyllic summer days, Gilmour and Waters pick acoustic guitars, as they did for this number during the rest of the 1970 tour. Wright—who barely sings at all during this show—plays tapes of birdsong, then adds two solos on the Farfisa organ.

For much of the program, the group's main instrument is actually echo. Each of the four players explores the space between notes with varying levels of delay, reverberation, and tremolo. All four drop out of the sound at various times, showing their predilection toward both jazz-type soloing and the creation of an independent, ever-flowing sonic space. Nature sounds add to the audio ambience. Gilmour creates space effects with his guitar slide; Wright feeds his keyboards through sound-altering units.

Watching the players' interaction shows how they effectively created space and tension, setting a mood with both "musical" (instruments, melodies) and "nonmusical" (found sound, Waters' trademarked "funny mouth noises") elements. Anarchy and beauty, hard and soft sounds, the clear-headed and the insane, coexisted in Floyd's world a long time before *Dark Side of the Moon*.

Mason's drum setup, including four tom-toms and five cymbals, shows how rock percussionists were expanding their sonic palette by 1970. Wright uses Hammond and Farfisa organ and, on "Cymbaline," a grand piano, something the group couldn't do in a regular live setting. Gilmour played a black Stratocaster, and Waters both a Fender bass (having dispensed with his Rickenbacker some time before) and a gong, which he pounded at various points with relish.

This special, viewed by tens of thousands of both stoned and sober rock fans across the U.S., did nothing to dispel the Floyd's growing reputation in the States as the ultimate "head" band. While the Grateful Dead's audience was more seriously drugged out, they were dancing half the time and certainly not listening too carefully.

Pink Floyd never induced its audience to boogie; the band was there to put on a *concert*, and until 1973, you could, at most halls, hear a pin drop at a Floyd show.

Underground Radio

Many college radio stations began playing experimental rock in the late 1960s and early 1970s. The growth of university radio, paired with a growing number of stations on the new FM dial playing "underground" or "progressive" music, led to increased exposure for contemporary British bands such as Pink Floyd, Procol Harum, Traffic, King Crimson, Yes, and Emerson, Lake, and Palmer that had no natural outlet on the AM Top 40 stations of the sixties.

Every major city in the U.S. had one or two "underground" stations, some of them affiliated with educational institutions but others establishing themselves as commercial outlets catering to a young, upwardly mobile audience. The rise in the 1970s of FM rock radio came due to an interest in increased playlists and improved sound. FM was in crystal-clear stereo; AM was echoed and monaural, as it remains to this day.

Pink Floyd, as a band conscious of sound, production, and texture, was a perfect match for the FM listening audience. Even as early as 1970–71, underground radio was all over the band.

The 1971 Concert Tour

The Floyd were extremely busy in these years, trying to break through to new audiences all over the globe. In 1971, for instance, along with recording *Meddle* and sketching out musical ideas with which to accompany a ballet, they played multiple short tours in England, Germany, Italy, and Switzerland, scheduled around stints in Scotland, France,

Holland, Japan, Australia, Hong Kong, Denmark, and Sweden; then they went to the United States.

The corner of 8th Street and 6th Avenue in New York is a really god-a-mighty outasite corner as corners go. No not the corner itself, it's a little further down that the action gets good. And the good action is supplied by a newsstand, one of only 4 such newsstands in all of New York to sell the *New Musical Express*.

Well there was this time around December '67 or January '68 when something really exciting occurred on the cover of the *New Musical Express*.

A brand new group got the cover and the group was known as Pink Floyd. Now if that wasn't some kind of a name then my name is Tony Kroll.

And besides their name was their clothes. Everybody was wearing clothes then, but there was something special about their particular choice of garb. One guy had a pair of floral curtains for pants; they weren't really a curtain but they *looked* just like it. Except that curtains don't have legs. Another guy had some sort of vinyl or plastic or something in the form of a jacket, you could tell it was a jacket because there was a shirt under it. If there wasn't a shirt under it, it would have been a shirt itself. And that was just the point; they were challenging the very concept of *clothing among other things*.

And one of the things was *music*. Everybody was doing weird stuff. But Pink Floyd was *consistent* about their weird whoppers as well as being *serious* about it all.

But there was still—at first—an aura of mere shenanigan attached to their whole routine. It all seemed like psychedelic overstatement. They had a cut called "Interstellar Overdrive." And the album was called *Piper at the Gates Of Dawn*, kind of one of those Procol Harumesque titles so big at the time. Well there was plenty of other overstatement on the album too. There was a touch of the Dave Clark Five in one cut and a touch of some poetry in another. There was a cut called "See Emily Play." "Emily" seemed like a natural, it looked like people were gonna eat it up, literally, right off the record. (Edible records even seemed like a not-that-remote eventuality at the time, such were the times.) But alas it

never got anywhere because people thought the title was actually "See Melanie Play," and even though Melanie wasn't around just yet most people were willing to use their imagination and prophesy Melanie's final arrival.

So that was about it for the first album. People still play it whenever friends and neighbors gather under one roof and the stereo is warmed sufficiently to make possible the hearing of such dandies as "The Gnome," "Chapter 24," "Lucifer Sam" (two years before "Sympathy for the Devil"). "Matilda Mother," "Take Up My Stethoscope and Walk," "The Scarecrow" and "Pow R. Toch." They still play it all right but by now it's scratched. It's scratched a lot more than their second album, *A Saucerful of Secrets*. Which may be *oh so trippy* and all that but it's just a lump of inner space.

It's not *inner* space anymore. Between albums they more or less decided that if anybody was gonna do outer space it was gonna be them. Well the Stones *had* done "2000 Light Years from Home" and all that but it was more or less a sure thing that the Stones wouldn't be sticking with it forever. So they grabbed it up and took it straight to their heart. (Several years later Jefferson Starship blasted off and—well the universe is big enough for everybody.) Well anyway they knew what the heart of the matter was and so they decided to redirect all that dull space swill getting kicked around at the time and turned it into something a bit more sinister. So they did this thing called "Set the Controls for the Heart of the Sun" which ain't a bad concept at all. I mean if you wanna die by fire instead of ice what's more fiery than the big golden ball in the sky that rises in the East and sets in the West?

But like often things spacewise would get a bit out of hand. So once in a while they'd switch gears and end up just in the general field of science fiction tiporamas. Or even some zoology anthropology like with that song they have called "Several Species of Small Furry Animals Gathered Together in a Cave and Grooving with a Pict." Then they decided to do an archaeological number and dig up the cuts from their old al-

bums. So they called the new disc of ancient stuff *Relics* (on Capitol).

Well that's the story behind the stories in their songs but what about their music? Well there are lots of bird calls and gongs, electronics, French horns, etc. Plus there's the basic band at the center of the whole thing. Which these days means David Gilmour on lead guitar. That's what it means. And also Nicki Mason on drums and tympani. Okay, and also Rick Wright on organ, harpsichord, piano, cello and harmonium. Is that enough for you? Well there's more, there's Roger Waters on bass and all those electron effects. They're all English and stuff like that and they all play LOUD. When they play live.

They play live in the U.S. every once in a while and in fact the first time they played New York they played the Cheetah the same night Donovan played Lincoln Center. And they don't play loud just to annoy all the silence fans. No

Between the planets electronic birds pipe at the gates of dawn, heralding

The Intersteller Thunder of Pink Floyd

by R. Meltzer

Influential rock writer Richard Meltzer penned a positive, if somewhat stream-of-consciousness, two-page article about Pink Floyd for *Circus* magazine in 1971. Too bad nobody proofread the article's title.

In support of the soon-to-be-issued *Meddle*, the band crossed the Atlantic for a five-week, twenty-seven-show tour beginning October 15 at the Winterland in San Francisco. For the most part, these gigs took place at college auditoriums and large halls, two environments in which the members of the group were comfortable.

Writer Lynn Van Matre described the band's 1971 oeuvre as "a sort of psychedelic Muzak" but noted that the music "oozed out in concentric circles, lulling and attacking the listener at once. Very strange, and very, very fine."

Breaking through to new ears in America was not only a matter of economic ambition for the group; it was also about maintaining some sanity. Nick Mason, quoted in Barry Miles's *Pink Floyd*, noted why the group didn't like to run through the same "old" songs for British audiences: "Being embarrassed of standing on a stage for the fourth year running and playing 'Set the Controls,' 'Careful of That Axe,' "Saucerful of Secrets' . . ."

Unlike most bands of the day, the Floyd did not use an opening act, preferring instead to command the stage with an array of instruments that was impressive (especially for the time), a quadraphonic sound system, a light show, and an increasing amount of stage effects.

Light Shows

Many American universities with planetariums or large theaters ran "light shows" in the 1970s at which recordings of rock music were played to the accompaniment of light projections, lasers, and films.

These events were not primarily educational, instead serving as opportunities for teenagers (some of them stoned) to "freak out" to their favorite current music to the visual accompaniment of flashing lights. At least all the freaks were in a safe place where they couldn't get hurt.

Of the bands whose music was played at shows like this, Pink Floyd was the one most suited for the academic settings of universities, planetariums, science centers and such. The members of the band, educated and well-spoken, were interested in machines, history, and science, and tended—at least in the early days—to attract a quiet, adventurous, respectful group of fans.

The 1972 Concert Tours

In mid-April 1972, following some recording for *Obscured by Clouds*, the band began its sixth U.S. tour, an eighteen-date journey that didn't go west of Chicago. The climax of the tour came with two shows at Carnegie Hall (May 1 and 2) and a gig at the Kennedy Center in Washington, D.C.

The Floyd used their patented 360-degree surround sound throughout the auditorium as well as an impressive light show. In addition, to help offset a somewhat sleepy stage demeanor that even their biggest fans were beginning to notice, they added some new visual effects, including a large flaming gong and sheets of fire emanating from buckets.

After returning to Europe for a series of gigs, then taking two months off, PF returned to North America in September with a seventeen-date western tour that included two shows in Canada and took the band to heartland states like Oklahoma, Kansas, and Colorado for the first time.

Around these tours, Pink Floyd—a busy bunch of bees—accompanied Roland Petit's ballet troupe, filmed themselves playing at Pompeii, appeared at more European shows, and finished both *Obscured by Clouds* and *Dark Side of the Moon*.

During these American shows, PF played much of that soon-to-be-classic disc. At first titled "Eclipse," the suite included most of the songs that ended up on *Dark Side*, but hardly with the arrangements or production sheen that fans would hear on the finished album.

The record came out in March 1973, the same time their *next* tour started in Madison, Wisconsin. By the time the tour ended, the Floyd had become "instant" stars.

4

Settle in Your Seat and Dim the Lights

What Were Pink Floyd Concerts Like in . . .

T hrough 1973, Pink Floyd was much more highly celebrated as a concert act than as a recording group. While many revere the band's first album, *The Piper at the Gates of Dawn*, some in the London underground felt at the time that it was tantamount to a sellout. Many people, even the fans who lined up to see the Floyd in concert, found albums like *More*, *Meddle*, and *Obscured by Clouds* to be incomplete or disappointing.

Theirs was a winding, confusing, often directionless journey, as the group tried hard to find its way on stage, but their spirit of adventure made PF's live act an embodiment of the psychedelic experience of discovery and celebration of both the positive and negative of life. The Floyd pushed the envelope constantly and their experiments should be acknowledged.

This chapter traces Pink Floyd's evolution as a live act, breaking their history as a concert attraction into ten segments.

1966: Making a Name

The nascent Pink Floyd was certainly not packing halls at this point; the band was just trying to impact a London scene suddenly teeming with pop groups.

So how *did* the Floyd first draw attention in Great Britain? By going "far out," both musically and visually, from what had come before in popular music. Colliding with London's underground, they found a friendly home for the notion of wedding avant-garde improvisation and

A suitably dramatic shot for a dramatic setting. Roger Waters bangs a gong at Pompeii. *Photofest*

sound to pop song structure and bathing the whole beast in liquidy, disorienting visuals.

Their music, constantly evolving in those days, was by mid-1966 a progression from traditional R&B toward a fully electric original fusion. The setting owed much to jazz, with its small combo of instruments and its focus on soloing and setting a mood, but the Pink Floyd was definitely what then was referred to as a "beat group." Syd Barrett was a fan of the Beatles, the Rolling Stones, the Byrds, Love, Bob Dylan, and even the Mothers of Invention.

At this time, the PF repertoire consisted of chaotic, barely-together twelve-bar blues progressions and enigmatic folk-rock songs by Barrett, both spiced with free-form noise during solo sections and between verses.

The need to move beyond R&B numbers like "Gimme a Break" and "Road Runner" asserted itself fairly quickly, as the players (especially Wright) got bored with hewing to the soul and blues conventions that hamstrung their desire to improvise. By mid-1966, Barrett was writing more material anyway.

Another catalyst for the move toward free-form improvisation is the simple fact that in the early days, the band really couldn't play (something various members of the band have acknowledged). Waters, still a frustrated guitarist, attacked his bass rather than romanced it, while Mason, not yet having been astonished by Cream's enormously influential Ginger Baker, was busy figuring out his drumming style.

Although he had to manage the transfer from acoustic piano to Farfisa organ, Wright was always the band's purest musician and, even in the early days, was responsible for "treating" his keyboard sounds and working with all sorts of electronic gadgets to project sound around the room.

Barrett, having watched AMM's guitarist Keith Rowe use a metal slide on his instrument, adapted the technique to his own playing. Soon Barrett had transformed his rudimentary blues-influenced guitar licks into an aggressive, experimental style that depended on echo, feedback, distortion, and especially volume to transport listeners to unfamiliar states.

Early Pink Floyd shows were *meant* to disorient, using volume, lights, waves of sound, and "nonmusical" elements such as feedback and echo to take the listener on a trip. "It's a definite realization of the aims of psychedelia," Waters said in 1966 of the group's stage show, even though Barrett was the only member of the group at this time to be fully enamored of the drug experience. In 1966, it was the people *around* the Floyd who were stoned.

The group's first experience was playing shows in the underground community, but Pink Floyd also worked out in the provinces throughout the later part of 1966 and by the end of the year—having become the hottest underground rock act in the country—played the Royal Albert Hall for an Oxfam anti-hunger benefit.

1967: The Pop Star Year

The Pink Floyd, by now a "name" band, had hired a lighting director (but did not have a roadie until later in the year; Rick Wright was still schlepping around the equipment for a few extra pounds per show).

Their sound was louder than nearly every other band—police noted a dangerous 120db level at one show—and their visuals unparalleled on the circuit.

The idea of projecting slides of dizzying liquid light onto the stage was born from a desire to re-create the visuals of the drug experience. Even those who did not partake of hashish and LSD were interested in the Pink Floyd's visuals, because they provided a synthetic trip; psychedelic London was all about pushing the boundaries. That the slides would crack under the intense heat of the projector, sometimes injuring the unlucky light technician, was apparently all part of the risk.

The group's light show had passed through several hands in the early years. Perhaps the first to project slides over the band were American fans Toni and Joel Brown, who did so in September 1966. John Marsh handled duties for a time, but Peter Wynne Wilson really helped push forward the band's visual component.

Using all sorts of tricks to create lighting effects—including stretching condoms and other materials over a slide projector—Wilson helped make Floyd's visuals as anarchic as their sound.

While most of their "underground" shows at the Marquee Club and UFO featured films being played before or after the group, the first Pink Floyd gig in which films were played *during* the group's performance appears to have come at the University of Essex on January 28, 1967.

The group's famous Fourteen-Hour Technicolor Dream (April 29, 1967) and Games for May (May 12, 1967) performances were groundbreakers. At the first show, Floyd played at dawn, as the light streaming through the Alexandra Palace's windows heightened the effect of their music.

Games for May, at Queen Elizabeth Hall, was the first Floyd appearance to feature a quadraphonic sound setup. The players had their "Arnold Layne" promotional film and other images projected onto themselves while performing. Nature noises were played from tapes, the band gave away flowers and had soap bubbles pumped into the crowd, and Roger Waters threw potatoes at a large amplified gong.

Besides the sound of vegetable on metal, what would you have heard at a Pink Floyd show in 1967? Probably not "See Emily Play," even after it became a Top 10 hit on the British charts. While the Floyd enjoyed their atypical hit single, they clung to their status as an experimental, "out there" live band. The group was more likely to play stretched-out pieces like "Pow R. Toc H.," which afforded the chance to set up a mood, solo over the chords, and glide to the finish in ten minutes or so.

Which is not to say that everyone enjoyed it. Some fans, wanting "entertainment" or the Top 40 hits they'd heard, went so far as to throw coins, garbage, or even beer mugs at the band. Roger Waters suffered a deep cut from a thrown penny at one 1967 show, and it was clear that not everyone—even in and around London—was prepared for Pink Floyd's unpredictable, sometimes chaotic stage work.

The band played several Scandinavian shows in September and found these audiences very receptive to the avant-garde pop concept. The Pink Floyd would spend a lot of time in the future courting European audiences.

But there was still this business of being a "pop star" to deal with. In late fall 1967, on the ill-fated package tour with Jimi Hendrix, the Move, et al., the Pink Floyd still attracted some screaming teenage girls who'd seen Syd and the group on TV's *Top of the Pops*. This was just one more head-busting torture for Syd Barrett.

The American tour had been no better, as Barrett was in sad shape, forcing the band to make.an early trip home and cancel the last several shows. While the reception was slightly better back in England around Christmastime, Barrett's mood and playing were not improving and the band chose to sack its leader.

1968–69: Back to the Drafting Board

With David Gilmour having replaced Syd Barrett early in the year, the now hitless and directionless Floyd had to start again from square one. They isolated their strength—their live show—and worked it, embarking over the next several years on an incredibly ambitious and both physically and mentally draining worldwide touring schedule.

While their 1968 set still included material from *The Piper at the Gates of Dawn*, PF also felt comfortable enough to play several songs—the most experimental, nonlinear ones, which speaks volumes about the direction they were headed—from the new *Saucerful of Secrets*. Since they brought their own light show with them to clubs and outdoor theatres, the Floyd often got more money than other bands.

The band returned to America in 1968 and enjoyed it more than the previous visit despite some equipment theft and hassles from more conservative-minded citizens. In addition, the group had found welcoming arms in Europe, playing the 3,500-seat Palazzetto dello Sport in Rome and Vissingen, Holland's famous Concertgebouw.

Since the musicians had no interest in, or chops for, duplicating the sound of their early discs, they instead focused on improvisation, stretched-out progressions, and the occasional use of the avant-garde (taped sound effects and speeches, early versions of what would later by called "sensurround," etc.).

Much of the group's 1969 tour was devoted to *The Man and the Journey,* an extended piece including excerpts from several previously released and yet-to-be-released Floyd songs. America did not see the Floyd in 1969, however, and missed this entire experience.

The Man and the Journey, a two-part show, attempted to build narrative from bits of various Pink Floyd songs. The first part, *The Man,* was a kind of *Days of Future Passed* done Floyd-style, without the orchestra or goofy Moody Blues lyrics.

The group used various songs and performance-art bits to travel through a typical British day, from one dawn to the next day. The players hammered and sawed to symbolize work, then were served afternoon tea on stage. The trippy "Quicksilver" was used for sleep, while "Cymbaline" signified a nightmare sequence.

The second half of the show, *The Journey,* featured less representative, science-fiction material and, apparently, some odd onstage behavior from people in costumes. One recording of *The Man and the Journey,* from September 17, 1969, makes the rounds in ROIO (Recordings of Indeterminate Origin), or bootleg, circles.

While no discrete songs came *from* the show, the project was still important to Pink Floyd's development. In the coming years, the Floyd—Roger Waters, in particular, with his lyrics—would concentrate on turning their work toward a greater overall concept rather than to stand-alone individual songs.

The Man and the Journey was also a critical stage because the band was, by 1969, already tired of playing "Astronomy Domine" and "Interstellar Overdrive." They were still having trouble coming up with enough memorable new material to supplant those two-year-old favorites, but at least in this newer piece were using material in new ways.

As befits their status as fussy sonic aeronauts, the Floyd had become more ambitious in their presentation of sound. Early in 1969 they debuted their 360-degree audio projection system (run by Wright from a joystick near his keyboard) that sent stereo sound at different times to six different speakers. This they called an "Azimuth" coordinator.

As an outgrowth of the band's avant-garde spirit and sense of humor, Pink Floyd also began using taped sounds on stage, including footsteps, birdsong, and crying babies. In addition, the band introduced tactics such as sawing wood on stage, eating, playing cards, etc. and poured money into better speakers, microphones, and amplifiers, maybe at the expense of a more outrageous light show.

While they never became a fully costume-oriented band like Genesis, the Floyd did at this point start to have friends come on stage in gorilla and dragon suits during their shows, even though these extra presences didn't do much except walk around the band. The use of minor pyrotechnics also became part of the group's live presentation.

1970–71: Hit the Road, Jack

In 1970, the group continued its ground assault on the world, playing more than a hundred shows in Europe, the U.S., and Canada. The next year, the foursome made their first trips to Asia and Australia.

Their hard work was beginning to pay off, as live shows and albums had given PF an increasingly strong reputation as *the* band to see while stoned. Pink Floyd now played larger halls, at least outside of the U.K. (But in England, in order to blanket the entire country, they still played smaller venues like the Lads Club in Norwich!)

With the increase in outdoor festivals came such jobs as the Open Air Festival in Hakone, Japan, and the Randwick Racecourse in Sydney, Australia. Their biggest show of the period was in Paris, in September 1970, at the Fête de l'Humanité, in front of an estimated audience of *five hundred thousand!*

Unfortunately, their new material wasn't providing much help to the live show. While PF often played the "Atom Heart Mother Suite," sometimes with brass section and choir, other tracks from the new album— "Fat Old Sun," "Alan's Psychedelic Breakfast," and "If"—were performed but once, and "Summer '68" not at all. Amazingly enough, by 1971, much of their stage show still featured songs released in 1969 or before (including what must have been a real snooze through Wright's "Sysyphus").

Their experimental edge came out during occasional performances of the new "Return to the Son of Nothing" (later known as "Echoes"), while occasional versions of "The Violent Sequence" from *Zabriskie Point* foretold the use of its melody in 1973's "Us and Them."

The Floyd's interest in sound—something they could control, at least at indoor shows—led them to continue to invest in good equipment. Visually, the musicians hadn't found a way to translate their vision from the clubs to the bigger stages. The varied places the band played made it difficult to have a consistent or groundbreaking visual component.

At a May 1971 gig at the Crystal Palace in London, the group introduced a huge inflatable octopus into the "lake" separating the outdoor theater's stage from the audience. Unfortunately, the volume of music at the gig, and perhaps the inflatable, killed a huge school of fish in the lake.

Late that year Pink Floyd did some of its most highbrow work, playing two gigs at the Festival of Classical Music in Montreux, Switzerland, in September, and then filming four days' worth of live material in the Roman Amphitheater at Pompeii.

A few days after that, their *Meddle* tour began in San Francisco. While Floyd filled out live shows with the side-long epic "Echoes," which helped them find their way forward as a recording act, they didn't play much else from the new album.

In spite of their reputation as a psychedelic band, not all the audience's senses were tickled at a Floyd show from this time; for instance, the band wasn't much to look at. The dusk of the Age of Aquarius brought to an end Waters & Co.'s interest in wearing attractive stage outfits. They had tried their best to look psychedelic and, later, hippied-out, through 1969 or so, but by this time the band had taken to wearing T-shirts on stage.

That lack of sartorial elegance, plus the primitive quality of their stage props and lights, made for a show that was probably more interesting with one's eyes closed . . . which contributed to the Floyd's reputation as a good band to trip to.

1972–73: Slouching toward Stardom

Continued success on the live circuit meant gigs at bigger, more prestigious, and more profitable venues, such as the Ford Theater in Detroit, the Hollywood Bowl, Carnegie Hall in New York, and the Spectrum in Philadelphia. That's not to say the Floyd enjoyed touring America

Stage left, Roger Waters attacks his Fender bass. Both he and David Gilmour played black Fenders with white pick guards on the 1973 American tour. Also take notice of Nick Mason's transparent drums. *Photo courtesy of Mark Campbell*

that much; they found Europe to be more personally comfortable and equally, if not more, hospitable to their music.

Perhaps the biggest problem the group had up to this time was the continuing lack of playable new music. Uninterested in road-testing material from *Meddle*, the band instead had spent the later part of 1971 trying out song fragments and bits that would end up on *Dark Side*. ("On the Run," for example, began as a guitar-and-drums piece.)

For their first live show of 1972, on January 20 in Sussex, of the Floyd presented the mostly formed *Dark Side* album. Differences between what was played live and what was on the album consisted of sound effects, a few lyric changes, varying tempi, and the lack of the saxophone and backing singers that would be added later.

The next month, they officially premiered the record—which wouldn't be released for almost a full year—to the press. By this time, Pink Floyd had finally dropped a few "old favorites" from the set but still played stretched-out numbers like "Set the Controls for the Heart of the Sun" and "Echoes."

During 1972, Pink Floyd played nearly a hundred shows, returning to Japan for a longer stay, visiting France (for shows backing Roland Petit's ballet troupe) and Belgium for lengthy sorties, gigging sporadically around England, and visiting North America twice more. Add to this the recording of two albums and you see that PF had a very busy year.

Of course, *Dark Side* became an immediate smash on release, and the group played the complete version of the album for all of its 1973 gigs. The band also, however, worked in several songs from *Obscured by Clouds* in its shows that year, which helped it dump even more of its pre-1970 material.

Augmented for the first time on an entire tour by outside musicians (sax player Dick Parry and three-piece backing singers Black Grass), the Floyd hammered their growing reputation home with a mammoth tour beginning in March in Madison, Wisconsin.

By this time, the band was playing the biggest or most prestigious hall in most cities it visited, filling arenas like Toronto's Maple Leaf Gardens, Radio City in New York, and huge Tampa Stadium.

During this time, the band also—as was its wont—squeezed in charity shows, playing two benefits for the homeless in London in May. The Floyd also played, in October 1973, two shows to help raise money for an old friend, Soft Machine drummer Robert Wyatt, who had fallen from a window and become paralyzed.

For the first time since 1967, Pink Floyd had a show that was as impressive visually as musically. With Arthur Max heading up the by now quite large road crew, the lights and effects really took wing. In addition to finally doing something with lighting beyond just raising and lowering a light plot on floodlight towers, the group now boasted a large disc (named "Mr. Screen") hanging behind Nick Mason's drum kit. This large disc, on which films were projected, also eventually gained trusses, lit itself, and rotated and moved.

The idea of having a plane crash into the stage during "On the Run" began this year as well; the collision first took place at the May 18, 1973 homeless benefit at Earls Court.

1974–75: Superstars

After several years of grueling road work, the Floyd stored away their suitcases for most of 1974.

They did play a seven-show French tour in June, then an indoor British tour in November and December. The latter portion of the year was spent relaxing and working on their next album. The December

14, 1974 gig at Avon would be the last time—with the exception of one festival show—that British audiences would see Pink Floyd until March 15, 1977.

The late 1974 British tour was far more difficult than one would imagine for a world-class band. The temperamental Arthur Max was proving difficult to work with, while Pete Watts, the band's longtime roadie, left the group in the grip of the drug addiction that would finally kill him in 1976. The concert sound improved, however, with new equipment and the addition of former Floyd recording engineer (*More*) Brian Humphries.

Once the by-now world-famous band finished recording *Wish You Were Here*—a project that took them far longer and caused more heartache than any of their previous albums—the Floyd set out for a nearly thirty-show, two-pronged North American tour, which began in British Columbia (one of three Canadian shows) on April 8. After covering the West Coast, the band took May off and came back in June to do the east.

For this tour, the band used more explosives than before and had new films shot, some including animation by Gerald Scarfe (who would go on to collaborate with Roger Waters on *The Wall*). These worked out far better than the band's new gimmick, a pyramid made of tarpaulin that had the nasty habit of blowing around in a heavy wind. The pyramid was soon discarded, allowed to blow into a stadium parking lot where loony fans tore it to pieces.

Their one European show of 1975 came on July 5 at Knebworth Park, north of London. For this huge outdoor gig, the Floyd, who usually worked alone, were joined by a rather strange set of supporting acts: the Steve Miller Band, Captain Beefheart, Roy Harper, Linda Lewis, Graham Chapman (from *Monty Python's Flying Circus*), and emcee John Peel.

The band's 1975 North American tour left them little time to prepare for this show, and despite a huge quadraphonic sound system and out-standing effects from designer Bill Harkin (who had a sixty-foot cable rigged up so that the "On the Run" airplane could fly over the audience before crashing into the stage), the show was rough.

Even before the Floyd came on, Knebworth was visited by clichéd "rock festival" problems. Roy Harper, added to the concert lineup at the Floyd's urging, threw a tantrum backstage and destroyed a trailer. The press were dissuaded from coming backstage (they eventually took their revenge in print). A fight broke out in the crowd during Beefheart's performance. The crowd also had a hard time hearing Lewis and Harper's sets due to poor sound. Finally, the skies were gray and misty for most of the day.

Floyd's set had its own troubles. A plan to have two RAF planes buzz the crowd at a preplanned moment went awry when the band delayed its start. During the opener, "Raving and Drooling," one of the band's speaker columns blew out. The resulting repairs and adjustments pushed Wright's electronic keyboards out of tune. This disaster led him to walk off stage at one point; he was forced to use a Farfisa organ instead of the

Pink Floyd recorded live
at Ivor Wynne Stadium
Hamilton, Ontario Canada
June 28, 1975

Dave Gilmour pictured on the back cover of a bootleg recording of a gig in the band's June 1975 Canadian tour. He is wearing a Montreal Canadiens hockey jersey, a sartorial choice that probably didn't go over so well, since the band played in English-speaking Ontario.

Hammond organ and his synthesizers for much of the gig, which altered the sound of the songs.

Waters' vocals were not sharp this day, which may have been due to the fact that many of the speakers and monitors ordered had arrived just the day before, which forced the sound technicians to improvise.

The audience members, however, seemed to enjoy the music, perhaps because most of them were fully baked (partially by the sun). Lights, smoke machines, and the doomed airplane gave visual flash, but the group did not feel it had performed well. The press, whom PF did not like (and who in turn did not like the band) agreed, administering a pillorying in the newspapers.

This rather dispiriting event was the last show that Pink Floyd performed for nearly eighteen months. It was also the last time the group played "Echoes" or *Dark Side of the Moon* as a four-piece band.

1977: Flesh Wounds

The release of *Animals* meant that Pink Floyd would undertake another world tour, this one (titled *In the Flesh*) the most spectacular but in some ways most painful of all.

Shows in mammoth stadiums were the order of the day. Beginning a twenty-nine-date European excursion in Germany, the group played Dortmund, Frankfurt, and Berlin before moving to Vienna, Zurich, Rotterdam, Antwerp, Paris, and Munich, then returned to Blighty for a series of shows at two venues: Wembley Pool, which hosted five gigs, and Stafford's New Bingley Hall, which opened for four.

From there, the group took three weeks before crossing the ocean, beginning a twenty-city, twenty-six-date North American jaunt in Miami on April 22. Pink Floyd played to more than eighty thousand at Chicago's Soldier Field, and filled other sports arenas such as Anaheim's "Big A," Atlanta's Omni, Cleveland Stadium, and the Boston Garden. The band then played a triumphant series of shows at New York's Madison Square Garden.

The use of a flying inflatable pig on the front cover of *Animals* had given the group, and its designers, the idea of using balloons as parts of their stage show. In addition to a dazzling array of lights and film projections, this tour boasted several inflatables: a Botero-looking nuclear family, cars, a refrigerator, and various pigs fitted with parachutes. Since many of these shows took place outdoors, the stage was covered with large umbrellas that helped protect the band from rain.

In New York, PF's four-night stand at Madison Square Garden was promoted by a parade featuring inflatable sheep and pigs.

For the first time since 1972, the Floyd did not use female backing singers on this tour. They were, however, augmented by sax player Dick Parry and guitarist Snowy White, who had appeared on *Animals* (you can learn more about them in "Make Them Do What You Want Them To"). White's presence was deemed necessary in order to help emphasize in concert the guitar-heavy focus of the new material.

Loath now to repeat old triumphs, the band had dropped most of the *Dark Side* material from the show, choosing instead to play the entire new album and all of *Wish You Were Here*. Pink Floyd did nod to its greatest triumph by playing "Money" and/or "Us and Them" as an encore.

This tour helped Roger Waters clarify his longtime feelings about the separation between rock star and audience, and fully form his vision of rock and roll concerts as warlike events.

The emphasis on playing hugely profitable shows at sports stadiums meant that the music was now second to the entire spectacle. The super-loud volume, explosions, and cheering crowds paying no attention to musical subtlety disgusted Waters in particular, although the remainder of the group wasn't overjoyed with the circumstances either.

Occasional sound and lighting problems beset the band, and Waters often shouted down fans who would scream, set off fireworks, or jump up and down even during the quiet songs.

As a result of various strains, Waters flipped in Montreal during the final show of the tour on July 6. In front of nearly eighty thousand people at Olympic Stadium, Waters egged on a crazed fan for most of the show. He drew his admirer closer and closer. When the fan climbed a fence separating stage from audience, Waters leaned over and spit on him. Gilmour was so disgusted by the turn of events that he refused to join the rest of the group for the encore.

This was Pink Floyd's final live show for two and a half years.

1980–81: Tearing Down the Wall

Many fans and critics consider *The Wall* to be Pink Floyd's crowning achievement. The live show concocted to stage the album, however, was so

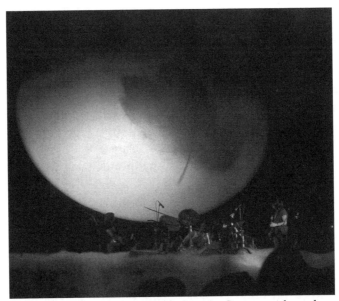

This shot, from a January 1977 show in Germany, shows how advanced and atmospheric Pink Floyd's live show had become in just a few years. The guitarist on the left is Snowy White; Dave Gilmour is out of view.   *Photo courtesy of Steve Leventhal*

complex that the band limited performances to just four venues and thirty-one appearances, so most fans never got to see it.

The album was first performed on February 7, 1980 in Los Angeles. It remained at the Sports Arena for six more nights. The entire entourage then moved to Uniondale, New York's Nassau Coliseum in February for five shows. After a long break, the band did six August presentations at Earls Court in London.

The following year, the whole kit and caboodle was transported to Dortmund, Germany's Westfallenhall Convention Center for eight nights, then went back to Earls Court for five more gigs that marked the final time the four-man Pink Floyd played a full show. Rumors have it that these shows were done, at least in part, to provide live footage for the movie version of *The Wall*, but the footage was scrapped.

The entire album—and *only* the entire album—was played at the shows, along with "What Shall We Do Now?," which had been left off *The Wall* (though the song's lyrics were still printed on the inner sleeve).

The recording of *The Wall* had been terribly traumatic for Pink Floyd. A stressed Waters had kicked the underachieving Wright out of the band,

Mason's marriage was crumbling, and Gilmour was frozen out of much of the album's creative process.

Wright *was* kept on as a work-for-hire musician to play the live shows, perhaps to help Waters deal with his guilt for firing the keyboardist, but more likely to stop the media from concentrating on a "Pink Floyd split" story rather than the *Wall* tour itself. In fact, in one of the best-kept secrets in rock annals, the press was not made aware that Wright was out of the band until 1983.

In addition to a stage set featuring movable rooms and a cardboard brick wall that was built up during the show, fully completed at intermission, and blown apart at the end, Pink Floyd went over and above other rock acts' shows, providing more eye candy.

Grotesque state-of-the-art Gerald Scarfe inflatables hung around the hall. Laser lights and fireworks (which caused drapes to catch fire on opening night) provided shock and awe. Animated images, again from Scarfe, thrown up on Mr. Screen showed hammers, judges, and fat, psychopathic wives.

The *Wall* shows also featured an entire "shadow band," clad in gray, who took the stage to start off the show while wearing life masks of the "real" group members. This technique was apparently utilized to emphasize the relative facelessness and public anonymity of Pink Floyd.

The "shadow band," which backed up the four-man Floyd throughout the show, featured Snowy White on guitar, onetime Gilmour bandmate Willie Wilson on drums, Andy Bown on bass, and Pete Woods on keyboards (veteran British session guitarist Andy Roberts replaced White for the 1981 shows). Four backup singers (Joe Chemay, Jon Joyce, Stan Farber, and Jim Haas) also augmented the band. These extra musicians allowed Waters to wander around the stage in his role as "Pink."

Gilmour was the tour's musical director, which meant that he was responsible for keeping the whole show going, cuing musical moments to stage directions, as well as playing and singing "Comfortably Numb" from a perch atop the wall.

Fans heard the music in unmatched concert fidelity; in addition to the already grand speaker system installed for all the shows, the band had speakers placed underneath the stands, which helped to convey various stereo and surround-sound effects, dialogue, and extra-musical noises.

Gilmour, perhaps trying to shed his old "scruffy hippie" image, had cut his hair to reasonable new-wave length. For much of the show, the band wore vaguely military-themed outfits, while Waters wore a T-shirt bearing the number one for much of the tour. (Perhaps this is the way the bassist and singer reminded himself that he was in charge.)

During the shows, band members made little contact; they could barely stand each other at this point. They had separate trailers, separate after-show parties, and separate entourages.

1987–89: Monsters of Rock

In the eight years since the Floyd's last live performance, the legend of their concerts had only grown. When Gilmour and Mason reorganized the band to record *A Momentary Lapse of Reason*, they were surprised at the size of the halls they could sell out on the album's concomitant tour.

The first leg of what seems to have been a never-ending tour began and ended in Canada, stretching from September through December 1987 and including sixty shows all over North America.

The venues were huge, including indoor basketball arenas like Atlanta's Omni (where the group was filmed) and the Rosemont Horizon outside Chicago, outdoor mammoths such as Denver's Mile High Stadium, Miami's Orange Bowl, and Cleveland's Municipal Stadium, and indoor behemoths like the Brendan Byrne Arena, the Hoosier Dome, and B.C. Place.

While that might have been enough for some bands, Gilmour & Co. were out for total domination, which required actually going *around the world*. So after five weeks off, the entourage geared it all up again starting in January 1988.

The Floyd flew to New Zealand to start the next leg. They played nine shows in Sydney, Australia, then eight more at Melbourne's Tennis Centre before journeying to Japan, where they did two shows at Budokan.

Following their triumphant Japanese appearances, they went back to America for more shows at ballparks and arenas. Then it was east to Europe for an especially crazy hop, filling football stadia in various countries (in France, they filmed portions of the *Delicate Sound of Thunder* tour document).

Finally, the bedraggled ensemble went back *again* to America for the end of the ninety-seven-show slog that, with a month-long break between trips to Japan and the United States, engaged musicians, staff, and crew for the first eight months of 1988. The final shows of the tour, at Nassau Coliseum (site of *Wall* shows), were also filmed.

The tour was so successful, breaking all sorts of box-office records, that the ensemble hit the road again in 1989 for the *Another Lapse* tour, a forty-show Europe-only jaunt. Playing twice at the Palace of Versailles and doing five shows at Moscow's Olympic Stadium were obvious highlight for the Floyd.

A worldwide satellite TV broadcast from Venice on July 15, 1989—the penultimate show of the twenty-two-month tour—*would* have been a highlight had the necessary logistics been worked out beforehand.

The band played a free concert for an estimated two hundred thousand fans from a boat sailing in a lagoon. Unfortunately, the volume of the show was said to have damaged buildings, and fans overran the city and slept in Venice's streets. The Italian army had to be called in to clean up the mess.

When it became clear that the city was at fault for not supplying the promised security and facilities, the entire government of Venice resigned.

By all accounts, the concert visuals were awesome. Lighting designer Marc Brickman received kudos for his excellent work with lasers and a rotating series of lights that moved around the stage.

Plans from set designer Paul Staples to open the show with the band emerging from a cricket ground built into the stage, proved a bit too hard to manage, but to compensate for this, the band built an even larger "Mr. Screen," and inflatable pigs, planes, and beds flew over the audience. The live sound was louder and of higher quality, with stronger speakers and improved technology that sent surround-sound effects around the concert halls.

Unfortunately, PF could not resist the urge to go "big" with the music as well, hiring a five-piece ensemble of session players and enough backup singers to make the audience forget that part of Pink Floyd's magic was that as a four-man band, it was capable of *sounding* like an orchestra.

This version of Pink Floyd made a slick, technically proficient but decidedly modern, clattering sound that lacked the smoothness or subtlety of the group's recordings, but certainly could fill up a big hall. Gary Wallis, the percussionist, had among the biggest racks of shakers, whizbangs, and dingdongs ever seen on a stage.

This twelve- or thirteen-person ensemble (depending on the number of backing singers) played a range of material from the Floyd's career, including most of the recent *Momentary Lapse of Reason* as well as "Shine On You Crazy Diamond," "One of These Days," chunks of *The Wall*, and the biggest hits from *Dark Side*.

1993–94: The Final Push

One-off charity concerts in 1990 and 1993 kept Gilmour, Mason, and Wright and their session pals in the performing habit, and the pre-sales of 1994's *The Division Bell* presaged another successful tour. This one went a staggering 110 shows and included new stops like Mexico City, Prague, and Ames, Iowa.

The venues again listed toward the huge: Arrowhead Stadium in Kansas City, Olympic Stadium in Montreal, Chicago's Soldier Field, DeKuip in Rotterdam, Barcelona's Montjuic Olympic Stadium, the enormous Cinecitta Studio grounds in Rome, and Strahov Stadion in Prague, a nine-soccer-field ground that was once the world's largest stadium in use and is now the training ground for Sparta FC and the Czech national team. (The Rolling Stones have played at Strahov as well.)

The band, including five extra musicians and four backing singers, played another assortment of new material and greatest hits. Pink Floyd also performed the full *Dark Side of the Moon*, for the first time in more than fifteen years, on several occasions. Nick Mason notes in *Inside Out* that the players could not use earpieces to monitor the sound from the stage, as the technology wasn't quite perfected, so they had to lug around huge monitor speakers.

Pink Floyd's stage set for this series of concerts was designed by Mark Fisher to resemble the Hollywood Bowl, and the usual effects were in place, including towers surrounding Mr. Screen that raised protective "rain curtains" over the musicians for outdoor shows. The large and complicated stage set resembled a labyrinth, which led to fears of *Spinal Tap*–like moments of confusion between various alcoves, trapdoors, and hallways.

Equally absurd was that this tour involved a sponsor. Volkswagen was brought on to help defray touring costs and ensure a greater profit. While car freak Nick Mason surely enjoyed touring the VW factory and driving prototypes, the decision to take on a sponsor was interesting for a band that had gone into paroxysms of guilt over the French soft drink

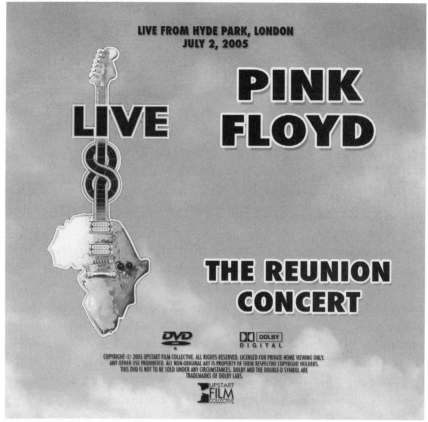

LIVE FROM HYDE PARK, LONDON
JULY 2, 2005

PINK FLOYD

LIVE 8

THE REUNION CONCERT

DVD   DOLBY DIGITAL

UPSTART FILM COLLECTIVE

While Live 8's primary goal was to raise money to fight starvation, it also achieved an aim many thought was nearly as difficult: bringing together Pink Floyd, at least for a day.

magazine ad they had done some twenty years previously (see "And Down the Hole We Fall").

Peter Wynne Wilson, who hadn't worked with the Floyd since the late 1960s, was hired by Marc Brickman to re-create his old liquid light projections, though, according to Mason, "technical advances actually made it more difficult to recreate the feel of the originals." The band also spent money on new films to accompany certain songs.

In another example of their dry British humor, PF spoofed the disco ball phenomenon by having one big ball open up to reveal a huge laser-light unit. The crowd, predictably, went wild.

"Wild" was also a good description of the North American show schedule, which had to be worked around World Cup soccer matches. At one point, the tour progressed from Toronto to Washington, D.C. to Chicago to Detroit to New Jersey over a ten-day period.

The apparently last full Pink Floyd shows ever staged were a fourteen-gig stand at Earls Court in London from July 13 to 29, 1994. These gigs were benefits for several charities, including Amnesty International, and one of them was filmed to help fill out the *P*U*L*S*E* tour DVD.

And Now?

The original foursome—with several sessioneers in tow—performed at Live 8 in 2005, perhaps capping the band's history as a four-man unit. Three of them, minus Waters, played together at a Syd Barrett memorial show, but there has been no serious talk of a Pink Floyd reunion.

In a Gary Graff piece published in *Billboard* on August 13, 2008, Gilmour averred, "The thought of going back to Pink Floyd just doesn't interest me." Four weeks hence, Rick Wright passed away, making the question rather academic.

A moment many never thought they'd see: David Gilmour, Roger Waters, Nick Mason, and Rick Wright reuniting for Live 8 on July 2, 2005, at London's Hyde Park.

Photo by Mick Hutson/Redferns

Ten Landmark European Pink Floyd Shows

- December 3, 1966: London (The "Psychodelphia vs. Ian Smith" Zimbabwe benefit)
- September 9, 1967: Arhus, Denmark (Their first full gig outside the United Kingdom)
- June 25, 1968: London (The first Hyde Park free concert)
- April 14, 1969: London ("More Furious Madness from the Massed Gadgets of Auximenes")
- June 28, 1970: Rotterdam, Netherlands (Kralingen Festival; footage from this show was used in the film Stamping Ground)
- June 17, 1981: London (The last four-man Pink Floyd concert)
- June 21, 1988: Versailles, France (Pink Floyd plays at the Palace of Versailles)
- June 3, 1989: Moscow (The first major Western rock gig in Russia)
- July 15, 1989: Venice (Satellite TV broadcast)
- October 29, 1994: London (The final Pink Floyd concert, not counting Live 8)

5

I Was There—
Mark Campbell

The 1972 and 1973 Tours Through a Fan's Eyes

by Mark Campbell

I became a Pink Floyd fan in late 1971 when I heard "One of These Days" on the radio. I quickly ran out and bought their *Meddle* LP and was impressed by the lush production and sonic effects,

A wide shot of the Floyd in Chicago, 1973. Note an early, smallish version of the band's image projection device, "Mr. Screen," above Nick Mason. This was the height of rock-show technology at the time. *Photo courtesy of Mark Campbell*

especially on "Echoes." Their '72 U.S. tour brought them to Chicago's Auditorium Theater in April and I was in attendance.

The small theater setting and Floyd's 360-degree sound configuration made for a memorable performance. Before the show, a free program, entitled *Eclipse: A Piece for Assorted Lunatics*, was distributed. We didn't know it then, but we were being treated to most of *Dark Side of the Moon* almost a year before it would be released in the U.S.

The now-familiar spoken word segments, the goofy giggling, and other *Dark Side* effects seemed to come from behind, above, and all around us, due to the band's high-tech (for 1972) sound setup.

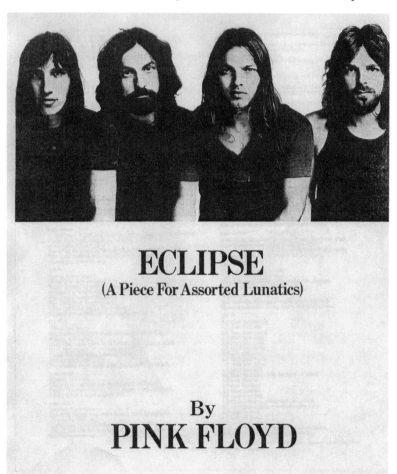

Pink Floyd distributed this brochure to fans attending the 1972 American tour. Included were the lyrics to the "Eclipse" suite, a project the band soon re-titled *Dark Side of the Moon*.   *Photo courtesy of Mark Campbell*

Following the *Dark Side* set, they performed several more current and past tunes, including "Echoes" and "Careful with That Axe, Eugene." The opera-house setting and superb acoustics made this concert, one of the first I ever attended, truly unforgettable.

The following year, in spring 1973, Pink Floyd returned to Chicago on their *Dark Side of the Moon* tour. This time, due to the band's increase in album sales and popularity, they played the much larger Chicago Amphitheater. I rushed out early and got great seats, in the eighth row. During the early '70s, little, if any security was used at concerts; Andy Frain ushers were present, but their primary role was to help you find your seat.

As a result, during the show, I was able to walk up to the very front of the stage, which was no more than four feet high, and take photos of the band. I captured a few excellent individual close-ups of Gilmour and Waters, as well as some decent shots of the entire stage from my seat.

What is striking about the photos is how little equipment is used and, by today's standards, how sparse their stage looks. In 1973, however, that stage set looked positively futuristic and extremely high-tech to us, especially the eclipsing sun device that rose up from behind Nick Mason's drum kit. The set list featured most of *Dark Side* along with other Floyd tunes from earlier LPs, but what I remember most is our close proximity to the band and the effects: the dazzling lighting, the surround sound, and that smoking, glowing, eclipsing sun.

Mark Campbell grew up in Chicago, listening to Top 40 radio in the late '60s and underground FM in the early '70s. He spent most of the next two decades in senior marketing positions at ABC Radio and Westwood One. Mark presently owns Marketing Spark, a marketing consulting agency in Chicago.

6

It's Been Just Like You're Gone

What Are Ten Great Syd Barrett Moments?

R oger Barrett was raised in an upper-middle-class setting with a classical British education and love and indulgence from his family. In his teens, he felt a strong pull toward the beatnik lifestyle. Given his artistic bent, in another time or place he might have become a painter, a professor, or a traveling acoustic performer.

Instead, Roger became "Syd," and fell headlong into—and helped create as well as personify—the swirling mass of culture that became psychedelic London. Influenced by beat music, blues, folk, high art, literature, science, the mystic East, and of course drugs, his brilliant imagination created, in a few short years, a body of work featuring striking highs and painful lows. Here are some of Barrett's high points.

"Candy and a Currant Bun" (1967)

Originally titled "Let's Roll Another One," this early live favorite—perhaps written during or in tribute to his idyllic dope-smoking Cambridge days—was a natural to be recorded in February 1967 at London's Sound Techniques studio. Joe Boyd produced the session, creating a delightfully gauzy, sticky sound the aural equivalent of chewy candy.

Re-titled as something a tad less drug-oriented after the band's management apparently received disapproving tut-tuts from BBC radio bluenoses, "Candy and a Currant Bun" featured Barrett (said to be angry at having to bowdlerize his lyrics) still toeing a fine line. He showed here a swaggering, macho attitude absent from the rest of his oeuvre and, in fact, absent in general from Floyd's decidedly unsexy career.

This upbeat celebration of girl-watching on a psunny psychedelic British psummer's day benefited from a representative Rick Wright solo and Syd's fast and furious guitar playing. Stretch the solo section out to five minutes or so and you have a pretty good idea of the band's live mastery circa 1966.

"Candy" wound up on the B-side of "Arnold Layne" (in fact, Wright's oft-maligned "Turkish Delight" solos for the two songs are nearly interchangeable). Even though it's great, this jet-propelled number wasn't even included on the 1971 *Relics* "rarities" compilation and remains unjustly obscure.

"Interstellar Overdrive" (1967)

Coming to life as a mishearing of the main riff from Love's 1966 garage classic "My Little Red Book" (itself a recasting—to the disgust of composer Burt Bacharach—of Manfred Mann's jazzier version), Barrett's supersonic spaceship guitar-riff-with-added-jam-session "Interstellar Overdrive" stands as the best recorded example of the Floyd's landmark improvisational attack.

Producer Norman Smith, bound by a need to capture a "commercial" product for EMI as well as a desire to allow "his" new group room to create and define its own sound, gave Barrett and the other Floyds plenty of leash, having them overdub an entire second performance directly *over* their first, then mixing the takes together. Such a recording strategy was quite revolutionary then, and remains so now.

While this process produced some anarchic sound, the cacophony wasn't absolute; the four Floyds were too good at reading each other, and too sympathetic in playing, to totally lose the thread.

All of Syd's stars were shining brightly on this recording. Using his steel slide, and his echo and reverb units, he coaxed supersonic bleeps, ear-charring feedback, and echoes of deep space from his guitar. The heights of psychedelic axe mastery he reached on this song have rarely been equaled.

Wright's organ wavered in and out, providing flying-saucer squeaks, atonal Eastern runs, and ghostly rumblings of passing asteroids. Mason, as usual, played off the others, providing spark when needed and simply stopping at times. His double-tracked drum roll, signaling the song's

Syd Barrett's 1965 book of illustrations and collages was excerpted for the fortieth-anniversary release of *The Piper at the Gates of Dawn*.

conclusion, is one of the piece's highlights. Finally, Waters' muscular bass teams with Barrett's guitar to drive the song; Floyd's future leader was already qualified to play elegant and dynamically interesting space-rock.

Barrett and Smith then mixed together the two complete performances, with Syd at times said to have simply moved the volume controls up and down to make pretty designs with his hands.

"Astronomy Domine" (1967)

While "Echoes," from 1971's *Meddle*, is known for moving the band's environment from outer space into the water, it shouldn't be forgotten that Syd Barrett, in the first song off the first Pink Floyd album, invoked both the stars and the "icy waters underground."

The first voice heard on a Pink Floyd LP is actually that of manager Peter Jenner, reading an astronomy text into a megaphone. The eerie effect perhaps evokes a distant space station's communicating with an astronaut. Barrett's clipped guitar and Wright's organ mirror the sound of an engine. Syd then picks out a note-bending riff and plows through a strange chord progression (E to E-flat).

Syd Barrett, with mirrored Fender Telecaster and *de rigueur* satin shirt, in late 1966.
Photo by Andrew Whittuck/Redferns

Barrett then quiets his guitar, allowing him to harmonize with Wright on the odd, hallucinatory lyrics, which invoke shades of green and blue: the colors of nature, the forest, the sky, and the sea. The key line in the song is "Floating down, the sounds resound around the icy waters underground," which seems attractive and sensual but actually lays out a scary picture of frozen waters in which few things can survive.

The wordplay is rich, offering no concrete meaning but a series of fascinating images that the spectral, spare music complements perfectly. Mason's aggressive drums serve as a lead instrument during the verses.

Like many Floyd songs from this period, "Astronomy Domine" featured a solo section that served, in concert, as a jumping-off point for a lengthy improvisation. On record, however, the quartet's playing is reserved, leaving room for the listener to imagine sounds as well as hear what is actually there.

The shimmering, echoing cymbal and guitar beginning at around 1:40 create some of the most psychedelic moments of sound ever put on tape by anyone, and the remainder of the understated but evocative instrumental section lays out the ground rules for a new kind of rock music.

Barrett's wild guitar work in the second half of the instrumental section was as innovative in its own way as that of contemporary stars

Eric Clapton or Jimmy Page. Syd was more interested in sound and the exploration of noise than the other two traditionally blues-based players, and wasn't afraid to play "bad" notes if they were part of his journey. The rest of the band, more traditional in their ways but conscious of the results coming from Syd's unusual process, followed his lead.

The sheer nerve of Pink Floyd's playing on *The Piper at the Gates of Dawn*, and especially that of Barrett, is virtually unmatched in rock and roll. Has any debut album featured a more adventurous palette?

"Take Up Thy Stethoscope and Walk" (1967)

This blues-based piece was actually written by Roger Waters, and from the get-go it indicates the bassist's rhythm-based approach (as well as his sarcastic anti-authority lyrical bent).

While it isn't a great *song*, "Stethoscope" isn't as dispensable as some critics have claimed. The lyrics are rather humorous, if odd, and the aggressive structure allows for the kind of free-form soloing that helped Floyd define its 1966 underground attack.

Barrett rarely played purely blues-inflected leads with the Floyd, but here you can witness the basic R&B influence in his guitar style during the vocal sections as he bends notes and leaves space around the vocals.

The lead guitar work during the improvisation section has little to do with the blues, however, and is especially intense. Playing a lightning-fast cascade of notes perhaps evocative of ace surf guitarist Dick Dale flying on a bad dose of biker speed, Syd whistles through the E major backing, using echo and tremolo to make his Telecaster sound even more astral.

The furious attack that Barrett and Nick Mason conjured transformed Waters' song into a brutal attack that must have been fairly amazing to see and hear in person. It's incendiary even on plastic.

"Lucifer Sam" (1967)

Melding the best of the blues, surf music, and British beat into one psychedelically wrapped package is tough work. But Roger Barrett didn't just accomplish this in one *song*, he did it in one *guitar riff*.

Barrett's guitar line for "Lucifer Sam" is so basic, so pure, and so catchy that you could believe it's always existed . . . but he had to invent it. His propulsive riff also provided a good structure over which Rick Wright could solo between the verses.

In addition to Barrett's economical guitar work, he also uses his voice to lend a sense of dread to a simple tale of his girlfriend's perhaps fiendish cat. The music sounds suitably demonic in its minor-chord gloom, but still chugs along and rocks harder than most other British pop of the time.

Syd's vocals are charged with emotion and he enunciates to emphasize both sound and content (*"Jennifer Gentle . . . you're a witch!"*), approaching affectation but not quite overdoing it. His frustrated cry in the chorus, in which he exclaims that there's just *something* weird about that feline, is both beguiling and troubling.

Following two intense verses and choruses, the solo section begins with Roger Waters' quick, cello-like bass runs. Barrett then brashly interrupts with slashing, stop-start chords before ceding again to Waters. Syd leaves space in what he's doing rather than playing quickly, and almost spastically, as he did on "Stethoscope."

"Flaming" (1967)

Another one of Barrett's fully unconventional but indescribably catchy pop numbers, "Flaming" stretches the idea of "catchy pop number" to include a full instrumental dropout; wide-eyed, drooling acid-trip lyrics; tinkling bells; tack piano; and a completely unconventional structure.

Our main character, perhaps Barrett himself, is lying stoned, by himself, on a blanket in nature, imaging himself sitting on a unicorn, communing with flowers, and traveling through space by telephone (oh, the simple joys of 1960s sci-fi!). One especially charming and fascinating facet of "Flaming" is Barrett's completely guileless delivery, which lends a palpable innocence to a narrative that a majority of the adult world would have found completely intolerable at the time.

"Flaming" is one of Barrett's greatest lyrics, serving as a crystalline description of the dreamy, sunshiny, mind-manifesting side of the psychedelic experience. Norman Smith's sensitive production features little sounds emerging from every corner of both the mono and stereo mixes.

It is far from the most famous or most oft-covered song on *Piper,* and "Flaming," with its pure pop smarts and flair for light melody, seems to exist in its own universe; it is difficult to imagine another artist doing much more with it, though it has been covered by avant-garde electronic artists Niki Mono and Nikolas Klau as well as played at gigs by 1980s American popsters Let's Active.

"Jugband Blues" (1968)

In the wake of British Top 10 hit "See Emily Play," this Barrett-penned track, recorded in October 1967, was briefly considered as a single; a spooky, psychedelic promotional film was even produced. Barrett's increasing instability, though, led the rest of the group—and management—to moot the idea of promoting "Jugband Blues."

While "Jugband" didn't make the cut as a 45, the band's feelings about Syd didn't stop them from using the song to pad their thin second album, *A Saucerful of Secrets,* despite Barrett having already been ousted from Pink Floyd. "Jugband Blues" was so strong, and the group so short of material, that including the song seemed a natural regardless of the awkward circumstances.

In retrospect, it's hard to see the lyrics as anything but a revelation of self-knowledge by a man slipping inexorably and tragically into the caverns of his own mind. In one short verse, Barrett acknowledges that he's "not here," acknowledges gratitude that his old shoes have been tossed out, and admits he doesn't even know who's written the very song he's singing. Imagine what he must have been feeling.

The band follows him along as best they can through the rambling verse and chorus, then a Salvation Army band–led instrumental break lends the number even more music-hall authenticity. The silly cacophony fits "Jugband Blues" like one of Syd's snug nylon paisley shirts.

(A BBC recording of the song featuring Barrett is even slower and more funereal, with the brass band replaced by the Floyd themselves playing kazoos in perfunctorily jolly fashion. Except that the entire enterprise is nothing approaching jolly.)

Following the brass interlude and an organ/guitar freakout, the Salvation Army reappears (for this section, Barrett apparently told the musicians to play whatever they wanted). The track then cuts to silence.

Singing lightly over Wright's spectral organ, Syd—perhaps unsure of what he's doing, perhaps knowing full well that he's messing about—plays

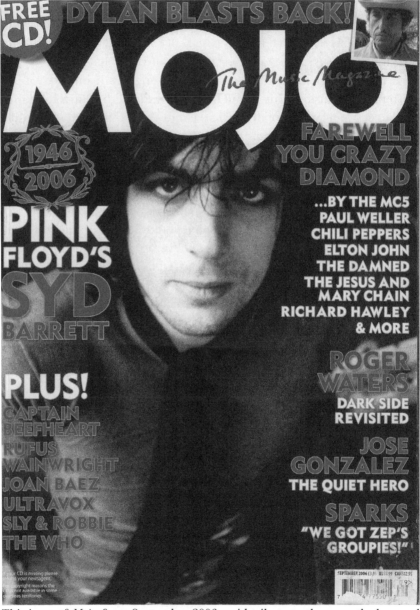

This issue of *Mojo*, from September 2006, paid tribute to the recently deceased Syd Barrett.

three different chord progressions on his guitar in the last four lines, singing with airy disconnection some of the saddest words in rock.

"Vegetable Man" (1968)

Placing a song never officially released by Pink Floyd on this list may not be quite fair, as the casual fan must make a concerted effort in order to hear it. But in this case, that effort is worth the trouble.

If Barrett ever made a *happy*-sounding song capturing his state of existential confusion, this is it. The jaunty musical backing combines the band's harsh, furious British psychedelic attack with a Kinks-like music-hall feel present in some of his other work.

Lyrically, however, "Vegetable Man" is as disoriented as "Jugband Blues"; Barrett describes his trendy psychedelic dandy pop-star look—his shoes, his clothes, his watch, his haircut—seeing himself only in terms of the objects that decorate him . . . but there's no "there" there.

A willing participant in the LSD scene of London, but also someone looking for a sane voice but surrounded mostly by opportunists, Syd by this time was quite aware of the vacant stare in his eyes, the growing corkscrews in his brain, his lack of real identity.

The track, among the last, if not *the* last, the Floyd recorded with Syd, sounds good, if unfinished, and was even considered as a single for a short time. Unfortunately, the rest of the band, perhaps feeling with some guilt that the song's narrative is just too painful to contemplate, has vetoed its release.

Come on. Put the darn thing *out* already, guys; it's great, it tells his story well, and it's no disservice to his memory. Or to that of his heirs. Or, for that matter, to the rest of us who'd like to hear it in full fidelity.

"Octopus" (1970)

While this *Madcap Laughs* track is Barrett's most straightforward solo rock song, even here he's fooling around with rhythms. The lyrics, which may be a goodbye song to a love interest (or a rejection of "civilization" for the pleasures of nature), are brilliant in places, but his voice is ragged and has trouble traversing the difficult melody.

In the second verse, Syd's voice drops to a lower register as he describes his happiness at being "lost in the wood," falling in volume as

Many photographers and interviewers ambushed Syd Barrett at his home in Cambridge, hoping to get some dirt on the former Floyd guitarist. This 1979 photo shows Barrett appearing far more "normal" than any scandal-sheet editor would have desired.   *Photo by Janette Beckman/Redferns*

well. Before long, however, he's returned to his high-register yelp: "The madcap laughed at the man on the border!"

A rockabilly guitar solo follows over some oddly timed backing, but Barrett's playing never resolves, instead simply fading back into another chorus.

Syd's lyrics in the post-solo verses are fascinating, but he delivers them in a near-shout, making it nearly impossible to hear the detailed text without assistance. The desperate, frustrated last verse references seeping seas, tropical winds, drones, squeaking doors, and, finally, isolation.

As the song began, so it ends: with an out-of-rhythm rhythm section fading out, leaving just a simple acoustic strum. It's hard to listen to too much of Syd's solo career, because of the intensity of such moments, but "Octopus" is about the best of his post-Floyd albums' chaotic pop-rocking material.

"Golden Hair" (1970)

Writing original music to a James Joyce poem probably would not have occurred to a lower-class or middle-class British musician, say an Ozzy Osbourne or even a John Lennon. But Roger Barrett's classical education and sensitive raising, and perhaps the courage of certain pharmaceuticals, led him to feel he could walk the path of the greats of the past.

Joyce's lovely ode to a classic blonde standing, unattainable, in her windowed tower served as appropriate material for the melancholy Barrett of *The Madcap Laughs*. Draping a sensitive acoustic guitar around the poem like a gauzy scarf, Barrett intones the lyrics with unsteady grace. A stately, quiet organ part and soft, rich vibraphone (both, perhaps, played by Rick Wright) add to the murky, midnight feel.

The effect is a singular mood befitting the song's gentle beauty. "Golden Hair" is Barrett's greatest solo track and a suitable memorial not to his mental illness, but to his ability to create beauty even in the depths of confusion and misery.

The most conventional—really, the *only* conventional—song on *Madcap*, "Golden Hair" was placed on side two directly before the album's most jarring number, the manic "Long Gone." This track ordering may not have been *purposely* done to reflect Barrett's changeable moods, but then again it might have been.

7

Count Me In for the Ride

What Are Ten Great David Gilmour Moments?

T ry as he might, David Gilmour just could not will himself into becoming a great songwriter. Despite his hard work, he couldn't write lyrics consistently, and worked much better in tandem—building music with Waters and Wright from the ground up—than on his own.

Gilmour's real strengths are as a singer, arranger, and guitarist; these abilities he has in spades. He created a signature sound informed by folk and blues but capable of epic sweeps, mournful, chiming simplicity, and inventive acoustic rhythms. Gilmour's oeuvre as Pink Floyd's guitarist includes classic moments—the four-note riff of "Shine On You Crazy Diamond," the corrosive playing of "Run Like Hell," the string-strangling squalls of "Echoes"—that belong in any encyclopedia of 1970s rock guitar highlights.

Caring much more about the sound of records than Waters, Mason, and even, eventually, Wright, the precise and very musical Gilmour carefully crafted the Floyd's mid-period and late albums into feasts for those who crave luscious sounds and invest time in careful, repeated listening.

Finally, his ability to deliver Waters' most paranoid, angry, depressed, or troubled lyrics with tunefulness and a sense of humanity gave Pink Floyd's work a much-needed spoonful of sugar. Is it a surprise that the group's music became somewhat more difficult to listen to once Roger Waters began singing more?

Here are ten of Gilmour's greatest performances.

"Corporal Clegg" (1968)

Upon joining Pink Floyd, Gilmour had to quickly acclimate himself to recording for a "name band" in fancy Abbey Road Studios. If this weren't enough of a head-smasher, the eccentric Norman Smith was manning the controls, and his bandmates were given, at the time, to recording cymbals backward with closely held microphones.

Adjusting to this kind of stardom wasn't easy for the more conventional Gilmour, who was especially puzzled by the idea of scraping a microphone stand against his guitar strings. ("I was all for music-ing things up a bit," he'd say years later.) With Rick Wright's psychedelic pop on one side and a bunch of band experiments on the other, the only straight-ahead rock song on *Saucerful of Secrets* was Roger Waters' "Corporal Clegg," the first evidence of the bassist's contempt for military types.

And Gilmour went to town. His lead vocal, tuneful and playfully sarcastic, carried the words, and he overdubbed a symphony of crunchy Fender guitars bathed in fuzz, high-level treble, and wah-wah. Though there's no solo, this is still a Gilmour guitar festival, '68 style: the only one, really.

"Astronomy Domine" (1969)

For the first several years of their career, the Floyd's reputation (and some would say performance) was far better as a live band than as a recording act. It is understandable, then, that after Syd Barrett's implosion and the relative failure of the band's 1968 recordings that EMI would have requested a document of Floyd's charms in concert.

While the recordings on *Ummagumma*'s live disc are not the band's only good ones from the era, they adequately document the Floyd's superb 1968–69 approach. Gilmour was still figuring out his role in the group, and playing an old Barrett number offered an opportunity for the guitarist to stretch out on material with which both he and the audience were familiar.

Gilmour's work on this version of "Astronomy" is a tour de force. Playing in a more wide-open and less clipped style than Barrett had, Gilmour—clearly not bound to the original arrangement—played a frenzied wah-wah solo and ran up and down the fret board with true daring. In addition, the stretched-out, trippy live arrangement offered Wright, Waters, and Gilmour a rare opportunity to engage in a plangent, extremely psychedelic three-part harmony.

"The Nile Song" (1969)

While Gilmour had laid out the guitar effects on "Corporal Clegg" from *A Saucerful of Secrets*, perhaps his first real all-out rocker came the next year. On the first side of the soundtrack to *More*, Gilmour ripped hard into this Waters lyric.

Probably the hardest rocking the band ever did, "The Nile Song" (remade on the same album with different lyrics as "Ibiza Bar") lacks brilliant lyrics, and appears to be completely minus the conspicuously non-rocking Rick Wright, but has an absolutely ferocious solo section featuring not only Gilmour's paint-peeling Hendrixisms, but also some atypically blast-furnace Nick Mason drumming.

Part of what makes this song special, and one of Gilmour's best, is that his strengths as a pure rock and roller—something the rest of the Floyd lacked—enabled the band to just turn up and play. This wild, nutty number, like *Obscured by Clouds*' "The Gold It's in the . . ." is essential for that very reason.

"Breathe" (1973)

"Breathe" was a whole new thing. Mason's drums, Waters' on-point bass, and Wright's lovely electric piano were alone enough to send the listener into the stratosphere, but Gilmour's pedal-steel guitar runs are still blurringly beautiful even today, thirty-five years following the album's release.

The pedal steel, which is played with both feet and hands while sitting down, is a staple in country and western music for its "weeping" tone. The guitarist uses his feet to play the pedals, which increase and decrease the volume of the instrument, and the hands play the guitar itself, which lies flat.

One hand picks the six strings, which are tuned differently than those of a "normal" guitar, and the other hand runs a piece of steel up and down the frets. The use of metal allows the player to glide across the musical scale smoothly and without stopping, producing a seamless series of ascending or descending notes and a consistent tone.

It took a versatile guitarist like Gilmour to subvert the normal country/western context of a pedal steel and fit the instrument's sound into a spacey rock ballad. The otherworldly sound of "Breathe" owes much to Gilmour's psychedelic use of the steel.

In addition, Gilmour provided some precise Fender guitar picking, adding a bit of folk influence, and a breathy, faultless vocal line. In all, "Breathe" rates among the band's greatest tracks, providing *Dark Side* with an effective, Beatlesque recurring musical theme that truly realized the aims of psychedelic music, completely manifesting the mind.

"Time" (1973)

Here is another example of Gilmour's work on *Dark Side* building his legend. "Time" features superb Roger Waters lyrics bemoaning the passing of time and lost opportunities, but owes much of its greatness to the guitarist.

The Floyd's axeman may have felt uncomfortable singing negative sentiments, but when he embraced the dark stuff, his sense of innate musicality carried the day. (See "Money" and "Dogs" for further proof.) Dusting off a rarely used harsh roar, Gilmour tears through the song's downbeat theme with, seemingly, no regrets.

His guitar solo shows a mastery of both the major and minor modes; the verse is in F-sharp minor, though it progresses through major chords, and the chorus descends from D major to C-sharp minor. Using touches of blues, straight rock, and even a bit of raga, Gilmour spins enough

David Gilmour at the band's March 7, 1973 concert at the International Amphitheater in Chicago.
Photo courtesy of Mark Campbell

melody both in the solo and under the verses' main melodic line to almost make the listener forget about lyrics. As is the case on the rest of the album, his guitar tone is also unparalleled in its clarity.

"Money" (1973)

Once again on *Dark Side*, the Floyd's guitarist was asked to turn his vocal cords to a series of grim lyrics, this time about greed: specifically, *who controls the money*. The passion of Gilmour's voice matches that of Waters' words, and the band here sounds as tight as a presidential security patrol.

"Money" is difficult to sing, not only because of the odd time signature but also because of a melody that runs up and down the musical scale. In addition, Waters' Dylan/Lennon-inspired lyrics pour out in a fierce torrent. But Gilmour manages just fine, putting emphasis in the right places with tunefulness and soul.

His guitar work on this song is among the best of the 1970s. His symphony of guitars is truly iconic, and his solos leave no room for improvement.

Gilmour doubles Waters' bass line, giving an appealing blend of one note played in two octaves. Also, his effective tremoloed B-minor chords add a physically tangible depth.

And there are his devastating guitar runs. Gilmour's first solo, a frenetic, bluesy sprint that emerges from Dick Parry's saxophone part, is heralded by a shocking shift to double time. Gilmour here features syncopated, daring bluesy note-bending and a kind of flashy virtuosity he rarely felt a need to show.

The band then drops the tempo, and, tense and controlled, Gilmour complements the restrained, tight, precise backing of his mates—dig Wright's wah-wah electric piano—with treble-heavy, slightly distorted, blues-informed picking with aggressive pulls and just enough sonic frosting that his guitar tone sounds "inside-out."

When Nick Mason kicks the band into another double-time tempo, Gilmour brings it all home with apparent ease. It's easy to simply nod at how good his playing is on this song without acknowledging the genius in Gilmour's head and hands; this is among the greatest solo sections in rock.

"Wish You Were Here" (1975)

The success of *Dark Side of the Moon* came with a heavy price: the gradual end of the Floyd's working partnership.

The band signed a new contract with Columbia Records (for American distribution) after *Dark Side*, meaning that they *had* to keep creating new music although they had lost cohesion and didn't want to spend time together.

Years later, Roger Waters claimed that the band, weighed down in a post-success depression, remained together only out of greed and fear. Waters was already feeling regret about his new life of fame and riches.

How did he react? Not too well. Songwriting for a follow-up went slowly, and the band ground to a halt in an odd attempt to record songs using only common objects like rubber bands and bottles. Thankfully the *Household Objects* project died a-bornin', and the Floyd eventually pulled together a new set of tunes, although their pre–*Dark Side* level of cooperation never fully returned.

Channeling his own demons, Waters wrote a great lyric about his own good and bad sides that also conveys the universal feeling of longing for another. Gilmour then grafted on to it one of the great riffs of all time. The layering of acoustic and electric twelve-string and six-string guitars gives the song a simple majesty that helps bring it beyond the songwriter's private concerns into something more beautiful and far-reaching.

Waters' magnanimous decision—surely a difficult one—to allow the more conventionally gifted Gilmour to sing the song made it that much more effective. On *Animals* and *The Wall*, Waters was far less inclined to allow anyone else to incant his lyrics, which might have felt more "real" to the songwriter but certainly provided many listeners with less pleasure.

"Dogs" (1977)

This spectacular epic is the only song on *Animals* in which Gilmour (or anyone other than Roger Waters, in fact) gets a writing credit. Surely Gilmour is the difference-maker on "Dogs," as his lead vocal, symphony of guitars, and arrangement are the lengthy piece's high points.

Gilmour's chugging acoustic rhythm—an extremely strange but seductive, threatening, even invigorating sequence of chords on a guitar tuned to an open D (rather than E)—introduces the song, and his vocal is excellent despite having to sing some real mouthfuls from Waters about stabbing people and dying of cancer.

"Dogs" began its life in 1974 as "You Gotta Be Crazy" and was featured prominently on tour that year, until the recording of *Wish You Were Here*. At that point, it was found lacking and did not appear on the album. One assumes, that since the lyrics were the most noticeable change between the early version and the *Animals* recording, the decision to delay the song came from Waters. The entire episode is said to have been a strong point of contention between him and Gilmour.

No matter the album or the writing credit, "Dogs" is an absolute tour de force for Gilmour, whose harmonized Peter Green / Eric Clapton–influenced guitar parts beginning at 3:48 and 14:16 are among Pink Floyd's most memorable sonic moments. His "wet," or heavily chorused, guitar tone perhaps reaches its apex here, as identifiable a brand as anything Pink Floyd does.

The eye-wobbling firestorm of oddly harmonized notes that come at 14:03, harking back to "Echoes," surely causes as much astonished bongwater-spilling from first-time listeners as anything in the group's catalog.

But in the middle of this progressive epic, Gilmour also shows gritty, punk-like spirit in his venomous soloing less than two minutes in. His picking during the verses and other solo sections also adds depth to the consistent, flowing acoustic strum.

When Waters takes over the vocal for the last verse and the odd, both *Howl*- and Roy Harper–inspired coda ("who was . . ."), the song slows down and loses much of its charm.

"Goodbye Blue Sky" (1979)

When Roger Waters wrote *The Wall*, he had to be persuaded—quite possibly by record company executives—to allow anyone else near the material. But he did cede the vocal on the lovely "Goodbye Blue Sky" to Gilmour.

Like Waters' older, acoustic-oriented "Cirrus Minor," "Cymbaline," and "If," "Goodbye Blue Sky" balanced elegant acoustic guitar picking with downbeat lyrics. Gilmour's typically gentle delivery—double-tracked during the second verse, last chorus, and fade—and signature guitar playing lent emotional resonance.

Following the worldwide triumph of *The Wall*, Gilmour would, counter to reasonable expectation, become further marginalized. He sang just one song on the turgid *Final Cut* and ended up asking to have his name taken off the harsh, ugly-sounding record.

It is rather amazing, in retrospect, that Waters felt that Gilmour's contribution was at all disposable. His vocals lent so much life to the group's 1972–77 material, and his guitar playing made the songs so much more accessible, that one would think that even the ultra-competitive and ego-driven Waters would realize the importance of his colleague's contributions.

"Comfortably Numb" (1979)

In Floyd's early days, Rick Wright and Dave Gilmour had established a special sound with their dual vocals. By this time, though, Wright was a mere cipher, on his way out, and Roger Waters had taken over singing most of his own lyrics. When Waters and Gilmour sang "together" on Pink Floyd songs, it was usually separately and rarely in harmony—yes, it's a built-in metaphor for their relationship.

Waters' high-register straining for notes didn't always work, and any time that Gilmour sang along, his tones made a song that much easier to hear (and the lyrical message easier to bear). Their trading off on "Comfortably Numb" works thematically and artistically, giving the band one of its last great moments.

Waters sings the verse, inhabiting the persona of a creepy backstage rock-and-roll doctor cynically checking out Pink to see if anyone's "home" before injecting a necessary dose of contraband medicine to get the rocker ready for the show.

Gilmour takes on the role of Pink for the resigned, narcotic chorus, in which, floating away on the clouds, he imagines himself as a young boy. But he realizes sadly that even the *dream* of youth, of tranquility, of freedom, is gone, and that the best he can do now is to shut off, to become numb, even as he has the eyes and ears of thousands.

"Comfortably Numb" is one of Roger Waters' best lyrics, one that touches on both his own struggles to retain his humanity and the tragedy that befell Syd Barrett way back when. Waters also deserves credit for fighting to include the orchestral backing.

Adding his piece to Waters' Dylanesque lyrics and delivery, Gilmour sings his lines with airy, tuneful regret and adds two anthemic guitar solos that ring with beauty. His first solo is busy and full of little shards of melody, bringing passion to "Comfortably Numb," which in its lyrics purposefully *avoids* any mood other than anomie.

Gilmour's first foray sets the table for what's to come; his second solo, biting and plangent and overflowing with passion, follows the second chorus. Keening like a wounded bird, Gilmour plays a solo among the greatest in modern rock, one that would cap the career of any great guitarist.

In addition to his solos, Gilmour also adds color with acoustic strumming and a slide guitar that echoes "Breathe," although the psychedelic haze of *Dark Side of the Moon* has dissipated by this point; as he sings so poignantly in the last chorus, "the dream is gone."

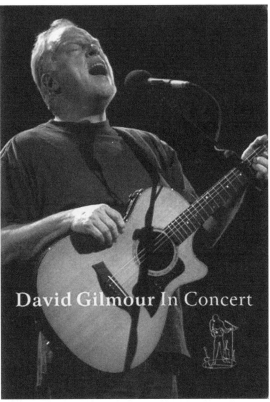

This DVD cover from Gilmour's 2001 and 2002 concert tour shows the passion with which he still plays his music, although his long rock-star hair of the 1970s is now just a memory.

8

Fling Your Arms Madly

What Are Ten Great Nick Mason Moments?

Nick Mason has taken plenty of stick—pardon the expression—for his drumming over the years. Sure, he's not the most technically awe-inspiring drummer in rock. His "slow four" drum tempo of the group's middle period is easily imitated and, as he himself has admitted, veers perilously close to cliché.

But his largely ego-free playing allowed the necessary space for the Floyd's music to unfold and develop. Mason's skills were far better suited to the group's dynamic than a flashy wizard like Carl Palmer or Bill Bruford would have been. He could range from simple timekeeping to wild pummeling of his kit to almost silent cymbal taps.

As has been said often by the other members of the group, Nick Mason was easily the best drummer for Pink Floyd.

"Arnold Layne" (1967)

Mason's aggressive, Ginger Baker–informed drums add a special kick to Barrett's narrative of a Cambridge knickers thief. Playing busily with his snare bathed in reverb, Mason serves as a lead drummer during the verses.

Following the first chorus, which he insistently powers along with a booming kick drum, Mason adds a crackling drum fill heralding Wright's organ solo and keeps up the pace during the frenetic keyboard workout. The solo sections of early Floyd material are short, but sweet, bursts of what the group sounded like in their live appearances: harsh and less than technically perfect, but brimming with energy and ideas.

Joe Boyd's chewy production establishes each member of the band at various points on the record. For instance, each time Barrett's vocal intensity rises, Mason is right there behind him with ominous, footstep-like drumming, signifying that Arnold won't escape the consequences of his actions.

"Take Up Thy Stethoscope and Walk" (1967)

From the first drumbeat, Mason owns this song, the first Roger Waters composition on a Pink Floyd record. Barrett's vocals and frenetic guitar are highlights, but Mason's forceful, mathematically minded introduction sets the pace for this odd bit of blues-influenced aggro.

Once the "freak-out" section begins, Mason goes into overdrive, laying down a vigorous backing. Mason's use of tom-tom was not a common tactic for rock drummers at the time. His furious thrashing of the drum kit was more than a match for Barrett and Wright's improvisations, and the percussive slant on the second half of the solo section is particularly stunning.

Giving Mason the outro to repeat his manic pattern may be gilding the lily, but the drummer deserved to open and close this one.

"Scream Thy Last Scream" (1967)

One of the few Pink Floyd songs to feature a Nick Mason vocal, this twisted piece of fairy-tale psych also sports extraordinarily silly sped-up vocals (complete with chipmunk-like giggles) and one of Syd Barrett's oddest lyrics.

Mason's real star turn on this one, though, isn't his recitation of Barrett's mad words. It's in the slow-to-fast buildup in the middle section. Moving from an absolute crawl to a crazed sprint, Mason keeps the beat with style, throwing in all sorts of fills. It's a spectacularly energetic performance, the kind of playing that gives the lie to the notion of Pink Floyd as unexciting, dispassionate, or bland.

Just to tie the package up, Mason delivers quite a capable lead vocal; had Syd Barrett not gone off his head in late 1967, this song might well have been released, although it certainly wasn't commercial enough to be a hit.

Unfortunately for the general music-listening populace, the group has declined for forty years to let this song out of the vaults. Former Floyd manager Peter Jenner, however, thought otherwise, and gave quality copies of this and "Vegetable Man" to bootleggers some two decades ago. Both recordings now travel freely among members of the underground community.

"Careful with That Axe, Eugene" (1968)

Beginning its life as a free-form live jam called, alternately, "Keep Smiling People" and "Murderistic Women" (it was recorded for a 1968 BBC session with the latter title), this largely instrumental piece, which evoked creepy horror-film music, was released on record as a B-side to the "Point Me at the Sky" 45 in late 1968. It also figured in the band's 1969 *The Man and the Journey* shows and remained a longtime concert favorite up to their 1973 worldwide breakthrough.

Live versions were always longer and even more intense than the studio recording. Mason would normally begin drumming softly, increasing his volume and pace slowly over several minutes, while Roger Waters would set a hypnotic one- or two-note motif on the bass. Wright's Eastern-inflected electric organ and Gilmour's sometimes sparse, sometimes chunky guitar inflections added a sense of foreboding to the tune, which due to Mason's controlled percussion work built up an almost unbearable sense of terror.

Finally, the axe murder referred to in the song's title becomes apparent, and the band tears into some of its hardest rock ever. Mason's drumming, both in live versions and on the 45 (which was re-released later on the *Relics* album), is some of his best, showing his mastery of tension buildup and release.

"Astronomy Domine" (1969)

The version of "Astronomy" on *Piper*, a truncated version of the Floyd's live-set tour de force, serves as a superb album-opener but doesn't really replicate what was happening on stage. The band finally got the tune down live in 1969 on *Ummagumma* with a group performance ranking among the best in PF history.

Mason, like the other members of the band, is able to veer on this extended number from ferocity to silence, playing the more intense sections with a powerhouse double-bass-drum approach influenced by both Ginger Baker and Jimi Hendrix drummer Mitch Mitchell. The complete percussion dropout during Wright's spacey solo is characteristic of Mason's unselfish approach, and his re-entry is galvanizing.

There's no film of this particular version of "Astronomy," but a clip from a 1968 Belgian show on YouTube shows the band's incendiary take on the song at the time.

"One of These Days" (1971)

The double bass guitar thrust of *Meddle*'s opening track is impressive, driving "One of These Days" along for three minutes in the absence of any steady beat.

During this buildup, Mason contributes backwards drum accents and a couple of bursts of kick drums. This is the kind of percussion work that presages the "buildup" used in house music.

Halfway through the track, during a guitar/keyboard lull, Mason incants, in a goofy, altered voice, "One of these days I'm going to cut

Nick Mason in 1970. He chose a double-bass-drum setup after seeing the one used by Cream's Ginger Baker.   *Photo by Jørgen Angel/Redferns*

you into little pieces," showing his ever-present sense of the macabre and humorous. Nobody else in the band could have carried it off.

After his vocalization, he *pounds* on the drum kit, crashing cymbals and propelling the song through more double-tracked Gilmour guitar strangling and Wright's piano rhythm and organ accents. Mason is playing as hard and intensely here, in a straight rock tempo, as he ever did.

Then, suddenly, the song crashes to a halt, refusing to overstay its welcome, instead giving way once again to the breezy sounds of the beautiful "Pillow of Winds."

"Obscured by Clouds" (1972)

While recording for *Obscured by Clouds* came during a break in the *Dark Side* sessions, the film scoring work was far less formal. The music shows this; in perhaps its last-ever truly relaxed recording environment, Pink Floyd recorded some fairly conventional (at least for them) early-seventies soft-rock . . . but with some adventurous and unusual touches.

The title track is one of the album's oddest. Following a long, dramatic, and foreboding keyboard fade-in, Mason's tribal electronic tom-tom provides a pulse. The band then appears, with Gilmour's guitar leads making clear the dread inherent in Wright's introductory drone. While this song's isn't one of the group's most famous, it features excellent ensemble playing and a forward-thinking percussion track.

Mason's simple but tense beat gives "OBC" good dynamics and an effective structure. Much of Mason's body of work stands outside the tradition of most rock drummers, since he usually used his left (snare drum) hand as heavily as his right (cymbal) hand, providing an "inside-out" beat that can envelop the listener with its trippy, backward sensibility.

The exploration of electronic percussion continued on "Childhood's End" on this album and with both "On the Run" and "Time" on *Dark Side of the Moon.*

"Breathe" (1973)

Dark Side's first proper song immediately lays out the territory: crystalline guitars and keyboards, thumpy bass, and a perfectly languid tempo that in itself is almost a theme of the album.

Mason's "slow four" drum work is as much a part of this album's magic as any other instrument, reappearing in several songs ("Time," "Us and Them," "Brain Damage") and serving as a link between them. This deliberate percussion motif provides the album with a druggy wave of crystal-clear cymbal and dry snare that implies urgency through its tense simplicity.

The delicate touch of drumstick on cymbal had rarely, if ever, been recorded this well, giving Mason's work an extra sheen.

"Time" (1973)

Despite being a "non-musician," Nick Mason was one of two Floyds (Rick Wright was the other) most interested in generating "new" sounds. Mason embraced electronic percussion with relish beginning in 1972. Both "On the Run" from *Dark Side* and the title track of *Obscured by Clouds* feature looped, electronically treated beats (which Mason referred to as "electric bongos") that later became central to Eurodisco and, after that, techno.

Mason also investigated, during the *Dark Side* sessions, a set of rototoms lying around the Abbey Road studio. These are drums with heads but no bodies, optimally used in a row since each drum head can easily be tuned to a certain note. Thus, using multiple rototoms allows the drummer to play "melodic" parts.

Mason's new discovery made its impact on "Time." The song's introductory clocks and chimes give way to a mechanized tock-tock of maddening simplicity, then the band enters slowly, with Mason providing booming, high-register rototom fills, a sound shocking at the time and one that still conveys tremendous power.

After this impressive intro, "Time" takes off. Some drummers might have played double time during the verse to pump up the beat or show off. Mason, instead, laid down a burning Jaki Liebezeit–style groove that is a lot more difficult than it seems. (Try playing along with it; a natural tendency would be to make it more complicated.)

During the chorus, Mason lays again into his patented slow tempo, then gets more aggressive during Gilmour's solo. His stylistic variation makes "Time" one of Mason's greatest moments on disc.

Asked by *Uncut* in 2003 to divine the secret of *Dark Side*'s enduring popularity, Mason jokingly replied, "I think it's the rototoms."

Nick Mason with his superb *Inside Out*, to date the only "insider" book written about the Pink Floyd.   *Photo by Brigitte Engl/Redferns*

"Dogs" (1977)

Any seventeen-minute rock song runs the risk of becoming turgid, and while "Dogs," arguably the centerpiece of *Animals*, has a couple of low moments, they aren't Nick Mason's fault.

Mason's drumming kicks in around 1:20, spare and simple, helping outline the earthbound focus of Waters' lyrics. The production of the bass and drums are, as usual on Floyd records, dry (lacking a lot of echo or reverb), allowing the keyboards and guitars to provide the color.

During Gilmour's first guitar solo, Mason provides simple but very effective double-time drum fills that are more conventional, and more rocking, than his usual MO. Spare drum accents also provide tension for several minutes after the band drops out during the repeated "stone . . . stone . . . stone" vocal section. Mason also plays excellent fills over the last verse, particularly coming in and out of Rogers Waters' pained vocal.

Perhaps the drummer's shining moment on this epic comes at 13:30, when his double-time drums kick in for a second time. Playing behind a typically lyrical Gilmour solo, he forces home the point that the Floyd could still rock when they saw fit. This section of the song lasts less than a minute, however, before drifting back into another "slow four" pattern, which Mason breaks up by not using the typical ride cymbal / snare drum combination.

It was around this time that Waters' working method began to grate on the other members of the band. Waters, who always *claimed* to want collaboration, found fault with his band members' song ideas, and as a result, Wright and Gilmour put their compositions on their *own* albums, which of course reinforced Waters' domination over the Floyd's direction.

As a result of criticism from Waters, Mason lost confidence in his drum skills, which soon began to suffer. By *The Wall* and *The Final Cut*, his playing was augmented by others. His confidence didn't really recover until the mid-1980s, and even on the band's 1986 "comeback" *Momentary Lapse of Reason*, many of the drum and percussion parts are played by session musicians.

9

Something in His Cosmic Art

What Are Ten Great Roger Waters Moments?

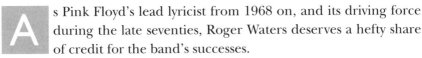s Pink Floyd's lead lyricist from 1968 on, and its driving force during the late seventies, Roger Waters deserves a hefty share of credit for the band's successes.

In his nearly twenty years with the band, Waters wrote a truckload of superb songs, delivered strong vocal performances, and played muscular bass . . . and, at times, surprisingly delicate acoustic guitar. Despite his hard-guy, strong-arm techniques, and his famously one-upping nature, Waters couldn't deny his basic humanity, and this quality comes through in his best songs.

Some of these selections may be too obscure, weird, or minor for some Floyd fans who revel in heavier numbers like "Eclipse," "Welcome to the Machine," or "In the Flesh." But each of these ten songs is intense, lyrical, and heartfelt, communicating the varying moods of the Floyd's most verbose and often most fascinating member.

"Let There Be More Light" (1968)

The first song on *Saucerful of Secrets* belonged to Waters, who wanted to take the opportunity presented by Syd Barrett's departure to lead the band—in his own way—toward the stars.

Feeling that he, not Barrett, was Pink Floyd's true science-fiction fan, Waters penned an impressionistic set of lyrics about a visitation of an alien ship at Mildenhall (a town in Suffolk in the southeast of England), most likely at the town's Royal Air Force base.

Mildenhall? Why *Mildenhall?*

Waters, as a fan of sci-fi and a careful, cynical observer of the military, may have found it interesting to bring the cosmic to a presumably prosaic, old-fashioned, hierarchical environment. "The servicemen were heard to sigh," according to the lyrics, when the alien being (in the form of, er, "Lucy in the Sky") is revealed.

The decision to set the alien visitation there may also relate to the use, since the early 1950s, of RAF Mildenhall as an *American* air force base, signifying intrusion into Britain. Roger Waters, an anti-nuclear crusader in the early 1960s with strong left-wing views, would return to anti-imperialist lyrics in the coming years.

Rather than falling into a misty psychedelic haze with the music, however, Waters instead drove the song with an aggressive bass style that he would employ regularly over the next few years. Playing a lead part, rather than a simple rhythm, Waters established the structure in which the other players would work.

The vocals on the song trade back and forth; Wright sings the verses with Waters whispering the lyrics underneath, while Gilmour takes the choruses. The solo section is truly skull-opening; as Gilmour uncrates a searing solo over Mason's insistent cymbal crashes and Wright's piano, a *separate song*, in the same key, emits from the right channel. (The album's mono mix, of course, does not feature this stereo effect.)

"Embryo" (1968)

Waters' gentle four-minute-plus track, recorded in 1968 but not released until 1970 (and then on a compilation album), eventually mutated into a twelve-minute Floyd concert staple, at least until they folded some of the track's subsonic sound effects into "Echoes."

This track is far more interesting than much of the other material the group was recording in 1968.

Rick Wright's keyboard playing gave the song much of its charm, with its ghostly organ and attractive piano run doubling Dave Gilmour's delicate vocal. All the instruments on this record are played with an admirable restraint, allowing the occasional shards of organ, piano, and percussion to glow through like a fire just below the earth's surface.

Waters, though, is the star. His lyrics show a wide-eyed innocence he rarely betrayed in the rest of the band's work, and the bassist's subdued

Roger Waters at the UFO Club, London, 1966. He was among the first notable musicians to use the Rickenbacker bass, appearing in public with it even before Paul McCartney.   *Photo by Adam Ritchie/Redferns*

instrumental contribution winds its way precisely through Mason and Wright's backing. At the song's end, Waters also adds sped-up vocals near the song's end, evoking the sounds of a baby.

"If" (1970)

How did the four remaining members of the Pink Floyd deal with the loss of Syd Barrett? By going on the only way they knew how: pushing themselves as musicians, writing what they were interested in, gigging incessantly, and taking on plenty of projects to find a new direction.

Amid their symphonic pieces, double albums, film scores, and ballet accompaniments, the first recorded evidence of the band's feelings about Syd Barrett emerged on side two of 1970's *Atom Heart Mother* in a simple, acoustic Roger Waters song.

(Waters had already written about Barrett. His 1968 "Incarceration of a Flower Child," never recorded by the Pink Floyd, was instead bestowed on Marianne Faithfull.)

"If," a lovely, folk-style ballad in the style of 1969's "Grantchester Meadows" (which Waters also sang), concerns itself with guilt and regret over the small and large cruelties of man, or in this case a *particular* man. The narrator sees himself as a late train, a flown-away swan, a lost soul who can't connect with people he truly cares about. Waters sings it himself with almost unbearable sincerity and frailty. Gilmour's pin-sharp electric guitar lines and Wright's churchy organ underscore the deep feeling.

It may take a leap of faith to assume the line "If I were a good man, I'd talk to you more than I do" refers directly to the fallen Barrett. But given that Waters had coproduced Barrett's first solo LP, it also takes a leap to assume that Barrett's solo career hadn't made a significant dent in Waters' psyche.

Waters had plumbed the acoustic guitar ocean before, notably with "Grantchester" and "Cirrus Minor," and would do so again. Even in his angriest, most bitter, least musical times, Waters would return to simple folk melodies for inspiration.

"Echoes" (1971)

In a musical sense, the epic "Echoes" belongs more to the "sonic architects" of the band (Wright and Gilmour), but Waters' lyrics here are among the best he ever wrote, and among the best to come out of the often non-cosmic, self-obsessed 1970s.

Although he swiped the lyrical cadence and some of the melody from John Lennon's epochal "Across the Universe," Roger Waters deserves credit for "Echoes." He writes here most enticingly about the simple humanity within all of us and how we can best reach our potential.

Waters snagged "inciting and inviting" from Lennon, but also referred to the Beatles in the elliptical line "And I am you and what you see is me." A huge Lennon fan, he ran here with the Fabs' legacy, expanding on the idea of love—of simple human contact—as a harbinger of something much greater, much more cosmic.

Heralding the grandeur of the morning sun while also celebrating the prosaic albatross, Waters lays out his concept: that all creatures are impelled by an unknown force to rise up out of the morass, whether it be physical or emotional, and become their greater selves.

The need for human interaction has always suffused Waters' lyrics, and here he claims that we need love and understanding *because* there is no one God, no one entity that calls us or forces us to do anything. Our instincts for connection, for contact, come from a deep place that we cannot understand but can access by simply throwing open the window and interacting with the world, talking to another person or singing to something as simple as a seagull.

"Free Four" (1972)

This may not be Waters' first song to show severe self-loathing ("If" contends for that dubious honor), but the amount of distaste in this lyric, for himself and others, is certainly noticeable.

As any armchair psychologist or music writer will tell you, self-loathing is just the other side of loathing for others, something Waters would soon explore. This, perhaps the band's darkest lyric to date, was Floyd's most commercial, catchiest song yet, at least to American ears. Waters may have enjoyed the irony in that.

Waters singing about the soldier in the foxhole (a reference to his father, lost in World War II) and everyone being "on the run" portends *Dark Side, The Wall*, and even *The Final Cut*. "Who is the master of fox-hounds . . ." is a typical Waters lyric about another theme that obsessed him: those in power and their motivations. The words about courtrooms

「来日記念盤」王者ピンク・フロイド！

夢に消えるジュリア

サマー'68 ★ ピンク・フロイド

JULIA DREAM/SUMMER '68

OR-2840 STEREO

Odeon RECORDS

This odd Japanese release paired "Julia Dream," a British B-side from 1968—and a fine, underrated Waters track—with "Summer '68," an album cut from 1970.

and drumbeats indicate this song as a step toward his future lyrical approach.

And yet "Free Four" is also bags of fun. The VCS3 synthesizer line is comically low and foreboding. The Gilmour guitar solo is typically great, adding real bile to an already caustic lyric. Was it a conscious piss-take to festoon such a grim lyric with handclaps, acoustic guitar, and a jokey opening? And did anyone bother to tell Roger Waters that if he hated the music business this much, he could always leave?

Waters wrote this song alone, while most of the rest of *Obscured by Clouds* is a collaborative effort. Since the Floyd were in the middle of taping *Dark Side* when they did this album, it's easy to toss off *OBC* as a contract-filling throwaway. But buried in this album are some of the band's least pretentious, most enjoyable songs, sporting some American influence, some good pop dynamics, and nearly the last vestiges of psychedelic experimentation.

"Money" (1973)

For the first song on the second side of *Dark Side*, Roger Waters (perhaps inspired by the influence of his left-wing pottery-artist wife, Judy Trim) wrote about the corrupting power of money and who controls the purse strings, bringing the allegory to an individual level rather than staying within some arch political framework.

The song's last verse hones in on the fine point, a working person being denied a raise. (And by the next song, "Us and Them," a hungry old man with no money has died in the street.)

Waters also was firing on all cylinders with his bass line, which provided the song with its singular and extremely catchy musical focal point. And despite its odd time signature, "Money" was a very commercial and convincing rocker featuring Gilmour's roaring vocal and arcade of guitars, Waters' on-the-mark bass, Mason's simple drums, Dick Parry's down-and-dirty sax solo, and a very psychedelic electric piano from Rick Wright.

Judy Trim's influence is also felt in the song's introduction. Waters recorded himself tossing coins inside of some of her clay pots, and then he interspersed the sounds with cash-register noises from the Abbey Road Studios sound effects collection.

The band had always used "nonmusical" ideas, starting with *The Piper at the Gates of Dawn*, but much of what made *Dark Side* so interesting sonically was the folding in of *different* sorts of effects—non-"natural" sounds like coins, footsteps, airplanes, and odd bits of speech—than the band had used in the past.

The success of *Dark Side* led Waters and the rest of the band to go whole hog with effects in future years, cresting with the "holophonic" sounds (i.e., sounds that actually sound like they are behind and in front of the listener) used on *The Final Cut.*

"Wish You Were Here" (1975)

While Waters' bile against the music industry suffused much of *Wish You Were Here*, the album's most effective song was a simple folk-inspired lament. More than anything else on the record, the title track conveyed the staggering emotional distance from others, and from his own true nature, that Waters felt at the time.

Though the band was now an international success, all the members of Pink Floyd were experiencing severe burnout in their work and in their relationships with each other. Waters' lyric carefully notes an individual who has lost his positive, life-affirming side and wants it back.

Even though David Gilmour, musical co-collaborator and writer of the riff, is the "star" of this song, with his majestic guitar work and haunting vocal, Waters deserves full credit for conveying his feelings in such a naked and affecting way. Writing songs is hard; writing good songs is harder; writing emotionally *real* good songs is the hardest of all. Later,

Waters admitted that "Wish" was one of the few songs he wrote the lyrics to first, with the chords coming much later.

This remains one of Pink Floyd's best-loved songs, and its simple, seemingly effortless majesty (the result, of course, of a lot of hard work) a contradiction to those who would accuse the band of lacking emotional resonance or the ability to convey a simple tune.

"Sheep" (1977)

Following a soothing and sweet-sounding electric piano intro from Wright, which nearly lulls the listener into a sense that all is well, Waters comes in full bore, making fun of the proletariat sheep who stand around stuffing their stomachs while the slaughterhouse awaits them.

(A quick sideline: Waters has the only songwriting credit on "Sheep." Does that mean he actually claims to have written the lengthy electric piano introduction? If not, then how much money did it take to "buy" Wright's songwriting credit to make Waters appear to be the sole song-writer?)

Waters, author of the caustic and sometimes funny lyrics, sings this well, finding in the E minor key a series of notes that felt comfortable and even sounded tuneful. The trick of electronically "stretching" his vocal at the end of each line makes Waters' voice sound that much stronger.

And for once in a Waters song, the oppressed win; the sheep eventually come to their senses and overthrow their oppressors. In a typical Floyd piece of understated humor, they master karate and throw off the rule of the dogs with a bloody uprising. The band builds to an uplifting crescendo, this time in E major, that heralds the revolution at hand. The track eventually fades into birdsong and then the album's closer, "Pigs on the Wing 2."

Despite the implied violence, "Sheep" is a surprisingly upbeat song, at least from Waters' pen, in that the people screwed over in his earlier songs ("Us and Them," "Money," etc.) finally get their revenge.

As is true for most of *Animals*, however, the production here is compressed and not particularly artful, especially considering the sonic gloss of the previous *Dark Side of the Moon* and *Wish You Were Here*.

The drums are devoid of high end and depth; this is a shame, since Mason's playing is pounding and inventive. Gilmour's muddy bass playing and Wright's mid-song synthesizers don't *sound* very good, but they do convey a sense of dread and anomie matching Waters' lyrics about the exploitation of the poor by the rich and powerful. Even Gilmour's guitar, at the song's almost celebratory end, is somewhat muted.

For a band coming off huge success with FM radio–friendly, sonically pleasing albums, to release a new album in 1977 of three songs, each over ten minutes long, bracketed by short intro and outro pieces was a move that certainly showed a screw-you punk *spirit*, even if the music itself wasn't punk.

"Hey You" (1979)

Here's a contradiction in Roger Waters' work: When he wrote his more personal, one-to-one songs—songs that could communicate to an audience outside of any greater "context"—and didn't try to be a spokesman, political commentator, or Great Artist, some of his greatest, most universal art came out.

Rarely has an artist issued such a naked plea for contact and understanding as Waters did here, in the guise of Pink, on *The Wall*.

It meant something, of course, that this song opened side three—the second disc—of the album, coming after "Goodbye Cruel World," in which Pink tries to escape humanity for good. Here, we begin with lovely acoustic picking, a fretless bass (also played by Gilmour), and some typical Wright electric piano.

Gilmour intones two verses before a Hammond organ buildup leads into a corrosive guitar solo, in which Gilmour references the melody of "Another Brick in the Wall." Waters then takes over for the bridge, which discusses the wall of isolation itself and its disastrous effect on Pink. Here, the album's "concept" works as well as it could: without love and human contact, Pink, like anyone isolated, is susceptible to the diseases of cynicism and hate.

As he had on other Floyd songs of this vintage, Waters sings the final verse after Gilmour has established the mood. That Waters has to strain to reach the notes is especially evocative, and his misery is palpable.

And like many of Waters' other great songs, this one's about Pink Floyd as well as about his concept. Musically, "Hey You" has clear references to "Dogs" and "Echoes," as well as "Another Brick," while the singer touches lyrically on his well-worn concept of being burdened by a great stone.

It's also poignant that by the time this album came out, Waters had already decided, perhaps correctly, that the isolated and troubled Rick Wright was no longer capable of delivering his innovative keyboard parts consistently, and had fired him.

"Comfortably Numb" (1979)

Combining a suitably narcotic musical setting with a gorgeous Gilmour melody and some of the saddest lyrics in rock, "Comfortably Numb" is a standout not only of *The Wall*, but of Pink Floyd's career.

And it's not really as far from "Echoes" or even "Saucerful of Secrets" as one might think. The musical elements that made the band great are still there—steady, hypnotic drumming, an army of guitars playing both velvety and sandpapery textures, a blend of vocalists, and a strong sense of both melody and harmony.

And for those who don't like "concept albums," it's still possible to get something out of the best that latter-day Pink Floyd can offer. The key is to forget about the song having to exist in any other context but its own.

Plenty of enticing elements emerge from listens to "Comfortably Numb." Waters' Dylan-sounding vocal during the verse, providing the narrative of a person escaping his isolation through drugs (and of course becoming ever more isolated through that very action), is jarring. The minor-chord backing adds foreshadowing.

But what comes next is not a doom-laden climax, but instead a section in a *major* key, where Dave Gilmour's beautiful voice brings the narrator back to a happier time apparently achievable only through artificial means. But rarely did drug-fueled isolation sound so enticing and beautiful . . . another classic Pink Floyd contradiction.

When Waters and Gilmour worked together vocally on *The Wall*, as they did here, on "Mother," and on "Hey You," they transcended their arguments and each of their respective weaknesses, forging instead a music of both beauty and tension.

Ten Things Roger Waters Doesn't Need

- Education
- Thought control
- Dark sarcasm in the classroom
- Arms around him
- Rick Wright
- Margaret Thatcher
- Ronald Reagan
- Animal rights activists
- Hip-hop
- Sinead O'Connor

10

The Music Was Too Loud

What Are Ten Great Rick Wright Moments?

It's easy to view Rick Wright's career in Pink Floyd as a disappointment. Intensely musical, and blessed with a facility for keyboards, an ear for lilting melody, and a tuneful, perhaps too-precise vocal style, the jazz- and classically influenced Wright had several opportunities to become the key songwriter and musical influence in the band, but never marshaled his skills long enough to establish a beachhead.

More skeptical observers, including Roger Waters, simply believe that Wright never had enough good ideas to take control.

His organ work gave the early Floyd much of its astral, shimmery live feel, and his bag of tricks included piano, clavinet, spinet, electric piano, trombone (!), and all forms of creamy-sounding early synthesizers. Wright also operated the group's live quadraphonic sound system, using a joystick to shoot sound around the concert hall.

By the time of *Wish You Were Here* and *Animals*, however, Wright was implementing synthesizers that now sound very dated, getting faux-French horn and string sounds that draw attention with their cheap tones. When Waters brought in the concept for *The Wall*, Wright had few ideas to contribute, and his personal problems made his replacement by session keyboardists, as well as *real* string players, a fait accompli.

But before being cast from Pink Floyd's ranks, he contributed some great music to the band's catalog.

One could argue, in fact, that Wright, more than Waters, Gilmour, or even Barrett, has been the one member of Pink Floyd most influential in the development of music. Certainly Barrett's pop songwriting skills have led to a new generation of singers and songwriters who claim his muse, and Gilmour's guitar playing has endured, and Waters' rock operas have their devotees, but Wright's keyboard playing has been extremely prescient concerning modern sound.

The mind-expanding keyboard tones on "Dogs" and "On the Run," for example, are nothing if not proto-techno, while "Obscured by Clouds" and the first movement of "Shine On" show the debt that new age and ambient music owe to the Floyd. Wright's cranky nature and his late seventies / early eighties wasted period helped erode his reputation, but his contributions to the best of Pink Floyd's music made the band's work much better than it would have been otherwise.

"See Emily Play" (1967)

This epochal psychedelic single may not have been the way the Floyd wished to have itself represented, but the British public had the good sense to make "Emily" a Top 5 record in the memorable summer of 1967.

Wright's keyboards played a major part in the record's undeniable magic. Procol Harum's Gary Brooker didn't like what he called in *Melody Maker* the group's "awful" organ sound, but on "See Emily Play," the rich-sounding Farfisa provided a solid underpinning for an otherwise spare arrangement. Guitars only enter the equation in specific spots.

Following the first chorus, Wright hammers out a lovely bit of classical frippery on a treated piano (or a clavichord?) that evokes the image of a stoned ballerina dancing at triple speed. This five-second bit may be the single most representative British psychedelic moment: Victorian, druggy, whimsical, and a little bit dangerous.

Wright adds a third part on an echoed piano during the choruses, tapping out A-flat/F-sharp/E in an alternate rhythm to the rest of the instruments. It's the kind of part that can get lost in a good arrangement until one tries to disassemble and identify the parts of a successful pop single.

Finally, Wright sings backup, his trademark winsome voice especially bleeding through on the fadeout.

"Astronomy Domine" (1967)

Syd Barrett opened *Piper at the Gates of Dawn* with an invocation of sea and sky, a theme the group re-explored years later. Four minutes, fifteen seconds of pure psychedelic bliss, "Astronomy Domine" takes off into the atmosphere with guitar, organ, drums, and bass establishing their

A poster advertising the May 12, 1967 gig that led to the writing of "Games for May," soon re-titled "See Emily Play." *Photo by GAB Archive/Redferns*

own space by playing in differing rhythms and fooling around with dissonance.

Wright wasn't given naturally to "freaking out," but he picked up on the Barrett brief quickly. His organ part included antiphonal notes, freeform rhythmic and tonal improvisation, and some good old fashioned Eastern runs.

In addition, Wright's somewhat arch pronunciation of Syd's lyrics adds a particularly English frisson. That the members of the band were well-spoken and from "good homes" was big news, and their very Britishness was special. Most British pop singers consciously lost their accents to sound American, but Syd's Floyd just *sounded* English, musically, lyrically, and in the way they sang.

"Matilda Mother" (1967)

Syd Barrett's bedtime plea to his mum—originally with lyrics cribbed from a Hilaire Belloc book but rewritten for legal reasons—featured trade-off vocals, Wright taking the mike for the first two verses.

(It's not clear why the group chose to have Barrett take over for Wright mid-song, but later on in the Floyd's career, Dave Gilmour and Roger Waters would share vocal duties as well.)

Once again, Wright's careful enunciation of Barrett's lyrics, augmented by Norman Smith's production, makes every consonant more than clear. The fussy vocal delivery endangers the already teetering-on-the-edge-of precious fairyland lyrics.

Not only did Wright's singing set an appropriate mood for "Matilda," it also balanced Barrett's wilder, untamed ranting during the "Why'd you have to leave me there" section and the last verse.

Wright also tossed in perhaps his best early keyboard solo. His organ playing evoked not only Eastern scales, but also the feel of ghosts being summoned from dusty, cold crypts. The playing during the fade is also chill-inducing, with echo making Wright's spectral work seem even darker. This is goth music without the attitude and silly makeup.

"Paint Box" (1967)

This vaguely disturbing narrative, perhaps Wright's most underrated work, features a jazzy piano-based arrangement and a lengthy solo.

Acoustic and electric guitars played by an apparently in-control Syd Barrett, Roger Waters' gulping McCartney-styled bass, and clattery Nick Mason drums add to the sonic palette, topped by Wright's unsettled vocal telling a short story with an undercurrent of dread.

Wright sings here of young adulthood, drinking in pubs with "fools," going through the motions of a social life when he would rather be doing something else. Eventually he connects with a young lady who wants to go on a date . . . but stuck in traffic, he's late, leaving his date angry.

This small slice of life was featured as the B-side to the Floyd's first outright flop, the "Apples and Oranges" single, and as a result wasn't heard by many people on its original release.

The original mono mix of "Paint Box," featuring a jarring, echoed piano part and a different, longer fadeout, was superseded by a shorter stereo mix issued on the 1971 *Relics* compilation. The mono mix was made available, however, for mass consumption—and re-titled "Paintbox"—on the 2007 three-CD *Piper at the Gates of Dawn* special edition.

"Remember a Day" (1968)

Wright's gift for ethereal vocalizing works very well with this (perhaps) idealized song of childhood. He, as much as Barrett, invoked the classic British psychedelic themes of lost innocence and easy days of youth both with his singing and his lyrics.

Adding to the stately feel is the judicious use of classically tinged piano, rather than his usual choice of organ. The sparse instrumentation (featuring producer Norman Smith engaging in some very Mason-like drumming) allows the vocals, and Barrett's unsteady slide guitar, to come forward.

Originally thought to have been recorded in February 1967, this track is now believed to have been taped that fall, meaning it was recorded after *The Piper at the Gates of Dawn* rather than having been an outtake from it.

Wright had been hoping, in the face of Syd Barrett's decline as a songwriter, to become more of a voice in Pink Floyd. But his songs were somewhat lighter (and his personality perhaps less scabrous) than those of the ultra-competitive Roger Waters. Eventually Wright was forced to accept a reduced role in the band.

"Summer '68" (1970)

This singular song in the Pink Floyd canon is a fascinating multi-genre exercise both twee and muscular, American and English at the same time. Lyrically, it's . . . somewhat under-evolved.

The title indicates a snapshot of Wright's experiences during the group's July-through-September 1968 American tour. Following a quick encounter with a young lovely, the protagonist is already acknowledging that he must move on and is saying goodbye "before we said hello."

As bad as this is, the song's narrator compounds the misery by cruelly asking the girl to tell him how she feels. The protagonist informs this perhaps professional groupie that he would rather be lying in the sun with his friends, and that tomorrow he will meet "another girl." (One wonder what Wright's wife Juliette thought of all this.)

It is said that following the group's 1967 American tour, all four members of the Floyd returned to England and immediately got shots

Waters and Wright attack the beat on November 12, 1970 in Copenhagen, Denmark. Wright's tie-dyed shirt is probably not meant as a target.   *Photo by Jørgen Angel/Redferns*

to combat recently contracted venereal disease, so the pleasures of the road were not unknown to them. Wright returned to the one-night-stand theme in 1972's "Stay."

Following a basic piano-led verse, the "How do you feel?" chorus is heavily compressed and bass-y. Following the second verse and chorus, "Summer '68" swerves abruptly into Beach Boys territory with layered harmonies, trumpets, and an orchestral swell worthy of Brian Wilson and Phil Spector.

Like most attempts at pop epics of the time, "Summer '68" gets lost in the middle. But it's an often spectacular attempt at creating a multi-part pop symphony, even if its lyrics give perhaps a deeper, and less flattering, view of the writer than he might wish.

"Echoes" (1971)

Following the debacle of *Ummagumma*'s "Sysyphus" and *Atom Heart Mother*'s fascinating but frankly bewildering "Summer '68," it was clear that Rick Wright was in a deep songwriting crisis. Then again, the entire band was struggling to come up with decent material, and another live album was out of the question.

The next major leap in the Floyd story came, then, nearly by accident. During Abbey Road recording sessions in January 1971, which the band entered with *no* new material (ah, the liberal recording budgets of those times!), they tried feeding instruments through various effects to come up with some inspiration.

The random playing of a piano note (B, for those of you wanting to try at home) through a Leslie rotating speaker produced a liquid effect that the band enjoyed enough to develop. The Leslie speaker, used on many pop productions of the period, adds an echoed, wet sound perhaps best heard on guitars: the Beatles' "Sun King," for example, or the introduction of Ringo Starr's "It Don't Come Easy."

Wright's piano sets the stage for the song, which was conceived and recorded as separate bits entitled "Nothing," then re-titled "Son of Nothing" and eventually "Return to the Son of Nothing" when performed in London early that spring. Eventually Waters added lyrics that both celebrate and mourn humanity.

Gilmour's guitar, reminiscent of a "whale" sound, and Wright's soulful, funky Hammond organ echo Waters' lovely lyrics, which mention and evoke the range of colors of the sea: green, gold, sandy brown, white, and above all, crystal blue. The *Meddle* album cover, with its image of an ear under water, is a great match for the sonics of "Echoes."

"Echoes" took six months of off-and-on work to record, but everyone in the band still points to it as perhaps their first truly pleasing post-Syd music. Pink Floyd was now forging its formula: Find an inspiration (perhaps by accident), develop the idea, hone it with precision into a crystal-clear, great-sounding product, and present it in an interesting package.

"Us and Them" (1973)

During their work on the soundtrack of Antonioni's *Zabriskie Point* film, Wright wrote a languid progression intended for the film's student protest sequence. Antonioni didn't like the piece, however, and it remained unused until 1971, when Waters needed backing for his apocalyptic *Dark Side of the Moon* lyric about war, poverty, and death.

Waters' lyrics fit perfectly with the somber music he had composed. David Gilmour's resigned vocal fit well atop Wright's unusual chord sequence and melody. The chord progression in the verse—a D to D6 to an unusual D minor with a major seventh—immediately alerts the listener that something other than the usual pop music, or even Wright's jazzy musings, is happening. The tasteful piano and organ work are appropriately mournful for the song's subject matter.

Wright also sang in the background, but his vocals during the chorus are somewhat lost among those of the electronically altered session singers. It's one of the only places on the otherwise pristine *Dark Side* album where the production becomes perhaps a bit too much.

Finally, Wright kicks in a mournful, classically inflected piano solo at 4:40. Unfortunately for the hapless pianist, the second half of this excellent solo is covered by one of the album's many spoken interludes (the "short, sharp shock" section).

"Us and Them" remains one of Wright's favorite Floyd tracks, and even Waters, loath to credit Wright for much of anything in the last thirty-five years, would tell *Uncut* magazine in 2003 that "the chord sequence is beautiful." It is quite interesting to realize that Wright's two major contributions for *Dark Side* ("Us" and "Great Gig in the Sky") comprise the saddest-sounding music on the record, and the songs Waters used to convey the concept of death.

"Any Colour You Like" (1973)

The only "jam" on *Dark Side*, this swirling, impressionistic head candy could be construed as the band's last great psychedelic moment. Wright's use of the VCS3 synthesizer, fed through a tape loop, to create echoey, mind-expanding sounds is still astounding.

While this song can be seen as disposable to the album's "concept," since it has no relation to Waters' lyrics, it's also a welcome space-out moment from the disillusioning *Dark Side* storyline. It's key to note that it's the only place on the album where the band isn't hewing to a pre-ordained concept from its bassist. Waters isn't even credited as a writer, most likely because he didn't do anything except play bass.

Wright and David Gilmour (who also contributes an abrasive guitar solo) were always happy to play music without undue concern about lyrics, which neither of them could consistently contribute anyway. The tension between their music-minded approach and the straight lyrical bent espoused, from 1971 on, by Waters is part of what made their mid- to late-period albums great, but also a major factor in tearing apart the band.

"Shine On You Crazy Diamond" Parts I and IX (1975)

The three "writing" members of Pink Floyd each provided significant pieces of the multi-part epic that began and closed *Wish You Were Here*. Wright's swirling keyboards bookend the album, setting a funereal mood.

In the first and last pieces, he does his best late-period work. Wright's introduction to "Shine On" includes languid synthesizer tones, acoustic piano, Hammond organ, and extra-musical tinklings of electric piano. This piece, in fact, has influenced keyboard and synthesizer players over the last thirty years.

Part IX, which closes the record with a swirl of synthesizers, is an appropriately somber summing-up of the album's melancholy, emotionally frozen mood. As the song fades, Wright plays the melody line from the verse of "See Emily Play." While much of Floyd's newfound fan base might not even have known the song, Syd Barrett never left the minds of the other members of the group for long.

Despite the band's success, Wright's genius was fading. He was displaying a lack of inspiration and did not write or play well under Waters' scrutiny. By *Animals*, Wright's musical influence had fallen to a distant second in importance to the layers of Dave Gilmour's guitars, and only rarely on the album did the keyboardist show his gifts.

Rick Wright in 1996, demons largely behind him and once again a member of Pink Floyd.   *Photo by Rob Verhorst/Redferns*

A Pink Floyd Live Top Ten

by Steven Leventhal

O f the hundreds of shows that Pink Floyd put on in their forty-year gigging career, it would be a fool's errand to pick out just ten great ones, or even a hundred. But each fan who has listened obsessively to shows from all of their eras has a list of favorites.

This chronological list of critical Pink Floyd concerts considers umpteen Floyd concerts and picks out ten with one eye on historical import and the other on group performance.

December 23, 1966: UFO Club, Tottenham Court Road, London

This date marked the opening of the UFO (pronounced "you-foe") Club, a key point in the emergence of the London Underground. This was the first of the "Night Tripper Evenings," where every Friday this Irish ballroom morphed into a psychedelic club.

The Floyd got the music and lights contracts, and would soon become the closest thing this anarchic scene had to a "house band." The club served as a major gathering spot of the London freaks, poets, good-timers, and political activists, galvanizing the new underground.

April 29, 1967: Fourteen-Hour Technicolor Dream Free Speech Festival, Alexander Palace, London

This massive festival was held to raise money for the *International Times*, an underground newspaper and early Floyd champion that had been busted for obscenity by the authorities.

This concert was perhaps the apex of the London underground. The Floyd headlined the approximately forty bands, poets, dancers, and performance artists, including the Pretty Things, John's Children, the Soft Machine, Dick Gregory, the Social Deviants, and Yoko Ono.

Pink Floyd, just back from Heathrow after playing a gig in Amsterdam earlier in the day, hit the stage just as the dawn's early light began to stream through the huge glass windows of the "Ally Pally." While the quality of the Floyd's playing during the gig is in question, clearly the drama and beauty of the moment, and the audience's steadfast love, carried the day.

September 17, 1969: Concertgebouw, Amsterdam, Netherlands

For their 1969 tour, which did not travel to America, Pink Floyd performed a conceptual music piece entitled *The Man and the Journey,*

which consisted of two album-length suites.

The show incorporated bits and pieces of many existing Floyd songs, as well as some that would appear on future albums. Their 1969 releases, *More* and *Ummagumma,* were represented by such re-titled works as "Daybreak" (a.k.a. "Grantchester Meadows"), "Nightmare" ("Cymbaline"), "The Beginning" ("Green Is the Colour"), "Beset by the Creatures of the Deep" ("Careful with That Axe, Eugene"),

This cover shot, from a 1969 live bootleg, shows Pink Floyd at the session that produced the cover of *Ummagumma.* Rick Wright is wearing the same sweater he wore on *Ummagumma*'s front cover.

Photo courtesy of Steve Leventhal

and "The End of the

Beginning" ("A Saucerful of Secrets"). The September 17 show was recorded by Dutch radio station VPRO.

April 29, 1970: Fillmore West, San Francisco, California

This show, a highlight of the band's third U.S. tour, includes an early performance of the "Atom Heart Mother Suite" without the brass section and choir that would appear on the album and in later concerts.

This night's performance was recorded and excellent soundboard tapes are in circulation. Pink Floyd played two encores, including a twenty-two-minute rendition of "A Saucerful of Secrets."

What's especially impressive about this high-quality show is that earlier in the day, the band had recorded their "Hour with Pink Floyd" special at KQED-TV in San Francisco.

July 16, 1970 and September 30, 1971: Paris Theater, London

With beloved disc jockey John Peel, a longtime champion of all forms of "new" music, as master of ceremonies, these two shows were recorded for the BBC.

Listening to the excellent recordings made of these gigs, one can compare two very different, extended versions of Dave Gilmour's "Fat Old Sun." This period represents the group's transition from the confused *Atom Heart Mother* to the clearer *Meddle*, with "Echoes" replacing "Atom Heart Mother Suite" as the show's centerpiece.

The soon-to-disappear-forever "Embryo" is the only other song that appears in both shows, which are widely circulated among collectors.

October 4–7, 1971: Roman Amphitheater, Pompeii, Italy

While not technically a concert, because it didn't take place in front of a live audience, several Pink Floyd performances in the ancient ruins of Pompeii, buried by a volcanic eruption in 79 A.D., were recorded live.

The fascinating *Live at Pompeii* film, by Adrian Maben, chronicles this recording, along with footage shot in Paris and in 1972 at the Abbey Road Studio during recording sessions for *Dark Side*.

Committing such longtime favorites as "A Saucerful of Secrets," "Set the Controls for the Heart of the Sun," and "Careful with That Axe, Eugene" to film, the four Floyds attacked their back catalogue with a passion bordering on fury. The final section of "Saucerful" captured here remains one of their greatest performances.

January 20, 1972: The Dome, Brighton, England

This show marks the first public performance of material from *Dark Side of the Moon*.

While some of the material had yet to be written, this gig does feature the band tearing through "Speak to Me," "Breathe," "Travel Sequence" (a very different, jazzy version of "On the Run"), "Time," "The Mortality

The Floyd on an oddly small stage during the early 1970s. By this time, they had graduated to playing large halls. *Photofest*

Sequence" (a very early take on "The Great Gig in the Sky" that bears little resemblance to the later versions), and a run-through of "Money," albeit without lyrics.

Dark Side was first performed for the press on February 17, 1972 at the Rainbow Theater in London. This Rainbow show indicates the rapid evolution of the songs, which would not be released for a year.

One good example of the album's development comes from a November 29, 1972 show at the Palais des Expositions in Poiters, France. In this show, one can hear a nearly complete version of the album without the characteristic backing female vocals or the saxophone of Dick Parry, who did not come aboard until 1973.

May 9, 1977: Oakland Coliseum, Oakland, California

Following *Dark Side* and *Wish You Were Here*, the band was more popular than ever in the United States. Consequently, to meet the demand for tickets, they began playing shows at outdoor stadiums, in addition to the indoor sports arenas they had booked on earlier tours.

So instead of playing their Chicago gig at, for instance, the Auditorium Theater, an indoor concert hall with good acoustics that seated a few thousand, they were at Soldier Field, a cavernous football field that seated nearly seventy thousand.

The shows on this tour consisted of the entire *Animals* and *Wish You Were Here* albums, plus encores of either "Money" or "Us and Them." This show featured both of those numbers as well as an additional encore, the band's last-ever performance of "Careful with That Axe, Eugene."

July 6, 1977: Olympic Stadium, Montreal, Quebec

This, the final show on the *Animals* tour, is the nadir of Roger Waters' mid-seventies sports arena tour diary.

As the show progressed, a crazed fan, egged on by Roger Waters, climbed up the netting separating the band from audience and screamed his "devotion" to Pink Floyd. In a gesture that Waters himself later described as shocking, the bassist walked toward the fan, further encouraging him, then spit in his face.

"I realized that what had once been a worthwhile and manageable exchange between us and them had been utterly perverted by scale, corporate avarice, and ego," notes Waters in the liner notes to the 1980–81 live CD *Is There Anybody Out There?*

This seminal event would be a key inspiration for *The Wall*. Waters came to see the huge, impersonal stadiums in which the band was playing as theaters of war: literal battlefields of struggle, violence, and groupthink in which audiences were tortured by blinding lights and high-volume sound.

The rock star-fan interface became, to Waters, one of warrior (artist) and victim (fan), and in this context, he didn't particularly like being a killer.

June 17, 1981: Earls Court Exhibition Hall, London

This show was the last of thirty live performances of *The Wall*. The tour is chronicled on *Is There Anybody Out There?*

In many ways, the live show was superior to the studio album, with a key extra song ("What Shall We Do Now?") and a spectacular bank of lighting effects, film, and props.

It was also a logistical and technical challenge that required a crew of eighty workers just to keep the staged theatrics cued to the music. Yet despite the now-fractured band's almost complete lack of communication, everyone involved somehow pulled off his part with, at worst, minor hitches.

In addition to being the tour-ender, this is also the final full concert that Waters, Gilmour, Mason, and Wright ever played together.

Steven Leventhal is a fifteen-year radio veteran. He is the host and producer of the syndicated radio show Psychedelic Time Warp, *and an avid collector of books and ROIOs pertaining to the psychedelic sixties.*

12

Point Me Down the Right Line

What Acts Influenced Pink Floyd?

L ike all musicians, the members of Pink Floyd have their favorite artists from the pop, rock, and jazz fields. Some of those artists— Jeff Beck, Aretha Franklin, the Who, Kate Bush, Herbie Goins— have little or no relation to PF music, but the Floyd do have plenty of musical forbears.

As Pink Floyd became more successful, and more sure-footed (some would say overly entrenched), they stopped sounding quite so much like others, and other bands in turn began to sound more like *them*, although *The Division Bell*'s "Take It Back" featured a riff that sounded familiar to anyone who'd heard Marillion's "The Realese."

Chuck Berry

All British rockers who reached maturity in the 1960s revere guitarist/singer/urban poet Chuck Berry. They love his conversational lyrics, which provided inspiration for both Bob Dylan and his acolytes, and Berry's matchless understanding of the classic rock and roll form.

Members of the Floyd adopt an interestingly aggressive stance, reminiscent of the Move or the Pretty Things, during a 1967 London photo session.

In his early 1960s days playing with Geoff Mott and the Mottoes, Syd Barrett was a devotee of Berry and other fifties rock and roll, as well as of progressive jazz and American acoustic and electric blues. Gilmour, as well, was a Berry fan, recording "Beautiful Delilah" on a 1965 demo disc with his Cambridge band Jokers Wild.

In its infancy, Pink Floyd played lots of Berry-style early rock and rhythm and blues, with Nick Mason recalling that "Motorvatin'" was a particular favorite (there is no such song; he is probably referring to the epochal 1955 recording "Maybellene"). Barrett's cocksure persona on early Pink Floyd material was surely influenced by the bluesmen he was listening to, but also by the exuberant and enthusiastic Berry.

In spite of this early influence, however, by the end of 1966 the group had shed its old-time rock and roll and R&B numbers in favor of more of Barrett's original and progressive material.

Miles Davis

Rick Wright—Pink Floyd's de facto musical director at least through 1973—painted with a wide palette of colors. He loved the classics and lost himself in jazz, particularly the work of Miles Davis.

Davis, one of the most important musicians of the second half of the twentieth century, helped create modern jazz as we know it. He helped bring the music from the post-bop of the late forties through the hard bop and cool phases of the 1950s, the Latin, boogaloo, and African rhythms of the early and mid-1960s, the experimental ambient sound of the late 1960s, and the rock and funk of the 1970s. Davis's horn playing was crystal clear, and his taste in assembling bands and his confidence in their ability to improvise led to a stack of incalculably influential records.

Wright noted years later that one of his favorite pieces ever was Davis's take on Gershwin's *Porgy and Bess*, and that the essential 1959 *Kind of Blue* album—which is on the top ten list of many a rock musician—was a key spark to the writing of the chord sequence that eventually became "Us and Them" on *Dark Side* after beginning its life as a piece written for *Zabriskie Point.*

Davis's pianist on *Kind of Blue* was Bill Evans, about whom Miles said in his autobiography, "The sound he got was like crystal notes or sparkling water cascading down from some clear waterfall." This approach

The Pink Floyd, clearly thrilled with the process of recording *The Piper at the Gates of Dawn* at Abbey Road Studios.

Photo by Andrew Whittuck/Redferns

describes the best of Wright's work with the Pink Floyd, where instead of aggressively forcing his way forward, he hung back and played with the space between the notes as much as he played the notes themselves.

Bob Dylan

The Great White Wonder's impact in England was as great as it was in America; in fact, "The Times They Are a-Changin'" was a hit single in the U.K. before Dylan cracked the U.S. charts.

An entire generation of British musicians, including Syd Barrett, David Gilmour, and Roger Waters, grew up believing in Dylan's example: that you could write from the heart and do it with a belief in classic folk-oriented song structure that owed much to the British folk tradition.

Barrett's Dylan inspiration was less directly stylistic than an impulsion to find his own muse as a songwriter, growing from his early folk style into the electric psychedelic guitarist he became with the Floyd. Syd worked easily in the Dylanesque stream-of-consciousness style, especially in his later solo work where the distance between the merely quaint and the totally unhinged was sharply compressed.

Gilmour and Waters, as more conventional and certainly more dependable talents, internalized Dylan's style musically (Gilmour) and lyrically (Waters). The folk picking of both players in the more pastoral Floyd songs was certainly inspired by Dylan's adoption of classic roots forms.

Sometimes the Floyd found real inspiration in Dylan's work, reaching back to their own folk traditions on songs like "Cirrus Minor," "Wish You Were Here," and "Goodbye Blue Sky." Certainly Waters' closing lyrics to "Sheep" ("Get out of the road if you want to grow old") owe much to "The Times They Are a'-Changin."

On occasion, the influence only reached as far as aping Dylan's sometimes droning, tuneless vocals and haranguing manner, as Waters did on *The Wall*'s "In the Flesh."

The Beatles

The Floyd never tried to *be* the Beatles or, as proper southerners, even *sound* like the Beatles, but the Fab Four's palette is unavoidably spattered over much of the Floyd's greatest work.

Sgt. Pepper's Lonely Hearts Club Band, the bible of summer 1967, gob-smacked musicians all over the English-speaking world, and the Floyd were no exception. Syd Barrett quotes musically from the album's title song in his subsequent single "Apples and Oranges," while Waters twice invoked "Lucy in the Sky with Diamonds": lyrically in "Let There Be More Light" and musically in "Point Me at the Sky."

Finally, the universal appeal and acceptance of the brain-melting "A Day in the Life" surely dovetailed with the Floyd's already strongly developed sense of *musique concrète* as expressed on the contemporary "Interstellar Overdrive."

Syd Barrett's replacement, David Gilmour, took much of his guitar sound in later years from the Alan Parsons/Geoff Emerick/George Harrison sonic palette of *The Beatles* (the "White Album") and *Abbey Road,* using the arpeggios of "Dear Prudence" and "You Never Give Me Your Money" as jumping-off points for his own playing, especially on *Dark Side* pieces "Any Colour You Like" and "Eclipse." Gilmour also stated that he enjoyed the picking on Cream's "Badge," which was actually played by Harrison.

This photo of the Beatles—from the taping of their *Strawberry Fields Forever* promotional film—comes from around the time that Pink Floyd visited them in Abbey Road Studios (March 21, 1967).

Roger Waters, as befits an artist with a bent toward "meaningful" lyrics, was a Lennon man, finding the classic "Across the Universe" compelling enough to use the lyrical pattern for 1971's groundbreaking "Echoes" and later playing "Universe" in his solo career. It would be fair to say that Waters also garnered inspiration and solace from the confessional songwriting style of Lennon's 1970 *Plastic Ono Band*.

Love

Arthur Lee, one of the first black hippies (if not *the* first, as he later claimed), headed this extremely important Los Angeles group. Moving from the folk-punk of their self-titled 1966 debut to the psychedelic chamber rock of 1967's *Da Capo* to the orchestral majesty of early 1968's *Forever Changes*, Love produced a startling trilogy of albums rarely equaled in their melodic invention and majesty by any group.

British musicians took to the group immediately; Led Zeppelin's Robert Plant was a huge fan of Lee, while the Move covered *Da Capo*'s standout opener "Stephanie Knows Who." In fact, Love was much more popular per capita in England than in the States. Syd Barrett stated that Love was one of his favorite American groups, along with the Fugs and Frank Zappa and the Mothers.

Barrett was turned on to Arthur Lee's aggregation through the good offices of Peter Jenner, who mentioned that a certain Love track (a cover of Burt Bacharach's "My Little Red Book") had an especially cool descending guitar and bass line that Syd ought to pinch.

Getting the tune a bit wrong, Jenner instead helped inspire the riff to "Interstellar Overdrive," which sounds very little like Love but turned into a launching point for one of the Floyd's greatest live numbers.

(Some, including Roger Waters, claim that the theme from British TV comedy *Steptoe and Son* is really the basis for "Interstellar Overdrive." While the first few notes are identical, and Syd was certainly aware of the song, the banjo-led music-hall/folk theme is a completely different animal, and itself sounds like Bobby Helms's late 1950s American hit "Jingle Bell Rock.")

The Kinks

The Kinks, a very British pop group singing in native accents about British things, were a major influence on Syd Barrett's writing. "Arnold Layne" is a character study as good as any of Ray Davies' work, while "Bike," "Apples and Oranges," and "Jugband Blues" also bear the mark of klassic Kinks kompositions like "A Well Respected Man," "Dedicated Follower of Fashion," and "Rosy Won't You Please Come Home."

Even after Barrett's departure, Pink Floyd retained some of the Kinks' sardonic humor in the "Mr. Pleasant"–styled "Corporal Clegg," and engaged in Davies' trademarked music-hall trompiness in later numbers like "St. Tropez" and "Free Four" before ditching it entirely.

Barrett's solo material also bore the stamp of a Kinks fan. "Here I Go" and "Gigolo Aunt" have that crunchy "Sunny Afternoon"/"Autumn Almanac" feel to them, and "Effervescing Elephant" has wordplay certainly worthy of Davies.

This is a Dutch picture sleeve of the Kinks' "Mr. Pleasant," a song that the Floyd may well have had in mind during the 1968 recording of "Corporal Clegg."

Gilmour, however, claimed not to be thinking of the Kinks' "Lazy Old Sun" when he composed and recorded (and played every instrument on) "Fat Old Sun" from *Atom Heart Mother*.

Cream

Guitarist Eric Clapton, bassist/blues harpist Jack Bruce, and drummer Ginger Baker were perceived in 1966—by the music press and by themselves—as Britain's finest in their fields.

The formation of this group marked one of the moments at which rock and roll became "rock"—when players were organized by other parties, when grown men with little in common and few personal connections grouped together to play rock music as a career move.

That said, Cream was indeed revolutionary and groundbreaking, especially live, where they wed a blues-based, power approach to improvisational techniques previously only found in jazz. And the members of the Pink Floyd loved the band's work.

Barrett told French music paper *Les Rockers* in 1967 that Cream and the Beatles were his favorites, and Nick Mason was especially impressed by Cream's live show. He found inspiration in Baker's African-inspired, jazzy, nonlinear but powerful playing and soon went to Baker's double-bass-drum approach.

But just as importantly, Mason felt motivated by Cream to do his own thing as a musician: "That night was the moment that I knew I wanted to do this properly. I loved the power of it all. No need to dress in Beatle jackets and tab-collar shirts, and no need to have a good-looking singer . . . the drummer wasn't at the back on a horrid little platform . . . he was up at the front," he wrote in *Inside Out*.

It must have been a thrill to the Floyd to play only their second show after officially turning professional in support of Cream on February 3, 1967 in Yorkshire. The all-night gig, the second of a nearly three-week tour away from London, included go-go dancers and a barbecue, an example of the old ways brushing against the new.

Cream, of course, only lasted through late 1968, a collection of large egos running rampant without any personal connection to get the players through tough times. But all three members of the band remained important musical figures in their solo careers, Clapton especially.

Following his decision to leave the Floyd, Roger Waters snared ol' Slowhand to play guitar on his 1984 *Pros and Cons of Hitch Hiking* album and subsequent tour, although Clapton apparently wearied of Waters' need for structure and quit the tour halfway through.

Jimi Hendrix

The influence of Hendrix on the British musicians of the late 1960s and beyond is nearly incalculable. While Eric Clapton, Jeff Beck, Davy Graham, Bert Jansch, and Pete Townshend had emerged as the land's most important homegrown guitarists, Hendrix—an American in London—showed up and topped them all.

What Hendrix had that more staid Brits didn't—or couldn't—provide was the thrill of the chase, the desire to entertain, and the raw nerve to do something like play "Sergeant Pepper's Lonely Hearts Club Band" live after hearing an acetate of the song once or twice, just days after its release. Or play guitar with his teeth, or behind his back, or stop his band (while on Lulu's live TV show) in the middle of one song and immediately start another.

David Gilmour loved Hendrix, going over full-bore to the Fender Stratocaster in tribute. Gilmour's tone also owed something to fellow Strat user Clapton, but the playing on full-on rock tracks like "The Nile Song," "Fat Old Sun," and "The Gold It's in the . . . " certainly echoes that of Hendrix.

While Pink Floyd was never going to be a full-tilt, rockin' ensemble, Gilmour's best work with the group echoed Hendrix in its surfeit of mystery and passion, two traits that Hendrix helped bring to modern rock guitar.

Fleetwood Mac

Peter Green's Fleetwood Mac was one of the finest-ever British blues combos. From the release of their first record in 1967, the Mac were loved for the fastidious musicianship, rejection of pop stardom, and dual-guitar interplay between Green and Jeremy Spencer.

(This Mac was very different from the version that hit big a decade later; while John McVie and Mick Fleetwood, the rock-steady rhythm section, gave the group its name, Christine McVie didn't join until the early seventies, and Stevie Nicks and Lindsey Buckingham well after that.)

This version of the group was Chicago blues-derived to the core, although Spencer idolized Buddy Holly and Green could write good, commercial rock songs. Much of the group's dual-guitar early output, especially their 1969 instrumental hit "Albatross" (a lovely, mournful instrumental echoing both classic blues and Santo and Johnny's 1959 "Sleep Walk"), would influence David Gilmour's evocative guitar lines in years to come, notably on "Echoes" and "Dogs."

Fleetwood Mac opened for Pink Floyd in summer 1968 at Steve Paul's "The Scene" in New York City. One would assume that the two bands propped up the open bar quite efficiently.

Chic

Most entrenched British rock musicians of the 1970s—who had grown up in the 1960s with James Brown, Sly Stone, and Motown as their idea of black pop—had a hard time with disco, which they felt was mechanized, soulless, and lyrically vapid. Much disco was surely that, but the best of the genre has aged far better than much of the British AOR of the seventies.

Chic—bassist Bernard Edwards, guitarist Nile Rodgers, drummer Tony Thompson, and singers Norma Jean Wright, Luci Martin, and Alfa Anderson—was enormously successful in the late seventies and early eighties and especially influential for a new generation of British musicians in both their stylish production and their ability to weave a danceable beat to strong rock-oriented arrangements.

Chic's hit records, such as "Le Freak," "Dance, Dance, Dance," and "Good Times," were funk rather than disco, because of a lack of overbearing string arrangements and the band's technique of keeping the tempo just slow enough not to be manic and silly.

When Bob Ezrin came on board with PF for *The Wall*, he saw it as a challenge to make this most album-oriented of bands a hit on the singles charts. He found a surprisingly receptive audience in the Floyd, who—although they didn't like disco—had no problems incorporating a more funky one-hundred-beats-per-minute backing to several of their songs (just as Queen did with "Another One Bites the Dust" a year or so later).

As a result, "Another Brick in the Wall" Part II, "Run Like Hell," and "Young Lust" all featured a strong disco/funk backbeat that owed much to Chic. The enduring nature of the New York band's work is part of why the best of the up-tempo music on *The Wall* hasn't dated.

Ten Classic Floyd Homages/Parodies

Kevin Ayers, "Singing a Song in the Morning"
The former Soft Machine bassist/guitarist recorded this Floyd-reminiscent piece in 1970 with Barrett playing lead guitar, but the track was unusable and Ayers had to do the guitar himself in Syd's style.

Kevin Ayers, "Oh! Wot a Dream"
This jaunty, charming 1972 single combines an almost "Pow R. Toc H." sound-collage opening with Rick Wright–style vocals.

Elvis Costello, "You Little Fool"
Costello provides harpsichord (forward and backward), Barrett-like electric guitar picking, and a careful arrangement to this charming '67-style pop song.

The Dukes of Stratosphear, "Bike Ride to the Moon"
XTC's side project plumbed the depths of great American and British psych, with Barrett's influence perhaps greatest here.

The Dukes of Stratosphear, "Have You Seen Jackie?"
John Leckie, PF engineer and Dukes of Stratosphear producer, says, "No specific [Dukes] track is *intentionally* Floydian but, yes, I guess the solo in 'Bike Ride to Moon' is a bit *Piper/Saucerful* with slide guitar and 'Jackie' has an 'Arnold Layne' lyrical homage."

Robyn Hitchcock, "Balloon Man"
His hands blew up like two balloons.

Robyn Hitchcock, "The Man Who Invented Himself"
This British singer/songwriter invented himself as a possibly saner Syd Barrett who sang about seafood.

Queensryche, "Waiting for 22"
This progressive metal band, Floyd fans all, covered "Welcome to the Machine" in 2007. This instrumental lays bare their debt to Dave Gilmour's epic style.

Television Personalities, "I Know Where Syd Barrett Lives"
This appealing 1981 single made the band's debt to PF clear, but when bandleader Daniel Treacy gave out Syd's home address from the stage, David Gilmour kicked the TVPs off his 1984 tour.

Zerfas, "I Need It Higher"
This utterly obscure Indiana quartet recorded a spectacular album in 1973; a standout track, "I Need It Higher" gets the downside of British psychedelia just right.

13

Make Them Do What You Want Them To

What Notable Guests Played on Pink Floyd Records?

T he Floyd served as a cloistered unit from their beginnings through around 1978, when Roger Waters asserted more control and began to bring in outside musicians to help him realize his particular vision.

Many of the people who assisted on Pink Floyd's records in the early days were friends or relations, rather than established top session musicians. Singer Clare Torry is discussed in "Down the Hole We Fall," and here you can read about several other outside contributors to Pink Floyd records.

Norman "Hurricane" Smith (Vocals on "Matilda Mother," "See Saw," and "Corporal Clegg," Drums on "Remember a Day")

Smith, who produced the first two Pink Floyd albums, passed away at age eighty-five in 2008. Smith was a fabulist, a ham, and an opportunist . . . but he was also an excellent arranger and record producer and a genuinely well-liked person.

Shaving his age from thirty-five to twenty-eight in early 1959 in order to get a job with EMI as an apprentice sound engineer, Smith—a former RAF pilot and jazz musician—soon mastered his craft and by 1963 became a chosen second-in-command to producer George Martin at Parlophone.

Working with the Beatles on their recordings from "Love Me Do" through *Rubber Soul* gave Smith the opportunity to develop his own ideas about recording, as well as the savvy and confidence to develop his own bands; he soon left engineering and branched out to production.

On the recommendation of pop impresario Bryan Morrison, Smith went to see Pink Floyd live. He didn't like the band's music, but he enjoyed the psychedelic light show and saw the potential in signing a group representing the "underground." Eventually EMI inked the group with the condition that staff producer Smith, rather than Joe Boyd, who had produced "Arnold Layne" and shared a wavelength with the band, be allowed to record the worrisomely erratic youngsters.

Despite being in his forties, Smith began to dress "mod" and adapted to the psychedelic era, although he wasn't a big fan of the genre. He did excellent work with both the Floyd and the Pretty Things, recording the latter's pioneering *S.F. Sorrow* concurrently with *The Piper at the Gates of Dawn*. Smith's brief from EMI was to produce commercial hit singles, while the Floyd and the Pretty Things were chasing something deeper. These clashes produced tension, but also led to catchy music that crackled with spirit and innovation.

Peering through the lens of time, Nick Mason (in John Cavanaugh's book *Piper at the Gates of Dawn*) gives Smith a good deal of credit for helping the Floyd become a recording act. Smith's skills as an arranger colored many of the treatments of Barrett's songs, and since the Floyd hadn't played a lot of *songs*—favoring extended improvisation during their live gigs—the album's combination of the progressive and the somewhat conventional is due in not insignificant part to Smith's pop *nous* and guiding hand.

In addition to his skills at arranging, engineering, and production, Smith is credited with helping create the vocal harmony for "Matilda Mother" and the later "See Saw," and chipped in backing vocals on both (as well as appearing on "Corporal Clegg" and "It Would Be So Nice").

Smith also unseated Mason from the drum chair on "Remember a Day," one of the standout tracks on *A Saucerful of Secrets*. Smith—who could also play piano and trumpet—contributed an excellent and very

Mason-like performance on the skins, giving Rick Wright's meditation on childhood a spare but driving rhythm.

The International Staff Band of the Salvation Army (Brass on "Jugband Blues")

One would assume that any member of the Salvation Army would have been through quite a lot. But could eight musicians in full Army gear have been prepared for the madness of Syd Barrett?

Dragged into De Lane Lea studio in October of 1967 to play on "Jugband Blues," the International Staff Band of the Salvation Army—which had been playing, in various forms, since 1891—had probably never heard music like this.

Although it's often said that the Salvation Army band was told to simply play whatever it wanted during "Jugband Blues," during the first portion, the "knees up" section, the horns follow the G to D to A to D progression carefully. One would assume that Norman Smith helped script this music for the full band.

It's only in the "freak out" section, following the full band drop-out, that the ISB was urged to indulge a perhaps previously unknown penchant for *musique concrète*. In this shambling song, Barrett and the Floyd used outside musicians both for planned music and a full-on experiment.

Perhaps that lucky stroke of insanity—one that happened to work this time—led Barrett, in his increasingly demented and contrary state, to suggest that Floyd add a banjo player, a sax player, and two female vocalists. This idea died in committee, and shortly thereafter, Syd Barrett was on the street.

Lindy Rutter Mason (Flute on "Green Is the Colour," "Party Sequence," "The Grand Vizier's Garden Party")

A ballet student as well as a musician, Lindy Rutter met Nick Mason in the early 1960s, and they married in 1968. Her move to New York City to study ballet at the Martha Graham Center meant that Mason became the first member of the Floyd to travel to America, visiting her in summer 1966.

As the Floyd were somewhat isolated from the "rock scene" due to their somewhat aloof upper-middle-class bearing as well as their general suspicions of the music business, the members of the band were largely ignorant of session musicians and the process of hiring them. Ms. Rutter was drafted to play flute on both of the band's 1969 albums.

Ms. Mason's blowing on an Ibizan flute gave *More*'s "Green Is the Colour" and "Party Sequence" some Incredible String Band–like hippie pastoral verité, while her lovely introduction and conclusion to her husband's drum suite on *Ummagumma* gave the limp "Grand Vizier's Garden Party" some of its only charm.

Dick Parry (Saxophone on "Money," "Us and Them," "Shine On You Crazy Diamond," "Wearing the Inside Out")

Parry, a friend and bandmate of Dave Gilmour's in Jokers Wild and the Soul Committee back in their 1960s Cambridge days, was a natural choice for the Floyd when they needed a saxophone solo for *Dark Side*'s side-two openers, "Money" and "Us and Them."

On the first number, he provided a honking, down-low, raunchy solo reminiscent of 1950s R&B, a sound not generally associated with Pink Floyd. "Us and Them" featured a jazzier, more lyrical solo as well as some extraneous blowing during some of the choruses.

Suddenly this obscure sometime session player/horseshoe maker was all over the radio on several continents. In addition to reprising his role as guest sax man on *Wish You Were Here*'s "Shine On You Crazy Diamond"—which in all honesty felt like a retread—he also joined the Floyd as a full-time live performer for all of their shows from 1973 through 1977. Following the exhausting six-month *In the Flesh* tour, Parry then spent two years treading the boards with the Who.

As an old friend of Gilmour's, he unsurprisingly sided with the Waters-less Pink Floyd when the three remaining members wanted to record again following *The Final Cut*. Parry appeared on *The Division Bell* and toured with the band in 1994. He also played solo shows with Gilmour in 2001, 2002, and 2006, and took the stage with the reunited Floyd at Live 8 in 2005.

Doris Troy (Vocals on "Us and Them," "Breathe," "Eclipse")

Born in New York, and famous for her 1963 R&B smash "Just One Look," Ms. Troy was more appreciated in the U.K., where in her thirties she became a much-favored session vocalist.

After a stint on the Beatles' label, Apple, resulted in two singles and an album (all of which failed to make noise on the charts), Ms. Troy continued to work on sessions for a wide swath of artists, including the Rolling Stones, Ringo Starr, Dusty Springfield, George Harrison, and even Joe Boyd–discovered folkie Nick Drake. Most people familiar with her voice, however, have heard her through her association with Pink Floyd.

As one of four backing vocalists employed for *Dark Side of the Moon* (the others are Lesley Duncan, Liza Strike, and Barry St. John), she contributes to the memorable harmonies heard during much of the second side. During "Eclipse," she also throws in memorable gospel-styled interjections echoing the lead vocal.

The stage show *Mama, I Want to Sing*, based on Ms. Troy's life (in which she played the role of her own mother), ran for fifteen hundred performances in Harlem and is now being turned into a major motion picture. Unfortunately, Doris Troy won't see it; the legendary vocalist passed away in Las Vegas in 2004 at age sixty-seven.

Roy Harper (Vocals on "Have a Cigar")

Roger Waters' bilious lyrics for "Have a Cigar" laid on thick his distaste for the music industry that had helped make him and his cohorts millionaires. Waters seemed to drain the pleasure from his work and focus only on what made him miserable about being a rock star, something that most of his fans would have given their eyeteeth to experience.

Once it came time to cut the track, Waters—just off a concert tour and feeling uncomfortable with his voice—didn't feel he could do the song justice. Roy Harper, a mate of the Floyd's who had appeared with them at the 1968 Hyde Park free concert and whose career was being handled (and records produced by) Peter Jenner, was hanging around Abbey Road Studios and apparently volunteered to take the vocal.

Harper, a fiery, iconoclastic, folk-influenced singer and songwriter a few years the Floyds' senior, had become a cult figure in the U.K. in the late 1960s and early 1970s for his epic compositions in which he laid out, in no uncertain terms, his disdain for imperialist politics, authority figures, and artistic pabulum.

Other artists revered the caustic but honest Harper. The Nice backed him in 1969; Led Zeppelin wrote "Hats Off to [Roy] Harper" to salute him; David Gilmour later played on his *HQ* album. He seemed to fully embrace Waters' vision on "Have a Cigar," laying down a vocal brimming with sarcasm, matching the none-too-subtle lyrics.

It is ironic that Harper, a much-respected but somewhat underground artist who did everything he could to ensure he wasn't ground into sausage by his record company, enjoys lasting fame largely from singing a song about the music industry on another artist's album.

Harper's key 1960s and 1970s albums have just been released on CD, most for the first time ever in America, by Koch Entertainment Distribution.

Snowy White (Guitar on "Pigs on the Wing")

Like many young British guitarists in the 1960s, White was transfixed by American blues. He left school in 1964, at age sixteen, and spent several years in Sweden plying his craft. After returning to England in 1970 and settling in London, he established connections with players like Peter Green and Gary Moore. Following a short stint with Steve Harley's Cockney Rebel, White spent some time laying down licks for folkie Al Stewart.

Having established a reputation for ability, reliability, and a friendly, easygoing personality, White was recruited by Pink Floyd in 1976 as an "augmenting" guitarist and bassist, meaning he performed with the band during the *Animals* and *Wall* tours. The first outside guitarist to appear with the Floyd on a regular basis, he also recorded a guitar solo originally intended for *Animals*' "Pigs on the Wing," but his work was deleted from all but the American eight-track tape version. (The entire song is available on White's 1996 *Gold Top* CD.)

After departing Pink Floyd following the first half of the original *Wall* concerts (documented on the two-CD live set *Is There Anybody Out There?*), White spent more than two years playing with Thin Lizzy. He has worked both with David Gilmour and in Roger Waters' band, and in recent years his hair has indeed turned snowy. Since 1993 most of his activities have centered around his own band, the White Flames.

Snowy White, the first "extra guitarist" to go on stage with Pink Floyd, during the English leg of the 1977 "In the Flesh" tour.   *Photo by Ian Dickson/Redferns*

Lee Ritenour (Guitar on "Comfortably Numb," "One of My Turns")

One would have thought that the entire history of Pink Floyd—its birth as an R&B act, its vault into the underground, and its rejection of much of the typical pop music jungle—would have precluded working with a lite-jazz session guitarist.

But Ritenour—who played on his first session on 1968 at age sixteen and had already released several albums of smooth, accessible jazz instrumentals—was one of the best technical guitarists around, and Waters and Gilmour wanted quality players on *The Wall*. Known as "Captain Fingers" in the business, he strummed along with Dave Gilmour on "Comfortably Numb" and added electric rhythm to "One of My Turns."

The sonic majesty of "Comfortably Numb" involves both Ritenour and Gilmour. The two play oddly strung acoustic guitars on the number; the third-, fourth-, and fifth-heaviest strings (G, D, and A) are tuned an octave higher than usual, which provides a lighter and more shimmery sound.

Fred Mandel (Keyboards on *The Wall*)

The Toronto-born Mandel first came to the attention of the rock world as a member of the Canadian band Lighthouse, which enjoyed a Top 20 U.S. hit in 1971 with an aggressive chunk of horn-rock entitled "One Fine Morning." He later joined Alice Cooper's band for the albums *The Alice Cooper Show* (1977) and *Flush the Fashion* (1980).

A talented hand with experience on all manner of keyboards, Mandel ended up playing Hammond organ on much of *The Wall* due to Rick Wright's refusal to visit Los Angeles for additional recording.

Like several others who worked on the project, Mandel was not credited on the album sleeve. It's interesting that Roger Waters wanted

The "real" Pink Floyd interacts with the "shadow band" during August 1980 London performance of *The Wall*.   *Photo by Rob Verhorst/Redferns*

to pretend that Pink Floyd was still a band that didn't need a batch of session musicians, while the reality of the situation was far different.

Following Mandel's experience with the Floyd, he went on to work in the 1980s with Queen (*The Works*) and Supertramp (*Some Things Never Change*) and spent five years in Elton John's band. He then began a career in film production.

The Beach Boys Contingent (Vocals on *The Wall*)

Perhaps the oddest pairing of all time of session musician and album: Toni Tennille and *The Wall.*

With the Floyd reduced to Roger Waters and Dave Gilmour, producers Bob Ezrin and James Guthrie brought in musicians who contributed keyboard, drum, and even guitar parts. Where once the four-piece band had been fully self-sufficient, Pink Floyd now depended on the services of hired hands, having become a corporate behemoth shorn of most of its already thinly sliced personality.

Hiring Bruce Johnston and Carl Wilson of the Beach Boys (some members of the group allegedly refused to sing on *The Wall* after learning its lyrical bent) was already enough irony for one day for this very English band. Then again, the Beach Boys—beset, of course by madness in their own ranks—had already added backing vocals to hit songs by Chicago and Elton John earlier in the decade.

But asking Toni Tennille (of "The Captain and . . .") to add her vocal contributions seemed utterly perverse. The good-time, very American sounds of the C&T produced several big hits during the 1970s, but never approached either introspective pomp-rock or improvisational space-rock. Eventually, things worked out fine, with the California singers adding a sunny quality to the gray matter of *The Wall.* (See "I Was There—Toni Tennille" for more detail.)

14

And Down the Hole We Fall

What Were Some of Pink Floyd's Key Missteps?

Most rock acts—even the huge, successful ones—make mistakes; see the Clash's *Cut the Crap*, *Bridges to Babylon* by the Rolling Stones, the Beatles' *Let It Be*, and Lou Reed's *Metal Machine Music* for further evidence.

Pink Floyd, as a self-contained enterprise largely distrustful of the music industry, made plenty of errors, some of them in the early days when, in Nick Mason's words, the musicians were being "hustled around trying to make hit singles." But they also stepped wrong a few times during their platinum years. Here are ten Floydian slips, things they might have done differently.

The Hendrix Package Tour (1967)

During the 1960s, the accepted career path for popular entertainers in England was the traveling package tour, in which several different acts played a few minutes each at every show. This concept comfortably embraced the early years of the rock era as well, because up through the mid-1960s, pop and rock bands played short songs.

One could view Pink Floyd's repertoire at the time—a lot of improvisation, strong avant-garde tendencies, and a couple of surprise hit singles—and figure that playing seventeen minutes a night in between other acts wouldn't necessarily be the best fit. Traveling all over England, where the notions of psychedelic music and free-form improvisation hadn't yet been explored, would be another red flag.

But having signed with Bryan Morrison's management agency, and with EMI, the group had wedged itself firmly into show business, and as a result had to do such things as write pop songs, play gigs when asked, and condense their act into small, digestible bites. One could see

Syd Barrett losing himself in the lights and sound at London's UFO Club.

Photo by Andrew Whittuck/Redferns

trouble coming down the alley, especially since Syd Barrett had begun to disintegrate before his friends' eyes.

On this tour, which began in London on November 14, 1967, the Floyd played just before the headliner, Jimi Hendrix, and were preceded by (in order) the Outer Limits, the Nice, the Eire Apparent, the Amen Corner, and the Move. The Move and Hendrix went over quite well due to their penchant for spirited playing, all-around entertainment, and outlandish (especially to the British) appearance.

While many Americans see 1967 England as a swinging, flower-power land, this was *not* the case outside of London and a couple of university towns. The United Kingdom of the mid-sixties was still stuck in the *early* sixties, a land of light entertainment, hit singles, and lager rather than pot (much less LSD).

The Floyd had returned from a disastrous American tour just days before, and perhaps predictably, didn't go over well, refusing to play "See Emily Play" and instead insisting on aggressive, improvisational noise that would have been a hit at UFO but not in the north of England. Already furious at Barrett for his behavior in America, the other three Floyds found themselves wondering how to save their quickly collapsing career.

Early in the tour, the group occasionally played an angry piece called "Reaction in G," and at times did "Interstellar Overdrive," but eventually switched to the new, nearly guitar-free "Set the Controls for the Heart of the Sun," largely because Barrett was too out of it to play much of anything.

As the band jaunted around the north and west country of England, where screaming girls begged for hit singles and drunken yobs out for a good time threw coins and beer at this bunch of London *artistes* who wouldn't even play familiar songs, Barrett was in a precarious state. Already miserable with the price of fame and taking too many drugs, Barrett didn't socialize much with other musicians on the tour—although Jimi Hendrix was apparently kind to him—and rarely even spoke to his own bandmates.

Sometimes he didn't bother to play his guitar or even tune it, opting to stand still and occasionally randomly clang the strings. Due to Barrett's antics, the other members of the Floyd would, as Waters later told Barry Miles, "come off stage bleeding because we hit things in frustration."

On at least one occasion the devolving guitarist didn't even show up for the gig, requiring David O'List of the Nice to stand in as the band played "Interstellar Overdrive." The tour ended December 5 in Glasgow, not a minute too soon for a shell-shocked Pink Floyd. Six weeks later, the band would play its last gig before firing Barrett.

"Have You Ever Read the *Evening Standard*?" (1968)

In their efforts to write that elusive post-Syd "hit single," the Floyd released Rick Wright's "It Would Be So Nice" in spring 1968.

Wright worked long and hard to make his first attempt at a 45 a surefire hit, and as a result "So Nice" is overly fussy and indebted both to Barrett's vocal style and the kind of *veddy British* lyric favored by Paul McCartney, Ray Davies, and, of course, Syd. Both Nick Mason and Roger Waters professed—after the record bombed, of course—to hate it, but then again neither of them was coming up with catchy material in 1968.

The original copies of the 45 referenced a leading British newspaper, *The Evening Standard*, in its lyric. Unfortunately the BBC banned the single, unfathomably deciding that the use of the newspaper's name was tantamount to advertising. That the group released a new version with the generic "The *Daily* Standard" dubbed in mattered not a whit, as any momentum the song had was already lost.

The entire episode was so miserable for the band that "It Would Be So Nice" wasn't even anthologized in England or America until 1992, on the expensive *Shine On* box set. Most folks who have heard it only became familiar with the single on a mid-seventies European compilation called *Masters of Rock*—and that version was in stereo, rather than the original mono.

The Studio *Ummagumma* (1969)

Following their patchy recordings of 1968—the cobbled-together *Saucerful of Secrets* and the failed singles "It Would Be So Nice" and "Point Me at the Sky"—and the just okay reception of early 1969's *More* soundtrack, Pink Floyd was in trouble as a recording act. So what's the solution? Why, release a *double album*, of course!

The folly of such a notion—even with one LP slated as a live disc—should have been apparent not only to EMI or Norman Smith (still nominally their producer) but to the four members of the Floyd themselves, since none of them had many songs to offer the project. But each, allegedly at Wright's urging, took half a side of an album to do whatever they wished.

Waters offered a pretty acoustic reverie, "Grantchester Meadows," as well as a sonic experiment in which he overdubbed his voice at several different speeds. The other three members of the group indulged their ambitions with multi-part "epic" "compositions."

David Gilmour's "The Narrow Way," composed mainly of tasteful guitar work and some buried vocals, at least indicated a few melodic ideas and was not as self-indulgent as most of the rest of the album. Waters reportedly refused to help Gilmour come up with lyrics for this piece.

Wright's "Sysyphus" was the keyboardist's big opportunity to establish himself as a key composer in a band dreadfully short of material. But he stumbled with this pretentious "suite," built around faux-classical piano, which was neither memorable nor groundbreaking. He admitted as much not long afterward.

Coming on the heels of "It Would Be So Nice," the failure of "Sysyphus" may have been destructive to Rick Wright's already fragile ego. For a while, he had been hankering to do something more than rock music . . . and when given the chance, he failed. After that, Wright composed little on his own for the band.

Mason's "The Grand Vizier's Garden Party" is an extended percussion track featuring a flute intro and outro played by his wife Lindy (who wasn't credited). It's grandiose and embarrassing, with an unprepossessing ambient atmosphere but little on the whole to recommend it.

The live tracks on *Ummagumma* nearly saved the album . . . but then again, isn't there something pretty desperate about a 1969 album relying on live versions of 1967–68 material?

"Atom Heart Mother" (1970)

Little more proof is needed of the mist in which Pink Floyd found itself following Syd Barrett's sacking than this twenty-three-minute multi-car pileup.

One would have thought that the misery contained in the *Ummagumma* studio album would have prevented the Floyd from again trolling the classical underbrush for a new direction, but apparently the foursome decided that what they really needed was a collaborator to make all their Royal Festival Hall dreams come true.

This meandering multi-part piece, some of which is the responsibility of Waters' collaborator Ron Geesin, has little to do with rock and roll. That would be okay if the piece were either good avant-garde or good modern classical, but there are few tuneful moments, and the sounds themselves aren't interesting enough to compensate for the dearth of melody, rock dynamics, or interesting playing.

A middling ambient, electronic section ("Mind Your Throats Please") sees the Floyd traversing a road they had more competently navigated on *More*, and the massed brass buildup nineteen minutes in is much ado about nothing. "Funky Dung" is *not* funky, at least musically. Wright's churchy organ backing up an almost tuneless massed choir adds extra pretense to the enterprise.

To be fair, Geesin received no support or respect from the older, more staid—in fact, combative—brass section, and was rushed into fixing a mistake in the sheet music that affected the beat in "Funky Dung." In addition, neither conductor John Alldis nor the brass section was familiar or comfortable with rock, or even jazz, and the tempo was a bit sluggish.

Perhaps the most interesting part of the entire piece to Floydwatchers is the use of a simple chord sequence (G minor to C) that three years later formed the basis for much of *Dark Side of the Moon*. For his part, Geesin would go on to do far more interesting work; he remains as contrary as ever and a fascinating conceptual/ambient musician.

The songs on side two of *Atom Heart Mother* are better; "Alan's Psychedelic Breakfast" is a slightly more interesting "experimental" work than the title track, and has more melodic ideas to boot.

Geesin, in collaboration with an Italian Pink Floyd tribute band (Mun Floyd), presented a new version of "AHM" in London in June 2008. The piece, this time given proper preparation, received good notices.

Not Paying Clare Torry More? (1973)

Session songwriter and sometime vocalist Clare Torry became famous for her singing on *Dark Side of the Moon*'s side-one closer, "The Great Gig in the Sky." Rick Wright's gospel-oriented piano piece, when adapted for full band and two tracks of screaming female singer, grew from a simple instrumental into a full-fledged meditation on death (and for those who don't enjoy it, a sonic approximation of same).

Ms. Torry, as per the rules of session work, was paid a flat fee (said to be thirty pounds) for her vocals and given credit for her work on the

Pink Floyd's ill-fated ad campaign for Gini Bitter Lemon tonic was meant to trade on the striking pyramid images used on *Dark Side of the Moon*.

album sleeve. She was not listed as a composer anywhere in the song's credits; at the time, this was completely accepted practice, and at no time in the next twenty-five years did Ms. Torry make public statements indicating that she felt aggrieved.

The group generally tended to keep to itself and work with people the individual members felt comfortable with, and as a result Ms. Torry remained a valued member of the Pink Floyd extended family, performing at solo shows both by Waters and Gilmour through the early 2000s.

In 2004, however, she sued Pink Floyd, claiming that her vocals on "Great Gig" constituted a melodic composition. (In recent interviews, she has stated that she *should* have pushed for credit back in 1972.) The following year, she won damages of an undisclosed amount, and now has her name listed on album credits as a co-composer of the track.

Ms. Torry has also performed with former Procol Harum organist Matthew Fisher, who also waited decades before filing suit against *his* old bandmates Gary Brooker and Keith Reid, claiming that his organ riff constituted a part of the composition of their worldwide 1967 smash "A Whiter Shade of Pale."

Those French Soft Drink Ads (1974)

The Floyd, committed to their vision of artistic integrity, wanted to do things their own way. They did, however, take one advertising gig during their time together as a foursome, lending their images and name to a print ad campaign for a French soft drink, Gini Bitter Lemon.

Four different ads featured photos of the Floyd in the desert, with a pyramid motif nabbed from one of the posters included in vinyl copies of *Dark Side of the Moon*. The photo was accompanied by the phrase "Gini . . . Pink Floyd . . . Gini. Un goût . . . une musique étranges venus d'ailleurs." Translated, it means, roughly, "A taste . . . a music coming from elsewhere."

Unfortunately, some of the Floyd's fans in France were disgusted by this relatively innocuous ad campaign. (What would those folks say now about Led Zeppelin, U2, and Sting shilling for iPods and gas-guzzling luxury cars?) Eventually an equally distressed Pink Floyd, who claimed never to even have tasted the drink, elected to donate the money received from the campaign to charity.

This is one of several Pink Floyd ads for Gini Bitter Lemon tonic. Note the band's seemingly deliberate anti-fashion.

Waters apparently later wrote a punning song called "Bitter Love" about the whole controversy. He and Gilmour averred that never again would they pawn their songs for advertising, but oddly enough the two had no trouble lending their name and images to brands like Guinness and Avis.

Years later Wright earned the enmity of the other group members by licensing portions of his "Great Gig in the Sky" for a pain reliever advertisement, but by the 1990s the band had signed up with Volkswagen as a tour sponsor. Funny how time changes things.

The Inflatable Pig in the Face of Punk Rock (1977)

The Floyd, as successful representatives of the sixties and early seventies, shouldn't necessarily have been expected to know what was (and wasn't) acceptable symbolism to a new generation of rockers more familiar with welfare and hopelessness than with the increasingly depressing emanations from the mouths of wealthy rock stars.

The use of a giant inflatable pig, however, as the emblem for their 1977 album *Animals*, was like a red flag to the bull of the fans and publicists of punk rock. Roger Waters and the album's designers, Hipgnosis, intended for the flying pig image to be both funny and relevant to the new album, which began and ended with songlets entitled "Pigs on the Wing."

The December 3, 1976 photo sessions for the *Animals* cover began at the Battersea Power Station in London. As photographers set up their cameras, a group of workers filled an inflatable forty-foot pig with helium, lashed it to guide wires, and sent it into the air like a kite. Unfortunately, after a good group of shots had been taken, the pig broke free of its restraints and floated off.

The humor of all this is clear, especially after various air traffic controllers reported the sight. But to young punks and those critics who already viewed the Floyd as a bunch of rich, out-of-touch whingers, a fake pig floating over dull old Battersea Power Station on a gray late-fall day stood as a symbol of boring, overstuffed music.

Despite the wishes of its detractors, however, the pig did not die, continuing to serve as a symbol of the band in both iterations. Waters used it for solo shows and the post-Waters Floyd did as well, although Gilmour, Wright, and Mason were forced to add testicles to their pig to avoid a lawsuit from their former bass player for trademark infringement!

The flying pig still generates plenty of news copy. On April 27, 2008, Waters and his band headlined the final night of the Coachella Festival in Indio, California. During the show, the band's giant inflatable pig—

festooned with political graffiti—was accidentally (?) released and flew away amid explosions and lights. Much of the audience probably thought that it was all part of the show. Two days later, shredded pieces of the pig were found two miles away.

Norton Warburg (1978)

Tax rates are punitive in Britain, and as a result the newly wealthy must find ways to invest their money so that Inland Revenue can't take it away. ("Should five percent appear too small," George Harrison sang, "Be thankful I don't take it all.")

This economic reality does not exist in a vacuum. Con artists use the system to exploit the rich, coming up with "investment" schemes that turn out to be nothing more than swindles: money poured into doomed companies, some of which is diverted back to the "advisers" giving advice to the poor saps being forced to "invest."

Pink Floyd fell victim to such a scheme in the late 1970s. Investment company Norton Warburg, run by Andrew Warburg, promised to help the group escape an eighty-three-percent tax liability on their income with various schemes.

So the company moved money from failed investment to failed investment—restaurants, manufacturers, loony inventors—with more and more of Pink Floyd's money disappearing all the time in "management fees," which went directly into Andrew Warburg's pocket.

All told, the Floyd lost more than a million pounds, according to Nick Mason, and were forced to become tax exiles for a year to escape Inland Revenue's claims on the money they had been swindled out of. Once the company's misconduct became clear, Andrew Warburg, seeing his little empire fall apart, escaped to Spain. He eventually returned to England in 1982 and spent three years in jail.

In order to help bail out the band, Roger Waters suggested two new projects: one about hitchhiking (which Dave Gilmour didn't find interesting) and one about a rock star building a wall.

Not Paying the Islington Green School Kids? (1979)

The decision to use twenty-three thirteen- to fifteen-year-old music students from the London Islington Green School as vocalists during the "we don't need no education" section of *The Wall*'s "Another Brick in the Wall" Part II was a classic move in the Pink Floyd tradition of extra-"musical" sound.

The massed vocals stated in plain English what many felt at the time to be the essential irrelevance of what passed for public education in an underfunded English system. The irony, of course, of schoolchildren singing the lyrics went right over the head of right-wing London news-papers like *News of the World*, who latched on to the song as an attack on all that was Good and Honourable and British.

The students' teacher, Alun Renshaw, was happy with the original deal proffered by the Floyd: free recording time at their Britannia Row studios. But the more hysterical press reports of the time covered all the bases, first attacking the rock group as unseemly for pointing out flaws in the system as well as "exploitative" for not paying the kids a wage, then pillorying the school's headmistress, Margaret Maden, who had been a Communist in the 1960s.

Eventually a slightly embarrassed but not unbowed Roger Waters arranged for all the kids to receive a free copy of the album and also paid the school a thousand pounds. But since the teacher had taken the kids to the recording session without the headmistress's permission (perhaps believing it wouldn't be granted), the school wasn't able to officially acknowledge that its students had recorded the song.

In 2004, a "royalties expert" named Peter Rowan filed an as yet unsettled claim for the twenty-three former schoolkids arguing that they are owed thousands of pounds of royalties on the record. His claim was based on the 1997 British Copyright Act, which changed the rules for how session musicians are awarded royalties based on radio airplay.

Going On Without Roger Waters (1986)

At some point in the 1970s, Roger Waters decided that he alone was Pink Floyd, regardless of the work that others had put into the band: Mason with his drumming and undoubtedly much-taxed diplomacy, Wright with his significant musical grounding, and Gilmour with his production and arrangement skills.

Never close during their best times, Gilmour and Waters scuffled more often as the band became more successful. Both have said that the biggest fights in the band grew from arguments about royalties,

David Gilmour, Nick Mason (standing), and Rick Wright pose for a promotional photo in 1988. While the three were happy to work together again, some Floyd fans wish they hadn't made *A Momentary Lapse of Reason.*

Photo by Patrick Hertzog/Redferns

songwriting credits, and such, with the bassist in particular still angry at his "generosity" in "giving" Nick Mason songwriting credits that he didn't "deserve" back in 1973.

One would think that having millions of pounds in the bank would ameliorate some of the anger, but within a decade, Waters was informing Mason that he'd be getting no royalties on *The Final Cut*, even though the percussionist had spent a lot of time generating and recording sound effects for various songs.

The direction of the Floyd's sound also was a huge sticking point. Gilmour's approach was always more about the music and the production, while Waters by 1972 was fully convinced that he was the only "idea man" in the band—which is a valid and arguable point. The band's commercial (and, most would argue, artistic) breakthrough came when all four combined their particular gifts.

Aside from any megalomania on Waters' part, there are good reasons for him to have felt that he was the band's most important, and perhaps only irreplaceable, member. Gilmour and Wright had recorded solo albums after *Animals* (perhaps feeling that Waters was bullying their material off the Floyd's albums), and neither Mason nor Wright had been fully reliable of late.

While Waters' grief and anger about his family, about Syd Barrett, about bad business deals, about war and starvation, and about the travails of his own band are understandable, he appears to have become as cruel and unfeeling as he accused others of being. The big bust-up came in 1979, when he fired Wright from the band.

Waters wanted Wright go to Los Angeles during a holiday to record keyboard tracks, as Columbia Records had offered Waters a bonus to turn in *The Wall* in time for a 1979 release. When Wright refused, Waters saw red and decided to make his move.

The bassist and songwriter threatened to impound all tapes from the project unless Wright was dismissed from the group. This threat worked, though it was a line in the sand that Waters may not have been legally or morally empowered to draw.

While both Mason and Gilmour accepted that Wright had become a liability, they didn't forget the cruelty of Waters' gambit. Things just got tougher, however, after *The Wall*, especially between Gilmour and Waters. Mason wrote in *Inside Out* that due to all the tension in the air, the very idea of doing another Floyd album after *The Final Cut* seemed unthinkable.

But that eventually changed after Mason and Gilmour decided to work together again in 1986. Waters had already put together a touring band and done shows made up heavily of Pink Floyd numbers, which made both drummer and guitarist energized enough to want to continue with or without their bassist.

When informed of their plans, Waters simply told Gilmour, "You'll never do it," which gave the remaining Floydsters all the impetus they needed. Waters believed that it was *his* decision whether Pink Floyd should continue or not, and announced to the world in 1986 that the band was finished.

Mason and Gilmour begged to differ. "The feeling was that it wasn't his decision to make," said Gilmour. Mason wrote, "[Gilmour] had perhaps suffered the most injustice [in the band]. Even I, not prone to confrontation, felt aggrieved that after twenty years I thought I was being told to quietly lay down, roll over, and retire."

The three Floyds' decision to continue was undeniably successful, at least commercially. Two studio recordings (1986's *A Momentary Lapse of Reason* and 1994's *The Division Bell*) and a live set (*The Delicate Sound of Thunder*) outsold Roger Waters' solo material by a wide margin.

These post-Waters PF albums are described by their former bassist as "a pretty fair forgery," relying on "deep" lyrics, epic song construction, and the kind of production and arrangement techniques that Gilmour had honed over many years with the Floyd.

Unfortunately, Gilmour and Wright were never prolific composers, and for *Lapse* they called in other songwriters to help them try and re-create the magic that was prime-era Pink Floyd. Most lyrics on the somewhat improved *Division Bell* are credited to Gilmour and his wife, Polly Samson. But neither album holds together like the band's classic material, falling too often into cliché and overproduction: They're the musical equivalent of middle-age spread.

15

I Was There— Ron Geesin

The Story of "Atom Heart Mother"

by Ron Geesin

I had been introduced to Pink Floyd's Nicky Mason by a mutual Notting Hill acquaintance, Sam Cutler, on the 14th October 1968. My wife and I soon became good friends with him and his then-wife, Lindy, and through them we met the other members.

By May 1970, the group was being pushed by its manager, Steve O'Rourke, and EMI to get another album out but was, by its own admission, a bit low on ideas. They had assembled the skeleton of a long work in separate sections on tape at EMI's Abbey Road Studios. It was called either "Epic" or "The Amazing Pudding"; all my scores show "Epic."

Since I was well known to all group members by this time, they brought a rough mix to me of the assembled sec-

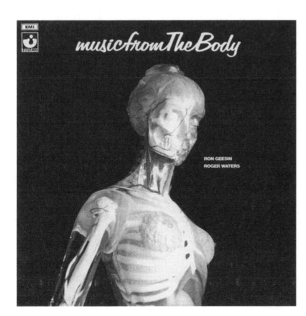

The Body, an odd, fascinating Roger Waters/ Ron Geesin soundtrack done in 1970, features an uncredited Pink Floyd on one cut, "Give Birth to a Smile."

tions and indicated that they wanted "a big sound" by means of other instruments played over a backing track. We settled on ten brass, solo cello and twenty choir (decided by budget). David Gilmour came to my studio in Ladbroke Grove, London, and played me a sketch suggestion for the first theme melody, followed soon after by Rick Wright, who did similarly for the start of the main choir section. The group then left me with the tape and went to tour America.

From mid-May to mid-June 1970, I formed the material, beginning by writing out a matrix of all the chords from the tape. Soon after the group's return, the sessions were arranged at Abbey Road from the 19th to the 23rd June to superimpose the brass, cello, and choir onto the master eight-track tape.

There was a fair amount of nervousness all round! The Floyds couldn't read music—I could, but slowly—so none of us really knew what was going to emerge. The brass players, "fixed" by the EMI system, proved very hard and cynical in contrast to those delightful experts from the New Philharmonia Orchestra whom I knew and preferred.

The EMI men, lips hardened by blowing all sorts of mediocre rubbish, soon sensed their naive prey and started asking provocative questions instead of being helpful. I was soon on the offensive, marooned on an ocean of parquet flooring.

My squaring up to hit a horn player signaled the necessary action of choirmaster John Alldis in taking over conducting from then on. Photographs of the sessions show that once removed to the control room, I was truly relieved.

At the end of the successfully completed sessions, in time at least, I said to Steve O'Rourke, "Well, that was a good rehearsal. When can we do it properly?" One reason was that, because of a misunderstanding between drummer Nicky Mason and myself, my part of the so-called "funky" section was recorded one beat earlier than I had written: I had taken beat two in the bar to be beat one. All I needed to do was move the bar lines one beat to the left, but there was no time!

Revisiting this work after thirty-eight years, I find that my part embodies a dilemma for and against: the opening section is a critical statement about the nature of so-called "progressive rock." The group's drone is on the tonic note of E, but my brass drones pull and twist in that tension up and down, never settling on it. In immediate contrast, I embrace David

Gilmour's first main theme chord sequence and wrap it around with a complimentary melody.

Do you know, in sound composition, if you time it right, you can put nearly anything next to anything else? So it is with the first effects section made by the group. You could interpret this as their exhibiting a love/ hate relationship with their own material, or mine! Here is a simulated 1800s cavalry charge ending with a motorbike, accompanied by a fog of trombones. The next challenge for me was the section for a lyrical solo instrument, cello in this case. Contrary to the more acid aspects of my work, I love a good melody and tried to do a good one here.

Coming to the main choir section, I am held on a lead with the bare minimum of chords. So, I stretch these as far as I can. Similarly with the immediately following "funky" section, except that I replace harmony with phonetics. By the time I had come to the return of the first theme, I muttered, "Not those old chords again!" so I wrote a completely new melody to make them, and me, appear fresher. The partially discordant ending is of course Geesin turning round with wry wink to say, "I'm not done in yet!"

It could have been titled "Floyd v. Geesin," "An Argument in E Minor for Soloist and Orchestra," "In and Out of Groove," "Atom Heart Bother," or even, as a German friend of mine used to call it, "Atom Cow."

The issued album was titled by this main work, which occupied all of side one. Each member of the group has at some time said nasty things about the album, including "a load of rubbish," but here I stress that I had nothing to do with side two!

Ron Geesin has been playing music with joyous abandon for most of his life. He describes his live improvisations as "sub-conscious flow," his studio music as "electro-melodic sound-painting," and his life as "chance careering."

His work has taken two main routes: pure expression, both in live performance and recordings, and music for films, TV and radio. Geesin plays fretted strings and keyboards and was an early advocate of using tape machines to augment or sometimes replace live musicians.

This essay, excerpted from the program of his June 14–15, 2008 performance of "Atom Heart Mother," is reprinted with thanks. Please visit his Web site (www. rongeesin.com), which is full of interesting stuff!

16

Yippee You Can't See Me

What Are Some Hard-to-find Floyd Tracks?

Pink Floyd recorded more music—singles, films, and tracks on outside projects—than its "proper" albums could contain. For various reasons, the songs listed below *were* released during the band's career, but are difficult to get hold of unless shelling out for fourteen-CD box sets or import reprints is your cup of tea.

All of these tracks, however, are worthy of exploration, either for historical or musical reasons. Many of these songs reflect patterns or ideas that the band would continue to explore. Some are just great pieces of rock and roll.

"Interstellar Overdrive" (1967)

Ready? Let's fasten our seat belts for a trip through space, time, and various recording, mixing, contractual, and record company follies.

The Floyd's first recordings as a four-man group were done with Joe Boyd and engineer John Wood at London's Sound Techniques in February 1967. Director Peter Whitehead filmed the band recording two songs; the footage was eventually used as part of the film *Tonite Let's All Make Love in London*, released that December (by which time Syd Barrett had nearly worked his way *out* of the Pink Floyd).

Whitehead knew of the Floyd because he had once dated Barrett's then-girlfriend, Jenny Spires, who persuaded the filmmaker to fund a recording session of this cutting-edge rock ensemble. The studio time yielded "Nick's Boogie," a nearly twelve-minute improvisation based around a Mason tom-tom pattern, and an early go at live favorite "Interstellar Overdrive."

Due to its loose groove, somewhat rough sonics, and single-take energy, the mammoth 16:40 track approximates the sound of Floyd onstage better than the outstanding but studio-cobbled final product released on *The Piper at the Gates of Dawn*. This early recording includes a lot of melodic ideas that are simply lost in the final studio version.

Both of these songs are currently available on the rerelease of the film soundtrack as well as the CD/DVD *London '66–'67*, but not on any "legitimate" album that Pink Floyd currently controls.

Once they signed to EMI, of course, Floyd rerecorded "Interstellar Overdrive" with producer Norman Smith on board. Smith gave the band a free hand, allowing Barrett to sit at the controls and mix together two complete takes of the song, and the studio version clocked in at a more palatable (though still outrageously long for the time) 9:42.

In July 1967, an early monaural mix of "IO" was issued on an EP (an extended-play 45 RPM disc) in France, but edited to 5:16. The song wasn't chopped up so much as truncated—the recording simply fades out without building up to the final coda. For anyone who's heard the final product in its entirety, this edit makes little sense. This version was made available on the 2007 fortieth anniversary triple-disc reissue of *Piper*.

That's not the only "Interstellar" outtake, though, on the triple-disc set. The previously unreleased take six is available as well. (A bootleg recording of take five of this song also exists.)

Take six, a complete run-through, is one of several attempts Smith and the group made at recording a more compact version without over-dubbing. It lasts "just" 5:04 and hews to the form of the released "IO," though with interesting variations in intensity and Barrett's playing. The ending is appropriately interstellar.

"Apples and Oranges" (1967)

Pink Floyd's time in the British hit parade, the teen music papers, and "fab" magazines was short. With "See Emily Play" just having slipped from the Top 10, and *Piper at the Gates of Dawn* recently released, the August 19, 1967 *Melody Maker* reported Syd Barrett was "suffering from 'nervous exhaustion,'" causing the group to cancel £4,000 of August bookings. At recent gigs, Barrett had refused to play, or sometimes strummed a single chord.

To make matters worse, Barrett wasn't generating commercial songs. (Early projected follow-ups "She Was a Millionaire" and "Scream Thy Last Scream" didn't work out.) Waters and Wright tried to supply singles, but "Paint Box" and "Set the Controls for the Heart of the Sun" ended up a B-side and an album track.

Shortly before the band's American trip in October, Barrett finished "Apples and Oranges," inspired by a girl at a supermarket in Richmond, southwest of London. The song was produced quickly, and it shows. Barrett's confusing and confused lyrics are complemented by piercing feedback, an unfocused arrangement and mix (the tambourine on the single mix is ridiculously loud), and a botched tempo change. Roger Waters later claimed that Norman Smith's production "destroyed" the song, but this evaluation seems rather harsh; the released take, while catchy in places and not without its charms, barely holds together.

"Apples and Oranges," released in early November 1967, had actually been heard the previous month on ABC's *Dick Clark's American Bandstand*, where Barrett gave an uninspired, halfhearted lip-synch performance as the other members of the band tried to cover for him.

Though it was procured by Tower (the Floyd's American label) for the show as an exclusive, the 45 was never released in the States. Its fate in the U.K. was little better; despite an upbeat *New Musical Express* review ("the most psychedelic single that the Pink Floyd have come up with . . . there's a catchy and repetitive chorus which should provide a reliable sales gimmick"), "Apples and Oranges" failed to dent the charts.

A 1968 film—post-Barrett—was shot for this already old song. Waters does the lip-synching honors, while new guitarist David Gilmour's face isn't seen until nearly two minutes into the clip. His white Fender Telecaster guitar gets a good view, however, perhaps as an attempt to make people think that Syd Barrett, he of the white Tele covered with mirrors, was still in the band.

"It Would Be So Nice" (1968)

"It was a lousy record."—Roger Waters

"Fucking awful, wasn't it?"—Nick Mason

These quotes, taken from Barry Miles's *Pink Floyd*, represent some of the most openly bitter attacks by one band member against another's work. No wonder Rick Wright was crabby so much of the time, with his own mates running him down in print after this failed 1968 attempt at a single.

While "It Would Be So Nice" may not be a classic, it's hardly worthy of the beating it's taken. The song is perhaps only "awful" if one believes that everything in life has to carry the self-important streak of *The Wall* or *The Division Bell* (or, for that matter, "A Saucerful of Secrets"). There is a place for "pop" in popular music.

The Floyd's not-me-fellas insistence that they did not enjoy making singles or being pop stars is simply hooey: successful men rewriting history and copping an attitude. (There are plenty of "we want to be rich and famous pop stars" quotes from 1966–67 to refute those later claims.) Pink Floyd fully embraced the idea of pop stardom until Barrett departed the band and the remaining four's *sheer inability* to write hit records forced them to adopt their later "album rock" strategy.

Had "It Would Be So Nice" or Waters' equally contrived "Point Me at the Sky" become chart items, the group certainly would have continued to release singles, and most likely would have been contractually required to do so.

Promotional films were produced for both of the band's 1968 singles. In "It Would Be So Nice," Wright, seeming somewhat embarrassed at his keyboard, looks to his bandmates for support. Waters simply raises his bored eyes to the heavens, Mason stares at something off camera, and Gilmour concentrates on his guitar.

"It Would Be So Nice" was never released on album in the U.K., or in the U.S. in any form, until 1992, when it was made part of the "First Five Singles" CD on the *Shine On* box set. Forcing a group's fans to pay big dollars just to hear a few rarities in good condition? No wonder people steal music on the Internet.

"Point Me at the Sky" (1968)

This was the band's second attempt at a single following the departure of Syd Barrett. This fable of a man inviting a friend to travel in his flying machine spelled the end of the group's attempt to write pop songs. After it failed, the Floyd didn't release a single in the U.K. for eleven years.

"Point Me," a spacey, Beatlesque confection—the chorus is a restatement of the refrain of "Lucy in the Sky with Diamonds"—features several sections edited together. The finished product sounded harsh and tinny on record, suffering from a poor mix that completely underemphasized the vocals, as well as a mediocre pressing. To this day, it is the only Pink Floyd song released at the time never to appear in stereo.

Though promoted with a short film of the group being flown in a battered old propeller plane, and a January 1969 BBC recording, this song went nowhere on the charts and remains unknown to many casual Pink Floyd fans.

The lyrics begin with a kind of come-on, as Henry McLean invites Jean onto his flying machine. But McLean wants to fly away not just for romance, but also because he's worried about the Earth, specifically starvation, pollution, and people generally being horrible to each other.

The idea of heading for the sky, perhaps from some deserted beach, to escape the miseries of the world is a recurring theme in Waters' early work, and suggests an increasingly negative worldview.

But once more, the business side of things messed up the message. Canadian copies of the single, on Capitol, were labeled "Point Me *to* the Sky"—indicating once again how little record companies really cared about getting the details right. This record was not released in America in any form at the time, and wasn't available in the States until 1992, as a part of the fourteen-CD *Shine On* box set.

This is Waters' first recorded lyric concerned with ecology, but not his last; he would soon write the anti-development lament "Breathe" for his collaboration with Ron Geesin, *Music from the Body.*

"Come In Number 51, Your Time Is Up" (1969)

Michelangelo Antonioni in 1969 was coming off the international success of his first color film (and his first in English), 1967's *Blow-Up*, an incisive dissection of "swinging London." He now turned his attention to America, but asked the very British Pink Floyd to contribute music to his new film, *Zabriskie Point.*

The music was recorded in Rome over what appears to have been a tense and problematic two-week period. The high per diems at least provided a few members of the band with the opportunity to drink fancy wines every evening. Antonioni was apparently very demanding and rejected a fistful of the Floyd's efforts from the sessions. (Much of this originally unissued material was released in 1997 on a bonus disc.)

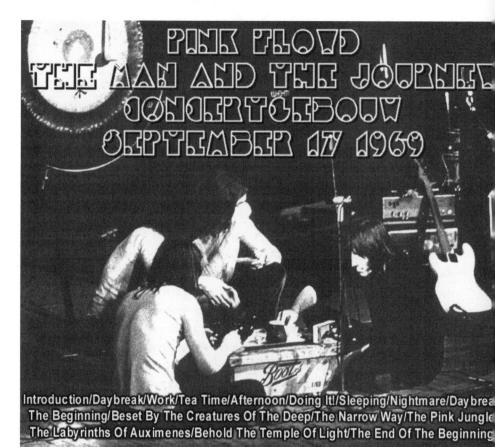

PINK FLOYD
THE MAN AND THE JOURNEY
CONCERTGEBOUW
SEPTEMBER 17 1969

Introduction/Daybreak/Work/Tea Time/Afternoon/Doing It!/Sleeping/Nightmare/Daybrea
The Beginning/Beset By The Creatures Of The Deep/The Narrow Way/The Pink Jungle
The Labyrinths Of Auximenes/Behold The Temple Of Light/The End Of The Beginning

This photo shows the band "sitting for tea," part of the 1969 concert presentation *The Man and the Journey*. Live recordings of the show have never been released legally, although some songs from it evolved into later Pink Floyd numbers.

Eventually one of the three pieces the director used was this rewrite of "Careful with That Axe, Eugene," an instrumental that had debuted in late 1968 on the B-side of "Point Me at the Sky."

Waters' octave bass notes and Wright's spectral organ set up an appropriately creepy backing to the film's conclusion, in which untrained actress Daria Halprin, grief-stricken over the murder of her lover, imagines the violent, fiery explosion of a fancy desert real estate development. The music's crashing climax at 3:04, with appropriate Waters scream and caustic Gilmour guitar, says more than any dialogue could to sum up the film's violent inner core.

"Crumbling Land" (1969)

The Floyd found it odd that Antonioni selected this track, which sounds like the American roots-rock represented by most of the remainder of the artists on the *Zabriskie Point* soundtrack, for his misunderstood yet fascinating film.

"Crumbling Land" is interesting both as music and for the fact that much of it sounds *nothing* like Pink Floyd. During the verses, Gilmour, Wright, and Waters appear to be channeling the three-part vocal harmony that Crosby, Stills, and Nash would soon make so popular. Waters' popping bass is atypical, and Mason's galloping drums could be the work of someone else.

Gilmour said, in Barry Miles's *Pink Floyd*, that "Crumbling Land" was "a kind of country and western number which he could have got done better by any number of American groups."

That may be so, but few C&W bands—especially British ones recording in Rome—would have included two dramatic organ- and timpani-led bridge passages. That and the stereophonic motorcycle effects in the fade are more emblematic of what Pink Floyd were doing at the time.

Another tune recorded at the film sessions, appropriately titled "Country Song," shuffled along in a bluesy/country vein, but again was somewhat mislabeled. This track didn't come out until 1997, on the *Zabriskie Point* reissue CD.

"Heart Beat, Pig Meat" (1969)

Tribal drums and keyboards form the backdrop for this anarchic spoken-word collage used in *Zabriskie Point*. The eerie and spare backing is the kind of atmospheric music that Pink Floyd did very well . . . and is a clear step toward the spoken-word collages that would inform *Dark Side of the Moon*, especially the female voice around 1:30 that sounds eerily like the airline announcer of "On the Run."

This track shows two important things about Floyd. It is evident from Antonioni's decision to use the band in his film that by 1969 Pink Floyd was seen, even by those outside of the rock inner circle, as a significant force in the growing field of progressive, even avant-garde popular music.

It's also critical to note that the band fished around endlessly for ideas to help convey stories in nonmusical ways. Think of how many times PF used the cries of seagulls, child's voices, snippets of mass media, and everyday dialogue to help convey a narrative. Even this "meaningless" track ended up influencing *Dark Side*, which both began and ended with a heartbeat.

"Embryo" (1970)

When EMI Records realized the value of marketing "new" rock in the late 1960s, the company chose to spin off several of its more progressive acts onto a custom imprint, Harvest. The new label issued a budget-priced compilation, *Picnic: A Breath of Fresh Air*, in 1970. This two-record set, intended to introduce fans to the label's artists, went out of print fairly quickly.

Picnic included Syd Barrett's "Terrapin," along with cuts by past and future PF pals Kevin Ayers, Roy Harper, and Pete Brown & Piblotko, but the most important track on the album for Pink Floyd fans was "Embryo," a stage favorite not released in any other form until more than a decade later.

Hipgnosis, who worked on most of the Pink Floyd's album designs from 1968 onward, designed *Picnic*'s cover. Containing anodyne images of a typical British day at the beach, it's not one of their best sleeves.

Those fans who investigated *Picnic*, however, found a delicate Waters number ranking among the group's prettiest pieces of music ever. Wright's lovely ambient piano and flutelike keyboard, and Gilmour's soft vocal and washes of wah-wah guitar, become sonic tendrils wrapping their way around the listener. Waters' swooping bass is echoed by occasional sped-up voices, which refer to his work with avant-garde classical composer Ron Geesin.

In 2007, a three-CD retrospective of music originally found on the Harvest label, simply called *A Breath of Fresh Air*, was issued. Though it also contains "Embryo," most of the other tracks do not duplicate those released on the original 1970 album. The Floyd fan who wants the track at a cheaper price is directed instead toward the 1983 U.S.-only *Works* compilation.

"What Shall We Do Now?" (1981)

This song was originally intended for inclusion on *The Wall*, but was eventually omitted. When the band went on tour to promote the album, Waters decided to reinsert the number, following "Empty Spaces" and preceding "Young Lust."

It's available on the double CD *Is There Anybody Out There? The Wall Live 1980–81*, and in its naked honesty is one of the most affecting latter-day songs that Waters penned.

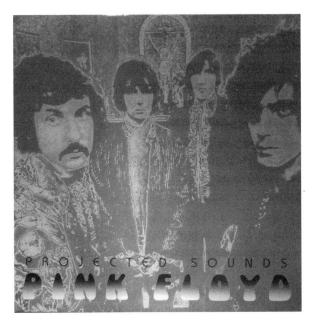

Over the years, Pink Floyd fans have snapped up bootleg recordings like this one in order to hear outtakes, unreleased songs, demos, and live records from Pink Floyd's entire career.

The lyrics concern the emptiness that comes with realizing your money can no longer provide joy, or even solace. The only thing that the singer doesn't seem to mention is love, and by the following song, the protagonist has begun to look for lust—a cheap substitute—instead of real human contact.

But "What Shall We Do Now?" is also a song about Pink Floyd, as discussed in "Engulfed in a Fever of Spite." Waters had been struggling with whether to continue the group for years, and was near the end of his rope. The desperation and anger come through.

"When the Tigers Broke Free" (1982)

With this single, Roger Waters confronted head-on—at least for public consumption—his father's 1944 death at Anzio. The song, also left off *The Wall*, was issued on the two-disc *Echoes* compilation and later tacked on to the 2004 CD reissue of the band's 1983 *Final Cut*. "Tigers" was also used in the *Wall* film.

It's far from commercial, but this single does effectively tell a grim story, with Waters' typically unadorned vocals accompanied by orchestral backing and military snare drums. His contempt for warlike thinking is clear from his sarcastic lyrics about the sacrifice of "ordinary lives" served up by British military brass just to hold on to a bridge and the line about the empty condolences sent to his mother from "kind old King George."

The gold-leafed condolence note, which Waters found years later in a drawer, shocked him, and his reveries of remembrance and staggering grief formed a major focus for his 1978–82 work. The "Tigers" referred to in the song were the tanks that broke through the Allied lines at the bridge and killed most, if not all, of Eric Fletcher Waters' company.

Whether or not Waters' music appeals, one can feel for his tremendous grief at having, as is stated in the closing lyrics, "daddy taken from me" not by the enemy . . . but rather due to decisions made by the high command of the British military.

Ten Mind-Blowing Floyd Sound Effects

- The toy box and birds at the end of "Bike"
- The seagulls in "Set the Controls for the Heart of the Sun"
- The mosquito in "Grantchester Meadows"
- The dripping tap beginning "Alan's Psychedelic Breakfast"
- The wind during "One of These Days" and "A Pillow of Winds"
- The football fans singing in "Fearless"
- The airplane crash in "On the Run"
- The clocks in "Time"
- Roger Waters' cash-register loop in "Money"
- The multiple televisions in "Don't Leave Me Now"

The Echo of a Distant Time

Do Other Bands Owe Something to "Echoes"?

I t's easy to maintain that "Echoes," from 1971's *Meddle*, is Pink Floyd's defining work. This 23:30 epic sums up the band's inner and outer space explorations with its sweep through funky rock, guitar heroics, a beguiling harmonic vocal line, and "turquoise and green" marine and sky sounds.

Bearing the distinct imprint of the Beatles in its tuneful verse sections and its lovely cosmic lyrics—and of early seventies British rock in an organ-driven, boogie-ish section—"Echoes" veers into singular territory during an extended section in which the band evokes the sounds of underwater life.

This epic is among the Floyd's most influential pieces, with its, er, echoes running through to Britpop, ambient house, stadium rock, post-punk, and, to Roger Waters' disgust, even musical theater. As unlikely a party as the Beastie Boys parodied the band's performance of "Echoes" in *Live at Pompeii* for their video "Gratitude."

The Electric Light Orchestra

Initially founded to further the work the Beatles began with mid-period psychedelic symphonies "A Day in the Life" and "I Am the Walrus," the Electric Light Orchestra was the brainchild of Roy Wood, songwriter and sometime singer of the Move.

(Wood's band, famous for catchy songs like "Night of Fear" and "I Can Hear the Grass Grow" as well as for antics like smashing televisions and dressing like 1930s gangsters, was among the Pink Floyd's "competitors" on the underground circuit and was also part of the Hendrix/Floyd late 1967 British package tour.)

After just one album, Wood departed ELO in 1971, placing the band in the hands of guitarist and composer Jeff Lynne, even more transparent a Beatles freak than his mentor. It makes sense, then, that ELO's biggest debt to Pink Floyd lies in "Echoes," which bears both musical and philosophical marks of the Fab Four's late-sixties oeuvre.

Jeff Lynne's major debt to "Echoes" is evident in ELO's 1976 classic symphonic instrumental "Fire on High," which begins with the same B-minor chord that Rick Wright intones on "Echoes" at 12:45. "Fire on High" also features similar overtones and harmonics over that single chord, takes some melodic ideas from the vocal line, and uses Gilmour's dramatic six-string explosion at 18:15 as inspiration for a very Floydian ringing, harmonic guitar line.

XTC

Characterized as punks early in their career, the manically energetic members of XTC—from Swindon in England's west country—were actually much too old to be truly "street," having been firsthand listeners to British psychedelia, hippie rock, glam, and even prog.

And they remained unashamed fans of early Pink Floyd, Pentangle, Genesis—and, at least in the case of bassist Colin Moulding, even Jethro Tull—despite the un-hipness of such forms of rock in the late seventies and early eighties.

The band's early work with John Leckie, who engineered *Meddle* for Pink Floyd and later worked on *Wish You Were Here*, afforded valuable lessons in studio techniques such as phasing and backward recording.

While XTC never recorded twenty-three-minute songs, its work does integrate psychedelic and progressive sounds. The close of "Echoes," with its frightening, otherworldly squalls and noises, is a very strong influence on XTC's equally apocalyptic "Deliver Us from the Elements," the last track on side one of the 1982 album *Mummer*.

Birdsong, Mellotron, and the sound of the breeze, major Pink Floyd reference points, also feature prominently on other songs from *Mummer*.

Later, XTC—working again with Leckie—recorded an EP and an album's worth of psychedelic homages under the name "The Dukes of

YCH, GARAGE, BEAT, POWERPOP, SOUL, FOLK... FOR PEOPLE WHO WANT MORE!

'S HIP! IT'S HAPPENING! IT'S...

Shindig!

1966

THE SAN FRANCISCO SCENE
*The Grateful Dead, Jefferson Airplane,
Big Brother & The Holding Company,
Quicksilver Messenger Service and more!*

*The strange tale
of the psychedelic
alter-egos of*

XTC

*"When I grow up
I'm going to be in a
band like Tomorrow"*

THE DUKES OF STRATOSPHEAR

05

9 771754 361006

BLUE ASH *The great lost power pop band*
THE STORY *New father/son acid-folk duo*
THE SONICS & THE ZOMBIES *Reborn on stage*

MAY-JUNE 2008
VOL 2 ISSUE 4 £4.25

LL THE HOTTEST NEW RELEASES AND REISSUES REVIEWED!

XTC's Andy Partridge, an unabashed Syd Barrett fan, worked with former Floyd
engineer John Leckie on two terrific psychedelic pop records released under the
name The Dukes of Stratosphear.

Stratosphear." Syd Barrett's work with the Floyd was a major touchstone for the two acclaimed Dukes projects.

Duran Duran

In the mid-1980s, "new romantic" dance-pop hitmeisters Duran Duran stood confidently atop the pop music mountain. Writing, playing, and even remixing their own material, they enjoyed five Top 10 U.S. singles in 1983–84 and experienced crowd scenes reminiscent of Beatlemania.

Duran guitarist Andy Taylor defended the group's videogenic, made-up, pretty-boy image in the early eighties by noting that he and his bandmates used video "like Pink Floyd used stereo." And he was right; MTV helped spread Duran Duran's music through a series of effective videos that painted the band as five too-hip denizens of a high-fashion, high-income lifestyle.

All hot things eventually cool down, and the former pinups found adulthood a difficult slog, falling prey to tax exile and drug problems, struggling through solo projects, and sinking into mid-level stardom during the hip-hop and grunge eras.

But even more predictable, perhaps, than their fade into obscurity was their 1993 "comeback" hit single, "Ordinary World," in which the former MTV stars sang, surprisingly affectingly, about *not* being stars. The truly astonishing thing about this gigantic worldwide hit was that few people seemed to notice that the melody of the verse was lifted from "Echoes."

U2

Coming along just a bit late for both punk and "new wave" in the early 1980s, the Irish quartet U2 was influenced by punk but avoided that movement's contempt for what had come before, instead using the bricks of 1960s and 1970s rock to build its sound.

While the group's rhythm section had energy, if not slickness, it was guitarist Dave Evans (a.k.a. "The Edge") whose singular playing gave the group much of its sonic identity. Certainly Evans worked several different angles, including classic rock, folk, and blues, but one of his biggest sonic influences is David Gilmour's Fender Stratocaster sound.

Like Gilmour, Evans plays spare guitar lines that he beefs up with digital delay or reverb to make his contribution sound bigger while actually remaining quite simple. It's a technique that takes courage, since most guitarists overplay rather than underplay.

Gilmour's choppy, effects-laden guitar tone near the end of "Echoes" is undeniably a starting point for U2, and the huge, chiming guitar climax is just icing on the cake. By the time of 1994's *The Division Bell*, by which time U2 was arguably the most popular rock band on the planet, Gilmour was using a lot of The Edge's reconstituted tricks to beef up his *own* guitar sound, particularly on "Take It Back."

Andrew Lloyd Webber

From the rock stage to . . . Broadway and beyond? Composer Andrew Lloyd Webber appears to have taken a big chunk of the melody of "Echoes" for the theme song from his 1986 show *Phantom of the Opera.*

While he lacks decorum, the dyspeptic Roger Waters has a point when calling foul on the world-famous stage composer. As he told *Q* magazine in 1992,

> I couldn't believe it when I heard it. It's the same time signature—it's twelve-eight—and it's the same structure and it's the same notes and it's the same *everything*. Bastard. It probably is actionable. It really is! But I think that life's too long to bother with suing Andrew fucking Lloyd Webber. I think that might make me really gloomy.

Of course, Waters shouldn't push too hard on such a fine point, since an uncharitable solicitor might object that much of the meter and some of the images of the "Echoes" lyric themselves come from John Lennon's "Across the Universe."

Webber also may have heard Paul McCartney's "Mary Had a Little Lamb," which uses a similar descending and ascending note structure. If so, that would be one of the stranger points of inspiration ever for the musical theater.

The Charlatans

In the late 1980s and early 1990s, British rockers such as the Stone Roses and Happy Mondays fused their grooves with the seductive rhythms of house and techno to form a new kind of psychedelic dance music.

Northwich, Cheshire's Charlatans, however, have lasted longer than most other groups from the so-called "Baggy" or "Madchester" movement, perhaps because they always had a better sense of rock's history than the others, and thus had more directions in which to turn after the acid house / rave culture burned itself out.

The band's early singles featured fat Hammond organ grooves and effects-heavy guitars, forging a classic but updated sixties feel, and a B-side, "Subtitle," featured a Farfisa part placing the song directly in *Piper at the Gates of Dawn* territory. In addition, the Charlatans' light shows owed more to Pink Floyd's 1966–67 visuals than to anyone else's.

The first Charlatans album, 1990's funky and psychedelic *Some Friendly*, owes much to keyboard-led rock classics from the late 1960s and 1970s such as Deep Purple's "Hush," the Doors' "Peace Frog," various Steppenwolf numbers, and even Delaney & Bonnie's "After Midnight."

But the band had a very strong feel for many of "Echoes'" components. The use of found sound on "109 Pt. 2" and "Polar Bear" and the slow, building grooves of "Believe You Me," "Flower," and "Sproston Green," which overflow with creamy Hammond organ, psychedelic guitar effects, aggressive bass, and winsome vocals, owe as much to "Echoes" as to any other influence.

The Orb / Steve Hillage

Guitarist Steve Hillage joined French/British anarchic hippy collective Gong in 1973 and stayed for three years. After he left the band, Hillage worked solo; the Floyd's Nick Mason produced his 1978 *Green* album.

He and his partner Miquette Giraudy have worked on numerous projects together over the past thirty years, including the ambient/progressive dance duo System 7 (called 777 in the U.S.) in the 1990s. System 7's floaty soundscapes hark back to Hillage's 1970s work, and the connection became especially clear when British techno artists the Orb remixed System 7's "Mia" in 1991.

The Orb—Alex Patterson and, less frequently, Kris Weston—is known for its remix work and love of prog, having produced an underground "trance" remix of *Dark Side of the Moon* in the early nineties, and its take on "Mia" reflected that influence.

Using psychedelic-sounding keyboards, a repeating note resembling that at the beginning of "Echoes," and a series of odd spoken bits about fishing, Patterson and Weston brought "Mia" underwater, creating a beguiling and fully psychedelic sub-sea environment that not only invokes the Floyd's masterwork but also shows its compatibility with more synthetic and "modern" sound.

Hillage and the Orb continue to work together on a loose basis in System 7, along with other techno DJs and sound architects such as Laurent Garnier and Carl Craig. Gong, also influenced by Pink Floyd's soundscapes, has also re-formed for short spells in recent years.

Mixmaster Morris

Morris Gould, a London DJ who began his career in the early 1980s, has worked with the Orb, the Shamen, System 7, and Spiritualized, among others. He has long professed a love for Krautrock, minimalism (i.e., Terry Riley, Steve Reich, and LaMonte Young), and all forms of underground dance music.

He produced some of his most 1970s-influenced work on the 1993 EP *Underground*, released under the name Irresistible Force. While the first track, "Underground," is Detroit techno with minimalist beats, "Flow Motion" shares more than a title with Can's 1976 album, and "Space Is the Place"—named after, but not reminiscent of, Sun Ra's soundtrack to

On this 1993 CD, Mixmaster Morris (as the Irresistible Force) blends ambient music and soft digital beats, invoking the spirits of such Old Masters as Can, Tangerine Dream, and Pink Floyd.

a 1972 film—is among the top ambient chill-out pieces of the era. "War and Peace Live" contains a keyboard fade filched from Rick Wright's 1969 dreams.

His Floyd influence is most notable, however, on that EP's so-called "ambient mix" of "Underground." Using a four-note motif played by a keyboard programmed to sound just like the one that began "Echoes," Morris uses swirly keyboards to establish a trance-like, psychedelic mood. He's invoking more than water "underground," however; in addition to the use of "Echoes"-like sub-sea-level effects, Morris is also replicating the sounds of the London Underground train.

Gould, known for his psychedelic outfits, lengthy live DJ sets, and admiration for Syd Barrett, continues to work sixties and seventies experimental rock into his work.

Node

One of the most evocative soundscapes of the past twenty years was created in 1995 by Node, a British ambient collective including electronic composer Dr. Dave Bessell, famed producers Flood (Erasure, Depeche Mode, U2) and Ed Buller (Pulp, Spiritualized, Suede), and Gary Stout.

"Swamp" is nearly nine minutes of swirling, murky underwater sound that is in some ways as frightening as it is beguiling, with primordial ooze dripping from both speakers and unidentifiable creatures peering out from behind the reeds.

Bessell told the author in 2008,

> Everyone knows "Echoes," and probably everything that you hear has an indirect effect on what you play. We were not consciously aware of a direct influence at the time we recorded it, but we did consciously go back to the working methods of electronic music of that period.
>
> So everything was jammed out live, mostly on old analogue equipment, and what you hear is what we played with minimal editing. So perhaps inevitably there is something retro about what we produced.

Node went on to record an album live at Paddington rail station in London, taking full advantage of all the ambient noise from passengers, announcements, and even rain on the station's glass roof, all following in the footsteps of *Dark Side*'s "On the Run."

The Flaming Lips

Lead Lip Wayne Coyne is a longtime devotee of what Pink Floyd produced both with Syd Barrett and after his departure. He told *Uncut* magazine in 2003 that the Floyd, on *Dark Side*, achieved "the type of mood we were hoping to get on [their 1999 album] *The Soft Bulletin*: a mood that says, 'this record is about death and isolation.'"

Among the Flaming Lips' biggest Floyd homages is "Pompeii Am Götterdämmerung" from their 2006 *At War with the Mystics* CD. The 4:22 track encapsulates the trippier side of PF's 1971–74 work, welding a typically psychedelic backing and Floydian progression to a harsher, post-punk energy.

Most of *Mystics* sports a strong progressive rock influence, with the disturbing instrumental "The Wizard Turns On" also owing much to the Floyd, including a nod to the opening piano of "Echoes" and an enticing Mellotron melody.

The Lips' trademark balancing of the humorous and the serious, often in the same song, even allows them to make fun of the notion of rock—in this case, represented by the grand conceit of playing "Echoes" in *Live at Pompeii*—as grand Wagnerian opera while also milking overdone pomp-rock, with all its clichés, for its undeniable effect.

18

I Was There— John Leckie

With the Floyd, Both as a Fan and as a Recording Engineer

by John Leckie

I got into rock and roll from Butlin's Rock and Calypso Ballroom and juke boxes in milk bars! Then it was the Jazz, Folk, & Blues Society at grammar school.

The first gig I ever saw was the Downliners Sect at Studio 51 in London on Sunday afternoon sessions. Then at age fifteen, I saw the Yardbirds at the Marquee in 1964, then saw *everyone* weekly at Klooks Kleek, 1965–69: John Mayall, Eric Clapton, Peter Green, the Graham Bond Organization, the Nice, Family, the Crazy World of Arthur Brown, Cream . . . plus Jimi Hendrix at the Roundhouse in 1967, the Who at the Starlight Ballroom Greenford, the Rolling Stones in Hyde Park, Blind Faith, etc. . . . and the Floyd. (Strangely, I never knew any musicians until I worked at Abbey Road; I'd always been in the audience.)

I first saw the Pink Floyd at London Free School on the same night that Cream played their second gig at Cooks Ferry Inn, Edmonton. It was 1967 and we went to see Floyd rather than Cream because we knew they were psychedelic and we wanted to see a "San Francisco"–style light show.

It was summer, so it was not totally black outside, and at Powis Square Nursery School. The audience sat on little kids' chairs (and occasionally jumped up and "freaked out," a move later known as "idiot dancing"). There was always competition between the Floyd and the Soft Machine amongst my mates.

A hirsute Pink Floyd around time of the *Meddle* album.   *Photofest*

I was big fan of *Ummagumma* and when I saw "Engineer: Peter Mew" on the credits and heard the record I realized, "That's what I want to do."

My career as a producer/engineer began at Abbey Road in February 1970. I had been shown around after my interview in 1969, and it all seemed pretty scary and technical, not unlike [the] BBC. [Abbey Road] called me back six months later and I got the job. It was a serious technical responsibility job but most of the people working there were *crazy* eccentric!

My professional relationship with the Pink Floyd was good. They were having fun and seemed to be allowing a lot of experimenting to get sounds . . . everyone was having their say. They were also still playing local gigs; during the recording of *Meddle*, I saw them at Twickenham Technical College.

I worked with the Floyd before and after *Dark Side*. Both their music and their circumstances had changed. The music was more rehearsed after *Dark Side*. The playing was more accomplished and yet the parts were simpler. It had more "soul" and less experimenting in sound.

My input on those records was minimal, I'd say. I was just learning, really, and flying by seat of my pants! I learned more than contributed anything artistically. Really, I just got the job done. It was good taking instruction from Roger or David and they were always super-critical on quality of sound before they went for a take. So I learnt a lot about listening.

During the time of *Meddle* they were experimenting all the time. "Echoes" and "One of These Days" were *all* experimental. "Echoes" started as "Nothing Parts 1–25" and each part was a snippet. Just like the piano coming out of the Leslie speaker starting "Echoes." There were also a few blues workouts.

After *Dark Side*, we spent time at AIR Studios doing the "household objects" thing but nothing came of it. We spent ages doing tuned wine-glasses, which I think Alan Parsons continued with later. There were also a lot of attempts at building up voices in long tape echoes one to two seconds apart. This technique later became known as "Frippertronics"! The same technique was used for the bass repeat echo on "One of These Days."

I don't know if I would have done anything differently had I produced their later records . . . like most recorded music, it's all gotten a bit too polished and I prefer a rawer sound. *DSOTM* is raw in its basic four-piece band setup. The whole of *Dark Side of the Moon* in 5.1 sound is staggeringly awesome on a big studio system! Back then, it was successful because it had *soul*, and it sounded great at a time when everyone was a hi-fi buff and it showed off their systems.

My personal faves? "Fearless" on *Meddle* has become one of my favorite songs, as it's loved in Liverpool; the La's and Cast both played it but those versions never got recorded. I also always liked "Pow. R Toc. H" because it was really spacey and cosmic. And "Interstellar Overdrive" is the recording most like them in the early days.

Have you heard this one? The riff in "Interstellar Overdrive" is the theme to *Steptoe and Son*! Imagine Syd watching telly at home and noodling on guitar and picking up on that. Coincidence, I'm sure!

We all know how Syd Barrett turned out. I worked with him a little bit late in his solo career and never got a real idea, in the studio, of his true talent . . . but he had charisma and, seemingly, lots of songs.

John Leckie is an internationally renowned record producer who has helmed projects for dozens of acts, including Radiohead, the Fall, Kula Shaker, XTC, the Stone Roses, Simple Minds, the Verve, Let's Active, the Posies, Baaba Maal, and Be-Bop Deluxe. He began his professional career engineering records by George Harrison, John Lennon, Yoko Ono, and Mott the Hoople, as well as Pink Floyd's Meddle *and* Wish You Were Here.

19

Bright Ambassadors of Morning

What Are Pink Floyd's Iconic Record Cover Images?

Since most of the members of the Pink Floyd were either art or architecture students, they were well versed in the importance of the visual. Their longtime interest and indulgence in light shows, lasers, and inflatable onstage characters indicates this. One of the first groups to have truly memorable cover images as a characterization of a collective identity, the Floyd took control of their own packaging fairly quickly, and had their own design sense in place by 1969.

Beginning with *Ummagumma,* the group's album covers served in part to define the music but were always a separate art concept as well. Every new Floyd album sported—*had* to have, really—an iconic image, and the band's development on this front is as much a story of designers Storm Thorgerson and Aubrey "Po" Powell, and their company Hipgnosis, as it is a story of Pink Floyd.

The Piper at the Gates of Dawn

Pink Floyd's debut album emerged in late July 1967, in the immediate wake of *Sgt. Pepper* and at the height of the public's fascination with psychedelia. The need, then, for an eye-catching sleeve and title were paramount for EMI, which had sunk a hefty chunk of money into its odd new band.

The July 8, 1967 *New Musical Express* reported that the album would be titled *Astronomy Domine,* and that Syd Barrett was designing the front

Vic Singh's superb cover photo for *The Piper at the Gates of Dawn.*

cover. Eventually the album was re-titled and the guitarist's drawing of an eight-armed beast— meant to represent the band—was relegated to the back of the sleeve.

In place of Barrett's work is a trendy but attractive cover photograph by Vic Singh, whose prism lens split each member of the Floyd into four. This trick effectively makes the image more disorienting and spacey, but at the same time more inviting, than a standard shot would have done.

Many record covers from the psychedelic era have dated horribly, because the ideas behind them weren't good to begin with. The Pink Floyd, on the other hand, had four interesting-looking people to showcase, clothes outlandish even by contemporary standards, a well-composed sleeve image, and a gimmick that made an already good shot even better. Score!

Ummagumma

The first two Floyd albums featured good sleeves placing the band firmly in the psychedelic camp. Their next project, the soundtrack to Barbet Schroeder's *More*, was packaged in a sleeve featuring an image from the film. Pink Floyd, to this point, had not featured a truly distinctive album cover.

The third album proper, *Ummagumma*, would be the first in which the Floyd moved forward in a graphically distinctive direction. Storm Thorgerson (see "Only a Stranger at Home") and Po Powell designed a cover using all four members of the group as essentially interchangeable props in an intriguing picture-within-a-picture illusion. This is an appropriate characterization, as the group never courted publicity as individuals or embraced the notion of "pop" stardom following Barrett's departure.

(Early versions of *Ummagumma* featured, leaning against the wall under the mirror, the soundtrack album to *Gigi*. Legal wrangling forced EMI and Capitol to paint the cover image a plain white on later pressings. Mint condition copies of the early pressings with the *Gigi* image are collector's items.)

The double album's inside sleeve featured conventional band portraits. Nick Mason conceived of the album's back sleeve photo: the group's instruments, amplifiers, and microphones laid out on an airstrip and assembled to look like an old airplane, in homage to a layout of an old fighter plane Mason had recently viewed in a magazine.

With the band's gong perched atop the transit van, and microphone cables curling out, the equipment looked less like a plane than like a giant electronic beast. Shots exist of the band members surrounding the gear, but the final image featured the band's roadies, Alan Styles and Pete Watts, flanking the equipment they would unload, set up, repair, and load back in every night.

A concert poster used in America in 1970 features an outtake from these photo sessions. Watts and Styles are sitting on the van in the background, while the Floyd crowd around their instruments.

Looking back from a 2008 perspective, it is rather amazing how *little* gear—two guitars, two basses, one drum kit—the band carried at the time, and as a result how hard the soundmen and roadies had to work to change broken strings, etc. during a show.

Atom Heart Mother

With Pink Floyd a standard brand among the U.K. rock fans by 1970, and a growing name in the U.S., the group responded with what would become a characteristic U-turn.

Rather than use their new record sleeve to evoke the Floyd's astrally conscious lyrics, or their improvisational technique, or their pioneering multimedia live shows, Thorgerson instead took a photograph of a cow in a field. The whole point was to produce something unrelated to the music.

For a band to eschew the normal post-psychedelic/hippie art of the day, and not even feature the name of the group or the album, was absurd, unheard of. A shocked higher-up at EMI, when presented with the notion of the cow sleeve, is said to have yelled at Thorgerson, "*Are you trying to bankrupt this record company?!?*"

Whether or not this tale is apocryphal, the sleeve was unconventional, but in retrospect perfect, an eye-catching image unlike anything else on the market. In a strange way it complemented the odd music the Floyd was making at the time, and its very difference made it stand out.

That the album went to number one in the British charts despite lacking a photo of the band did not go unnoticed by the Floyd, or indeed by other rock groups or album designers. The world had changed from the pinup culture of the 1960s; rock and roll fans had shown themselves fully capable of growing along with their bands and accepting new kinds of sleeves.

Never again would Pink Floyd feature their pictures on a front cover, and never again were they asked to.

Relics

Between the releases of *Atom Heart Mother* and *Meddle*, the Floyd released their first compilation, a ragbag of singles, rarities, and album tracks entitled *Relics*. This album was many fans' first exposure to early tracks such as "Arnold Layne" and "See Emily Play."

Emerging from EMI in May 1971, *Relics* featured a cover illustration from none other than former student draftsman Nick Mason. The drummer supplied a piece he had created back in architectural school—an odd-looking contraption including several musical instruments—that he called "a fantasy homage to illustrators Heath Robinson and Rowland Emmet [sic]."

Robinson (who died in 1944) and Emett (who lived until 1990) were both famous British illustrators specializing in fantastical machines, but while Robinson simply drew his goofy creations, Emett actually built some of his devices, which ended up in museums. Americans may find familiarity by relating Mason's device to something drawn by Rube Goldberg.

Not all Pink Floyd fans, unfortunately, were able to see Mason's intriguing cover. EMI Australia and Capitol (in the U.S.) released the album with far more conventional, and less interesting, sleeves featuring "first world" architectural artifacts. In 1996, the CD and LP reissue featured a photo of a real-life version of Mason's prototype, commissioned by Storm Thorgerson.

Dark Side of the Moon

Rick Wright apparently suggested that the new Floyd album have a "simple, clinical, and precise" image, according to the text of *An ABC on the Work of Hipgnosis.* The idea of basing the cover on Pink Floyd's groundbreaking light shows came from Thorgerson and Powell; up until now, their covers had rarely referenced the group's massive concert appeal.

Even this beautiful, seemingly straightforward image of a prism of light, however, is bathed in illusion. The angle at which the prism resolves on the back cover is physically impossible, and the colors emerging from the prism do not exactly relate on the color wheel.

The level of importance to which album sleeves had grown by the 1970s is indicated by the package; the inside and outside sleeves are designed so that two of them can be placed end to end when opened up to form a longer picture. (Roger Waters is given credit for helping design the inside cover, with the heartbeat emerging from the color bars.)

As a bonus, the album also included two posters and two sets of stickers. The album's success guaranteed that millions of teenagers would have Pink Floyd images on their bedroom walls for years. Soon, other bands began competing to give away the most swag with their albums.

Dark Side of the Moon's success was a perfect storm: a fine album and a memorable cover image for a band poised to raise their game one level and take advantage of an opportunity for a new superstar rock act in a fallow time.

The album's success was also a demonstration of Capitol's ability to push an act forward once it decided to do so. Feeling that *DSOTM* was an extremely commercial record, Capitol spent more time and money marketing it than they'd spent on most of the Floyd's previous albums combined.

The disc's cover image—spacey, high-tech, but simple and inviting—has been so successful in the last thirty-five years that it's been parodied and imitated but never approached in terms of what it evokes while actually saying so little.

A Nice Pair

When *Dark Side of the Moon* exploded to the top of the American and British charts in a way few had dreamed possible, EMI/Capitol chose to exploit the suddenly bankable band's back catalog by repackaging the first two Floyd albums. Knowing they were about to lose the band to Columbia made Capitol that much more determined to milk the escaping cash cow.

The Piper at the Gates of Dawn and *A Saucerful of Secrets* were hence stripped of their original psychedelic sleeves and instead placed in a custom-made double sleeve that bore the perverse humor and surrealist tendencies of the Hipgnosis team.

Using suggestions from members of the group and other Hipgnosis employees, Powell and Thorgerson came up with thirty-six different photos, some of which illustrated phrases like "a frog in the throat," "a fine kettle of fish," "laughing all the way to the bank," etc. Other images were just interesting photos of the band, while others showed arresting scenes such as a glittery theater lobby or a freaked-out, stoned hippie with cartoonish glasses.

The rarely displayed Floyd humor was evident in some of these photos, such as the group posing as part of its football team or wearing fake vampire teeth. The double-album package could have been cynical, but the involvement of the Floyd and Hipgnosis at least ensured that the enterprise was carried out with some taste and humor.

Wish You Were Here

Pink Floyd, now an internationally known supergroup, had carte blanche from new label Columbia to put together another grand package for a new album. But a simple redo of *Dark Side* would not serve.

The new album's theme of emotional and physical absence, especially in those who possess star-level talent and/or success, shone through to Hipgnosis, who developed a series of associated designs based on their reading of Roger Waters' lyrics.

For starters, the album appeared in the record racks wrapped not in the clear cellophane of the day, but in opaque blue. The necessity of identifying the group and the album on the sleeve led Hipgnosis' graphic designer of choice, George Hardie, to develop a special sticker.

The arresting image on the cover of Pink Floyd's *Wish You Were Here*, developed by Hipgnosis, is iconic enough that concert promoters used it for several years on the band's concert tickets.

The decal had to accurately convey the album's contents, since it was the first thing the prospective buyer would see. The circular sticker featured a drawing of two shaking robotic hands imposed over a background sliced into quarters, each a depiction of an element (air, fire, water, and earth). The "natural world" depicted here, then, serves simply as a backdrop for mechanical, forced interaction.

What was inside the package more openly reflected the album's lyrics. The Floyd and Hipgnosis didn't use a gatefold sleeve. But while *Wish You Were Here* lacked a garish foldout cover, it wasn't short on impressive images, each one again relating to an element.

The "front" cover featured two men shaking hands, one in flames; this image was shot at a deserted Hollywood sound stage, with the burning man in a special fire suit. (The idea of "getting burned" in business was on the Floyd's minds.) On the back cover, an empty suit, standing in a desert, holding a briefcase covered by Pink Floyd images, represented the faceless businessmen responsible for "selling" the band.

Inner bag pictures included a veil blowing through a British forest and a diver seemingly executing a perfect jackknife into a pond—but leaving no ripple. These striking, arty images offered, as did their live-show effects, a visual dimension to the Pink Floyd's music that the band themselves refused to provide in their outward appearance.

Animals

Despite Roger Waters' lovely opening and closing "Pigs on the Wing" sections, the music contained within 1977's *Animals* may have been Pink Floyd's most downbeat and violent to date. But the lighthearted cover image did lend the band perhaps its most permanent symbol: Algie, the flying pig.

None of Hipgnosis' initial cover ideas (one of them a shot of a young boy walking in on two adults copulating) appealed to the band. Instead, Roger Waters' vision of Battersea Power Station, near his then-home just south of the Thames River, provided inspiration that the designers accepted although they harbored some reservations. "Was it not intrinsically silly?" Thorgerson later asked in *The Work of Hipgnosis*.

The creation of the cover is the stuff of legend. The shot of the pig flying over the obsolete power station was originally scheduled for December 2, 1976, but bad weather and problems in hooking up a huge inflatable pig forced a one-day postponement. Photographs were taken of the power station and a cloudy sky.

The following day was troublesomely windy, and before any shots were taken, a restraining wire snapped, sending the already floating Algie out of control and the entire Pink Floyd crew—group members, eleven cameramen, and eight film crew members—into a panic.

A giant flying pig hovering above London would certainly have been strange, but it's probable that not very many people actually saw the dirigible. (The legend has expanded to include stories of panicky airline pilots calling their towers reporting flying pigs.) Algie eventually descended harmlessly in Kent, north of London, later that day, coming to rest in a field.

Algie was retrieved, repaired, and photographed on a third day. Eventually, photos of the pig from the third shoot were grafted onto a shot of the power station from the first. Several descendents of Algie went on to grace live Pink Floyd shows in subsequent years, and Roger Waters continues to use flying pigs on stage today.

The gloomy sky over the mammoth, defunct power station accurately represent the misery and dread of Waters' worldview in the late 1970s. The sheer goofiness, however, of a gigantic inflatable pig above London, during a time of punk rock and the Queen's Silver Jubilee, showed the group's all-too-rarely-displayed sense of humor, as well as Hipgnosis' ever-present surrealist sensibility.

The inner bag and foldout cover held lyrics and seemingly unrelated photographs that actually connected to the album's thematic concepts. In a continuation of a fad that had begun in the mid-1970s, the album's labels were also specially designed.

The Wall

While the lyrics and themes of the band's 1979 exorcism-cum-rock album were grandiose and overblown, the cover of *The Wall* was an exercise in simplicity. It had to be, because Storm Thorgerson was no longer in the picture.

Roger Waters canned Thorgerson after the designer failed, apparently, to properly credit the bassist for the concept of *Animals*. Circumstances—many caused by Waters himself—had led the group away from its old way of working, and besides, the Floyd's lynchpin had a new artistic collaborator: illustrator Gerald Scarfe.

The band had first worked with Scarfe after the release of *Wish You Were Here,* hiring him to do animated film to be projected on screens on the subsequent concert tour. The esteemed illustrator, who in 1981 married actress Jane Asher (a former fiancée of Paul

The design for *The Wall*—done by Gerald Scarfe and crew, not Hipgnosis—produced many memorable images, including the interlocking hammers seen on this sticker, meant to represent tyranny.

McCartney), had first drawn attention in the late 1960s with his mostly unflattering caricatures of public figures in British satirical publication *Private Eye*. His style was certainly far removed from the rock world of the time.

Album covers of the late 1970s seemed to contain either garish stadium rock fantasies, disco-oriented flash, or the somewhat arch take on pop art of the new wave and punk bands, with little room for minimalism, particularly the kind that made such post-psychedelic releases as *The Beatles* and the Rolling Stones' *Beggars Banquet* so arresting.

As usual, the Floyd reflected the lyrical content of their album with an innovative cover; this time, it was a minimal image of cinderblock bricks. A landmark in its simplicity, *The Wall* became the latest in an iconic set of sleeves. But this one, unlike its predecessors, was not surreal, fantastic, or lighthearted. It was harsh, spare, and devoid of color, like much of the music contained inside. Scarfe's dyspeptic drawings and album credits occupied much of the space, but the wall motif was carried through as well. The inner sleeves for both albums featured the lyrics, also inscribed in Scarfe's unmistakable hand, over the same cinderblock pattern.

Unfortunately, liner notes on early pressings of the album did not mention, even once, Rick Wright or, more seriously, Nick Mason.

A Momentary Lapse of Reason

The Floyd's first album without Roger Waters demanded a strong cover image. The remaining members of the band reached out to former colleague Storm Thorgerson, who was happy to be involved after having been excommunicated by Waters.

Much of the disc was recorded on David Gilmour's houseboat, making a water-related cover image appropriate, and the "vision of an empty bed" lyric of "Yet Another Movie" gave the designer an idea.

Eventually the cover image used involved more than seven hundred fully made but empty beds—yes, all seven hundred were real—shot at Devon's Saunton Sands, a southwest British coastal town popular with surfers. It's also a frequently used location for film and photos; in fact, a portion of Alan Parker's *The Wall* had been shot there in 1982.

Thorgerson's final product is a textbook Pink Floyd image: surreal, dreamlike (more so than usual given the sleeping motif), related to the album's lyrics, and utterly removed from the daily lives of most Pink

Floyd listeners. Like it or lump it, eighties or not, this dinosaur was not going to adapt to survive.

Pink Floyd—either oblivious to or not worried about their reputation for being overblown—also floated a helium-filled bed over the Thames River as part of the campaign to announce the subsequent tour promoting the album.

This sticker was placed over the black (or blue, depending on the country you lived in) wrapping of Pink Floyd's 1975 *Wish You Were Here* album. Designed by George Hardie of Hipgnosis, the sticker carries the album's theme of automation and forced interaction dominating the world.

20

Engulfed in a Fever of Spite

Didn't Pink Floyd Have a Lot of Self-Referential Songs?

F ew bands have used their songs to air as much dirty laundry as Pink Floyd. (At least the players didn't sleep with each other, thus avoiding painful Fleetwood Mac–style drama.) The post-breakup barbs flying between Waters and Gilmour, both in interviews and songs, rival those coming from the Lennon and McCartney camps in the early 1970s.

Syd Barrett's emotional collapse led him toward a completely naked style of composition, while Roger Waters took John Lennon–style bare-wires confessional songwriting to new heights (or lows, depending on your taste) after *Dark Side of the Moon.*

The Floyd's records have contained political polemics, ecological paeans, anti-business diatribes, and the occasional love song, but also material referring directly to band politics, the vagaries of stardom, and the personalities of various Floyds.

"Vegetable Man" (1968)

What could it have felt like to be Syd Barrett, a gifted but still very young painter/poet/songwriter with schizophrenic tendencies suddenly thrust into pop stardom amid an almost deadly trifecta of untested hallucinogens, sycophantic hangers-on, and the pressure of producing hit singles?

Even as Barrett began to suffer the effects of an acid-for-breakfast diet, which threw his youth and emotional instability into greater relief, he was capable of holding on to some of his gifts. "Vegetable Man," written as an attempt at a single but never released, has some of the most heartbreakingly personal lyrics ever written, inspiring reflection, humor, and pathos.

The clothes, shoes, and haircut Barrett assumes in order to be a perfect pop star represent what he has become in the public eye. The pressure of stardom and its attendant requirements was eating away at him, and he could tell he was losing contact with himself.

As the song continues, and the band becomes even more engulfed in a frenzied psychedelic haze, Barrett finally calls a halt to the proceedings. Over a lightly played backing, he intones: "I've been looking all over the place for place for me. . . . But it ain't anywhere."

He was so right.

"Cymbaline" (1969)

The Pink Floyd's gigs in the north and west of England during 1966 and 1967 were often disastrous, as the band played for drunks, soul fans, and teenyboppers unready for anything experimental. America was worse.

The band's forays into Europe had been slightly more successful and far less harrowing, but the relative ease of cracking the Belgian and Dutch market didn't remove the sting from Roger Waters' pen. The first audible evidence that the band's bassist was tired of the pop-star game, and all the compromises involved therein, came with this track from 1969's *More* soundtrack.

With David Gilmour singing, the words—referencing managers interested more in publicity than in taking care of their charges—come across far more sweetly than they might have had Waters taken the microphone, but there's no way to sugarcoat the bitterness in the bassist's horrified lyrics.

The feeling of abandonment that the Floyd felt at the hands of overmatched and overcommitted managers Peter Jenner, Andrew King, and Bryan Morrison in 1967–68 colored the group's attitude toward the rock and roll business forever.

Considering some of the ensembles the Floyd wore in the 1970s, this is a relatively dapper picture of the group. *Photofest*

"Free Four" (1972)

The early seventies were sometimes rough for the Floyd. Despite a growing fan base around the world, their albums were patchy, their tours expensive, and their leisure time scarce. They still hadn't found the key to utilizing their talents.

But during the recording of *Dark Side of the Moon*, Roger Waters' "concept" piece, the band grew confident that they were laying down memorable music with a sonic sheen heretofore unheard on their records. So at least there was cause for optimism.

It's odd, consequently, that this track, recorded in France for the *Obscured by Clouds* soundtrack during a lull in the *Dark Side* sessions, was one of the group's darkest pieces ever, though on a surface level it was one of the happiest-sounding.

The good-timey beat, both Kinks-like and reminiscent of *Meddle*'s "St. Tropez," gives the track plenty of punch. "Free Four" was, in the face of its remarkably negative lyrics about death, gloom, and the abuse of power, the group's biggest American radio hit to date.

For the first time on record, Roger Waters confronted his father's death in World War II and the powers that drive innocent men—foxes, in his metaphor—to die at the whim of and for the pleasure of the hunter. Waters, assuming the guise of a babbling old man on his deathbed, also discusses the hard slog that was their endless gigging schedule: "All aboard . . . maybe you'll make it to the top."

"Brain Damage" (1973)

The idea that this key *Dark Side of the Moon* track is related to Syd Barrett can be traced mainly to the lyric "The lunatic is on the grass," said to relate to the idyllic image of a guitar-strumming Barrett sitting on a Cambridge green. It's the kind of lovely teenage reverie that Gilmour and his wife Polly Samson also described in "High Hopes," the last track on 1994's *The Division Bell*.

Waters didn't know Barrett all that well in his early days; that honor went to David Gilmour. When he did return to Cambridge in 1962 after attending college in Manchester, Waters, already political, was involved in the Campaign for Nuclear Disarmament movement and hanging around with people his own age, rather than guys a couple of years younger like Barrett and Gilmour.

But despite his terrifying competitive streak, Waters knew a great singer and songwriter when he saw one, and couldn't help but be affected by Barrett's emotional instability, even though he relished the opportunity to show his mettle as a songwriter (and eventually did).

But "Brain Damage" is not just a song about Syd Barrett; it's also a song about Roger Waters.

Waters admitted later in *Uncut* that "seeing the ravages of [Barrett's] schizophrenia at close quarters" was the inspiration for the lyrics. But regardless of the song's grim outlook, Waters is actually expressing hope for the human condition, and showing empathy; he's stating that he knows that any of us could go mad, could lose it, and that he's willing to talk about it if *you* are.

Unfortunately, he couldn't talk about it with Barrett by this time, and the assorted pressures of the world would begin raining down into Waters' head shortly after *Dark Side* went to number one around the world.

"Shine On You Crazy Diamond" (1975)

It's odd that the Floyd would have used the main track on *Wish You Were Here* to tread the same ground—the illness and debilitation of Syd Barrett—he'd already visited on *Dark Side*.

While the goofy laughter and honking sax feel like leftover tricks pulled from the *Dark Side* bag, Waters' lyrics are much less empathic this time around and far more pointed in their indictment of Barrett's actions.

"You wore out your welcome with random precision," Waters sings, referring to Barrett's infuriating onstage gig-ruining of late 1967 and his seeming bent on destroying everything the group had created up to that point. But even then, Waters—as he did while looking in the mirror on the song "Wish You Were Here"—has hope, calling for Barrett's goodness and beauty to re-emerge, to reassert themselves, to shine.

And in a way, Barrett had re-emerged, though in a disturbingly corporeal form.

On June 5, 1975, while the band was mixing tracks from *Wish You Were Here*, a fat, hairless, vacant-looking roustabout in ill-fitting clothes showed up, uninvited and carrying a plastic sack, at Abbey Road Studios. Nobody could quite figure out the stranger's identity for several minutes, until it dawned on someone that this nearly unrecognizable figure was Syd Barrett.

While the tubby, bald Barrett, mad as ever, brushed his teeth and jumped up and down in place, the other members of the Floyd and their staff veered between shock and tears at the appearance of their onetime colleague. That David and Ginger Gilmour had just been married hours before just made the day even stranger.

After some odd conversation with members of the group and their entourage, and a short stay at the Gilmours' wedding reception, Barrett disappeared into the night, never to be seen by his former bandmates again.

"Have a Cigar" (1975)

The various indignities visited upon Pink Floyd are recounted on this *Wish You Were Here* track, with guest vocalist Roy Harper playing the role of a sleazy, sycophantic, greedy record industry insider more interested in selling plastic discs than in the actual process of creativity or the people responsible for it.

The band actually did hear the question "Which one's Pink?" from various music biz types during their early days, and their recent lucrative negotiations with Columbia Records had led them to understand just how much money they could make (and eventually did) by focusing on the business side of their music and by treating their work as "product."

Perhaps feeling as guilty of greed as he accused the music business of being, the always self-analytical Waters fought an internal battle for years over whether he should continue to participate in Pink Floyd, but didn't choose to leave (and, in his eyes, break up the band) until completing *The Final Cut.*

"Nobody Home" (1979)

Short one song for a particular spot in *The Wall,* Waters showed his mettle as a deadline-buster, penning these scabrous lyrics literally overnight at Gilmour's behest.

Perhaps fusing the various troubles of Syd Barrett ("the obligatory Hendrix perm") and Rick Wright ("a grand piano to prop up my mortal remains"), Waters here painted a picture of a pathetic, barely-alive rock-and-roller from his experience of watching the Floyd's unraveling tapestry. This being the album's only real piano-based number makes the reference to Wright even clearer.

But once again, Waters—who had struggled earlier in the seventies to give up cigarettes and hashish, and may by then have been inhaling quantities of cocaine—is writing about himself as well as about others. For himself and others, no mercy was on tap.

When, exactly, did Roger Waters lose his sense of empathy, even for himself, and move into territory so utterly black-and-white? On *Animals'*

Clad similarly, the four-man Floyd presents a united front departing the stage at Earls Court, London, following a 1980 performance of *The Wall.* By this time, Rick Wright had been booted from the band amid much bad feeling and re-hired as a session man. This news was kept private for several years.   *Photo by Peter Still/Redferns*

"Dogs," he had nothing but vituperation for a music industry shark who saw the world as a friendless, dog-eat-dog place.

But by that time, perhaps feeling a need to take the helm of a listing ship, and infuriated by others' personal problems interfering with the work of the Floyd, he was already treating some of his fellow band members badly.

Though *The Wall* is full of bile for everyone and everything that gets within shooting range—Pink, his wife, his teachers, his parents, his girlfriends, his audience, his handlers, the music business—Waters went the full length with the project anyway, taking the album on tour despite the fact that he'd already kicked Rick Wright out of the band, and that what remained of Pink Floyd was falling apart.

Was Waters, in the end, as cynical and manipulative as he accused the rest of the world of being on *The Wall* and *The Final Cut?* Only his analyst knows for sure.

"What Shall We Do Now?" (1980)

Originally left off *The Wall*, but later released on the *Is There Anybody Out There?* 1980–81 tour CD, this powerful and tragicomic litany of the options available to the rich for relieving their boredom is also one of Roger Waters' most affecting lyrics about the band.

Referencing his band members' spending and working habits, he sings, "Shall we work straight through the night? Shall we get into fights?" Gilmour and Mason, with their interest in road racing and new instruments, are the clear targets here, while Waters brings himself into the story with his pugilistic nature and obsessive work habits.

Waters also mentions touring the East, getting diseases, taking up drink, and breaking up homes as options; the members of Pink Floyd had done all of these things. It's not likely, however, that he was speaking from personal experience when he asked about "keeping people as pets."

"Poles Apart" (1994)

The Division Bell is a more cohesive album than *A Momentary Lapse of Reason*, mainly because the songs are better, the production clearer, and the participation of Mason and Wright greater.

"Poles Apart," the album's third track, talks about the two departed members of the Floyd: Syd Barrett and Roger Waters. Using a steel guitar reminiscent both of Barrett's "Interstellar Overdrive" anarchy and of the magical spell cast by Waters' "Breathe" is a neat trick, and typical of Gilmour's arrangement skills.

In the first verse, Gilmour sings, for the first time, about his own guilt at not doing *something* to help Syd Barrett out of his emotional instability. As usurper of the Floyd's guitar chair, Gilmour did his best in later years to take care of his friend's financial needs but apparently never get rid of the sense of unfairness that things had gone "right" for him and "wrong" for Barrett.

The second verse begins with Gilmour not-so-subtly addressing Roger Waters with a "Hey You," then goes on to accuse the former Floyd bassist of poor leadership and paranoia.

Following a fairground-ish musical section that sounds like a diseased cousin of "Being for the Benefit of Mr. Kite!," Gilmour wraps up by declaring that he's free of the sadness he'd felt about both of his former colleagues. But if anything that Waters says about Gilmour's bottled-up, passive-aggressive nature is true, then Gilmour's veracity in this lyric is questionable.

"Lost for Words" (1994)

The desire to "Keep Talking," expressed in *The Division Bell*'s previous track, apparently has come to naught for Gilmour and co-lyricist Polly Samson. Because this song, which begins with a slamming door and mournful keyboards, couldn't be much clearer about the futility of two sworn enemies discussing *anything*.

Is the lyric line aimed at Waters? Is he "wasting [his] time on [his] enemies . . . engulfed in a fever of spite" and "stuck in a world of isolation"? The use of acoustic guitar in the backing recalls the lovelier, more pastoral side of the Floyd's mid-period work, but Gilmour is certainly *not* telling Waters that he wishes he were here.

After laying out a narrative about the uselessness of hanging on to anger at an enemy, Gilmour in the last verse attempts a reconciliation with awful results.

It's not known whether Gilmour, Mason, and Wright actually asked Waters to rejoin the band, or if Waters even told anyone to fuck himself, but the audio of a boxing match in the song's middle section makes it clear that the two sides were in a competition, something that Waters could surely understand.

Ten Interesting Pink Floyd Cover Versions

- "Point Me at the Sky," Acid Casualties
- "See Emily Play," David Bowie
- "Money," Elkie Brooks
- "Have a Cigar," Foo Fighters
- "Candy and a Currant Bun," Half Japanese
- "Wish You Were Here," Wyclef Jean
- "Matilda Mother," Paul Roland
- "Comfortably Numb," Scissor Sisters
- "Breathe," The Shins
- "Lucifer Sam," True West

21

Matter of Fact, It's All Dark

ark Side of the Moon is full of magic.
The Floyd's 1973 album is majestic, carefully played and sung, and produced as well as other great rock records from previous years, notably *Abbey Road*. On this LP, each group member is at the top of his game and all four are perfectly balanced.

Dark Side blends classic songcraft with 1973-brand audio engineering that somehow hasn't dated in ways that later Floyd technical innovations (string synthesizers, vocodered vocals, honking saxophones, processed guitars, synthetic drum kits) quickly did.

Much of the LP's appeal comes from its being the right record for the right time: a glossy, radio-ready sonic experience with huge corporate muscle behind it, hitting the market when the moribund post-Beatles rock and roll world was ready for something new.

Some feel that *Dark Side* is overrated by and overplayed on classic rock radio. As great as "Breathe," "Us and Them," or "Eclipse" may be, the argument goes, the album's *individual* tracks don't necessarily dwarf "Arnold Layne," "Astronomy Domine," "Dogs," "Wish You Were Here," or "Echoes."

One argument against *Dark Side* is that the lyrical motif doesn't always fit into the concept about the pressures of "modern life," whatever that is, and the "concept" starts to fall apart late in side one. And even in his greatest moments, Waters still wrote from a post-teenage perspective, penning lyrics about the unfairness of life's trials that adolescents of all ages connect with.

But *Dark Side*'s words ring truer than many of his others. Waters' lyrics leaven the inevitable gloom and misery with some compassion and hope, unlike much of his later work, which has the optimism of a root canal.

Just as important to the album's success as Waters' lyrical concept, however, is the album's *musical* concept. The use of various elements of the album in the overture-like "Speak to Me" informs the listener that that this will be something other than a collection of songs. "Breathe," the album's centerpiece and key theme, is reprised at the end of "Time" and "Any Colour You Like." And Waters sums it all up with "Eclipse."

One assumes that Gilmour and Wright played a bigger part in the flow of the music than Waters, but *Dark Side* is and sounds like a group effort, and that's what's important. And it's not overdone or strained, like some of the group's later conceptual work.

Another key is the use of backing vocalists, which gave the Floyd an extra helping of soul that they desperately needed. Waters' precise observations are spiced with backing vocalist Doris Troy's often wordless ululations. Having more people making the music than just the four-man Floyd also helps communicate the sense of partaking in a shared experience, one with the feel of a spiritual ceremony.

And even with a few arguably mediocre moments, and an occasional loss of continuity, the album has an undeniable flow. Each song features fascinating arrangement touches, and the choices of instruments gives variety and sonic color. The pedal steel guitar and delicate cymbals on "Breathe," the VCS3 tones, treble-heavy percussion, and Farfisa pattern in "On the Run," Waters' thumpy bass on "Time," the tremolo guitar and sax solo on "Money," the Leslie guitar on "Brain Damage," and the Hammond organ in "Eclipse" seem to sum up much of the group's experimentation, advances, and strengths to that point. Every piece of the album fits, though not all the pieces are perfect.

For many years, the band had been trying to combine the composed with the experimental, and *Dark Side* actually made the promise of this idea real. A perfectly balanced narrative between sound and non-sound, music and non-music, endlessly flowing, this was in most ways their peak as a working unit. They four players jelled on certain tracks on their next three albums, but never with as much humanity, humor, or adventure.

The extraneous sounds on *Dark Side* differ in one key way from the band's previous use of "nonmusical" effects: the sounds are all of the man-made variety. Clocks, airplanes, an explosion, and human voices figure here, rather than seagulls, breezes, or insects. This appears to be a manifestation of Roger Waters' desire to move out of the natural world, psychedelia, and outer space toward a more inward, experiential focus.

The album's gorgeous packaging set another standard. The rainbow contrasting with black evidences the constant pulsing of life and vitality even in the darkness. And for an optimist, that's the point of the album: even acknowledging the blackness and misery of the world, there is still beauty, color, life, and love.

It is telling, though, that while *Dark Side* ruminates on death, war, age, economics, famine, lunacy, and religion, it lacks lyrical content about romantic love, companionship, family, or children.

"Speak to Me"

Serious musical works such as operas, operettas, and even popular musicals feature an overture, a composition at the beginning of the work that includes various melodic ideas from different parts of the piece.

"Speak to Me" does just this, beginning with a simple heartbeat, incorporating backward sounds, spoken-word excerpts from other pieces of the album, the clinking coins of "Money," airport noises from "On the Run," and Clare Torry's screaming from the "Great Gig" session, which cascades into "Breathe," the album's main theme.

This 1:30 piece caused a lot of misery in the Floyd camp years later, when Roger Waters grew to regret his "choice" to "award" Nick Mason, who assembled the collage, a cowriter's credit. (The band's negotiations around songwriting credits were famously stressful.) Mason claims that he fully deserves credit for creating a new piece by assembling the sounds on this song; Waters claims that the drummer didn't do any original work.

(A similar argument marred the *Final Cut* sessions. Mason spent hours assembling sound effects for the album, only to have Waters inform the drummer that the work didn't merit either a production or songwriting credit.)

The Floyd broke ground here with this early version of "sampling." In "Speak to Me," the band is forcing listeners to consider whether a sound collage is an original composition. Such a question foresees the growth of hip-hop, with its dependence on samples, and mash-ups, using various elements in the service of one final product.

"Breathe"

Emerging from the sudden deluge of sound at the end of "Speak to Me," Dave Gilmour's "wet" guitar introduces "Breathe" as all tension falls off the cliff. Nick Mason's drum pattern establishes a languid pattern for the band to build around.

Gilmour's innovative use of steel guitar, in a completely non-country-and-western context, affords the already dreamy song a spacey, psychedelic feel, and Wright's delicate electric piano notes fall like raindrops on glass. The two also combine their voices to bring home Waters' lyrics with the most pleasant delivery they could muster.

Waters had written about breath before, but this time the impetus sprang from personal urgency rather than a concern for the environment. In his lyrics, he rejects the psychedelic notions of the "imagined" experience, arguing (softly) that what you sense is all there is.

Marrying this grounded sentiment to such dreamy, psychedelic music is what writers like to call "ironic." The contrast between the reverberated, echoed, processed sounds of Gilmour and Wright's instruments, their tuneful vocal harmony on the chorus, and the dry, unadorned drums and bass of Mason and Waters has rarely worked better in rock; the airy feel never carries the song away, because the rhythm section anchors it, though with restraint and a sympathetic sense of space.

Even here, however, the message ends with not just foreboding, but the certainty of "an early grave" due to the assorted stressors of the world.

Waters here seems to be focusing on the unfairness of it all. He later stated in interviews that he didn't fully understand until his late twenties that life was to be *lived, right here and now,* and it's not a rehearsal. Perhaps this lyric is part of his understanding that time goes by too quickly and that death *always* comes too soon.

"On the Run"

Of all the *Dark Side* songs, this is among the most narrative, even though nobody sings a note; sound effects tell a story of an unordinary day at an airport.

Amid a seductive electronic rhythm that feels twenty years ahead of its time, footsteps rush through an airport terminal amid relentless announcements of impending departures. The departure, of course, is soon revealed to be that of the passengers on an airplane that crashes right into the terminal. But even this tragedy does not bring an end to the running footsteps.

The Floyd's seemingly endless global travels of the early 1970s engendered in them a fear of and disgust with flight, which only years later Gilmour and Mason, and manager Steve O'Rourke, dealt with by actually learning to pilot airplanes.

This track has few "conventional" sounds. Rick Wright fed a series of Farfisa organ notes into the VCS3, a voice-controlled synthesizer originally developed by the BBC Radiophonic Workshop, one of Britain's earliest labs exploring electronic music. The VCS3 also generated what sounds like a hi-hat cymbal. Gilmour and Wright fooled around with the VCS3 loops to get them at the appropriate speed, and Gilmour and Mason added backward guitar and cymbals.

(Once *Dark Side* was history, Rick Wright unfortunately began to spend more time with newer synthesizers than with analog keyboards. The decision to replace the creamy Farfisa and Hammond organ textures with synthesizers that quickly sounded obsolete changed the group's sound, and not for the better. The VCS3, created with analog rather than digital equipment, is and sounds like a real musical instrument rather than a machine.)

Adding to the creepiness of the keyboards is the use of vocal drop-ins. "Here today, gone tomorrow," intones Roger Manifold, a Floyd roadie nicknamed "The Hat." Manifold, and several other band friends and work colleagues, were interviewed by Roger Waters on various subjects, and their answers were chopped up into pieces and used at various points on *Dark Side*.

Waters came up with various questions, including "When was the last time you were violent?" and "Are you afraid of death?" to ask musicians, studio employees, and band hangers-on. Paul and Linda McCartney were among these, but apparently their answers were far too guarded to be helpful, as the closest PF got to having a Beatle speak on the record was Henry McCullough, at the time playing guitar for Wings.

This song, with its energetic, psychedelic, sexy rolling beat, was so effective that many people who don't know or care for Pink Floyd have heard it. Many rock radio stations used the song in the 1970s and 1980s as background music, either for lead-ins to news, time-fillers, or as ambient sound behind promos or prize giveaways.

"Time"

The recessing rumble of collapsing airplane debris suddenly gives way to a symphony of alarms, chimes, and bonging grandfather clocks from a recording that engineer Alan Parsons had made at an antique shop.

Parsons was working on a demonstration tape for a quadraphonic sound system, and the clocks were so well-recorded that the Floyd chose to use them. The introduction, another example of "found sound" that says more than words could, offers a rude awakening after the seemingly endless reverberations ending "On the Run."

Following a maddening computerized tick-tock, Mason's plangent rototoms and some deep, foreboding chords on piano and guitar imbue the song with almost a nasty, threatening mood. The echo and reverberation used on the piano and rototoms give the feel of being in a great room, listening to some ancient rite. It's one of the eeriest parts of the album, and among the most effective.

Soon the piano introduction gives way

Here is an example of the high quality of Pink Floyd shows available on the bootleg market. This is actually not a video presentation, but rather a DVD audio of extremely high sonic fidelity from a 1974 *Dark Side* concert.
Photo courtesy of Steve Leventhal

to one of two straight-ahead rockers on the album. Gilmour uses an atypical growl for Waters' urgent lyrics about living life while you can; the guitarist's vocal delivery harks back to 1969's "The Nile Song." His first of five great guitar solos on the album is just as corrosive, drenched in reverb and distortion. Guitar lines veer all over the sonic spectrum, while Mason, Waters, and Wright jam with admirable restraint. (This number rarely sounded full enough in concert.)

The invention continues as the Floyd use backing singers (background singers had worked on *Atom Heart Mother*, and had accompanied the uncredited Floyd on "Give Birth to a Smile" from Waters' *Music from the Body*) to give the whole sound depth and soul. For some reason, the band chose to feed the singers' voices through a tremolo effect.

The melody and setting of "Breathe" return as Gilmour reflects on coming home after a long day and sitting beside the warm hearth. This lyric, which could just as easily have been written about a medieval farmer, is the only true moment of respite found on the album. Waters' words reference villagers gathering to hear "softly spoken magic spells," which leads to the side one closer.

"The Great Gig in the Sky"

The album's original concept called for a piece on religion at this point in the proceedings, and that's the brief Rick Wright worked under when composing this mournful, classically tinted piano progression. At first it was to be called "God," then later, "The Mortality Piece."

The band recorded an instrumental track of drums, bass, and piano, then things stalled a bit. Pink Floyd had no idea what to do next with the rambling track, but knew that it needed an extra something. The notion of lyrics was a nonstarter, but session singer Clare Torry was called in on the off chance that she could provide some gospel inspiration.

Torry's singing, along with Waters' use of tape-recorded thoughts from Abbey Road Studio's doorman, Jerry Driscoll, transformed "Religion" into a meditation on death and dying. Perhaps the most effective musical moment in the song is Gilmour's overdubbed steel guitar, which again states the "Breathe" theme.

Many listeners find this song the weak link in *Dark Side*. One could argue that Waters' concept—again using "found sound" and non-lyrical elements to convey a message—does not fit the music and, in fact, transformed the original point from a meditation on religion to something much more insular and defined. Or maybe the problem is just that after nearly five minutes, it all becomes slightly annoying.

The Floyd's use, in *DSOTM* concerts, of two or three backing singers—who went at the number more soulfully—made live versions of "Great Gig" significant improvements over the studio recording.

"Money"

Only after *Dark Side of the Moon* did the Floyd sign a new record deal from Columbia, become millionaires, and see their group dynamic completely unravel. So it's a bit unfair to claim that Waters' acerbic words about money are hypocritical. At the time, Waters was already aware where most of the money was in rock and roll: with the businessmen, not the artists.

Some years later, Roger Waters would get more pointed in his diatribes about who had the money in the music industry and, oddly, would fight even harder with his own bandmates to get what he considered his fair share. Here, Waters, just angry at inequality, lashes out at those who control money and, therefore, power.

Beginning with a hand-constructed sample of cash registers and coins thrown into his wife Judy's pottery, "Money" then builds into a seven-four time signature that Nick Mason found very difficult to play, but did. (For a man accused of being tone-deaf, Waters did a heck of a job constructing this composition.)

"Money" is iconic rock and roll right from the get-go, with its slinky Dick Parry sax solo, superb Gilmour guitar breaks, and dynamic tension created by the airtight rhythm section and the supple wah-wah on Wright's electric piano.

Rarely did these musicians ever sound more in control of what they were doing. The solos are outstanding, the tempo aggressive, and the band uncommonly funky. Gilmour's vocal tears the paint from the wall, and his guitar work—the solos, the spare rhythm lines, the use of tremolo at various points—is among the best in rock annals.

The change in time signature from seven-four to four-four at the end of the song is rather scary, as if even the song has had its individuality hammered out of it and, like all of us, is now marching in lockstep to the drumbeat of capitalism, right into the military world of the next song.

"Us and Them"

The spoken bits about violence ("cruising for a bruising") lead into the album's most languid piece, which, probably not coincidentally, sports the most pointed, outward-glancing lyrics on the record. Waters writes about the difference between the enlisted men and the generals, the privileged and the hungry, with both anger and empathy.

Gilmour sings about the military men who see soldiers not as humans, but simply as data points on a large map in an endless game of give-and-take. The lack of compassion trickles down to the man in the street, who has no time for the poor and the indigent.

What we get from our leaders, Waters seems to be writing, is what we become.

And given the song's theme—emotional absence—it is appropriate that on "Us and Them," the lead instruments are really reverb and echo. All the sounds swim, including the muted bass and faraway drums. Most of the album feels more intimate than this song, which makes sense

The 1973 version of Pink Floyd, performing on the *Dark Side* tour. The four-man band is augmented by backing singers (left) and sax player Dick Parry (second from right) on what is likely a version of "Us and Them."   *Photo by David Redfern/Redferns*

because the lyrical concept here is the most disconnected and least personal on the disc. The entire feel of "Us and Them" is far away, as if in a hallucination or a fog.

The piano part is nearly perfect; Wright's playing was rarely better. He adapted a song originally written for a scene in *Zabriskie Point* for use with a set of Waters' lyrics, and the Miles Davis–inspired piece is at once jazzy and funereal. Once again spoken excerpts from interviews grace the song, this time unfortunately cutting into the second half of Wright's piano solo.

Among the few flaws on the album is the production on this number, which goes from grand to grandiose. Dick Parry's sax solo begins lyrically but ends with atonal squalling amid dozens of tracks of backing vocals and an unidentifiable, overpowering mass of sound. The whole package eventually stretches the listener's ability to sustain the heaviness. Everyone's wailing at top volume and top intensity, and the listener can easily lose the thread.

Waters would expand the lyrical theme of this song, perhaps the most depressing on the album, into the next couple of Pink Floyd projects, which concerned themselves with political and economic exploitation, insincerity, and emotional absence.

"Any Colour You Like"

The swirling VCS3 tones and crunchy guitar of "Any Colour" are a 1970s take on the old Floyd sound, as the quartet orbits the planet Psychedelia for the final time. But the spacey tendencies, intricate rhythms, and stop-start guitar solo mark this as accessible progressive rock as well. On stage, the Floyd would extend this jam for several minutes before beginning "Brain Damage."

In addition to serving as superb ear candy, "Any Colour" was a spectacular way for rock fans to show off the kind of high-tech sound systems that they were purchasing by 1973. Among *Dark Side*'s biggest selling points, in fact, remains its unprecedented sound quality.

While the Floyd produced the record themselves, Alan Parsons played a huge part in the engineering and Chris Thomas, who like Parsons had worked with George Martin and the Beatles, was called in late in the proceedings. The Floyds, however, especially Dave Gilmour, are hesitant to give Thomas much credit.

The song's F to G progression is similar but not identical to that of "Breathe," and following the guitar solo, the band once again runs through the chorus section of the album's main theme to bring the whole enterprise back to center, and back to the lyrical concerns at hand.

"Brain Damage"

This is Roger Waters' first lead vocal of the album. For the protagonist, the album's various pressures—work, poverty, violence, war, organized religion—have taken a toll, leaving in their wake a poor young lunatic.

It's impossible, of course, not to think of Syd Barrett when considering this song, since "the grass" is said to be a reference to the greenery of Cambridge. But Waters is using his experiences with Syd to get at something more universal, especially since he is talking about lunatics being in the newspapers. He's also saying that the lunatic is in *his* head, as well, and that it's potentially in all of ours.

Waters later addressed his own "split personality" on the title track from the next PF album, *Wish You Were Here*, and the turmoil in Waters' own head informed the future Floyd projects as well.

Musically, "Brian Damage" has plenty of links to Syd, from Gilmour's folky electric picking to Wright's heavily tremoloed Farfisa organ, which provide suitably '67 touches. Goofy laughter and more interview excerpts pepper the song, once again keeping the "found sound" concept at close reach.

One thing many people miss about this album, given its rapturous reception by rock radio, is its avant-garde quality. How many top-flight rock acts at the time were using sound effects, melodic "themes," and interview excerpts on their albums? Of course, the whole cake was much more palatable to the masses when tastily frosted, immaculately boxed, and festooned with a swirling Day-Glo ribbon. But Pink Floyd still deserves credit for pushing rock music forward without losing the way.

"Eclipse"

Wright leads off the album's final track—the summation of the entire enterprise—with a swirl of Hammond B-3 organ. That, plus the three-four tempo and the female backing vocals, announce this as the Floyd's attempt to capture the feel of the classic R&B and soul music most of them loved.

A somewhat Beatlesque ("Dear Prudence") descending chord progression frames the lyrics, which restate in a more didactic and precise fashion what Waters wrote in "Breathe": that what you do in life, what you experience, is what there is. As Waters told *Uncut* magazine in 2003, "There's a camaraderie involved in the idea of people who are prepared to walk the dark places alone. You're not alone! A number of us are prepared to open ourselves up to all those possibilities."

Calling the last song "Eclipse" indicates the moving from light to dark, life to death, sanity to madness. But even in this last song, Waters is pleading his case for truly living life: Pay attention to reality. There ain't no little green man on Mars, even though there is a dark side to the moon.

The use, following the song's end chord, of Jerry Driscoll's quote about the moon being all dark is intended as a joke, a palate cleanser, but since Waters was in charge of the use of interview excerpts, the choice probably reflects at least a shred of Waters' true feelings.

It is particularly interesting how Waters, who liked to take credit for Pink Floyd's science-fiction focus (and diminish Barrett's role in same), found his greatest financial and perhaps artistic success by turning inward and viewing outer space as a symbol of death, insanity, and isolation rather than as a metaphor for discovery and hope.

22

Why Can't We Blow the Years Away

What Are Some Forgotten Gems from the Floyd Collection?

aving recorded a dozen albums, four film soundtracks, and a passel of singles, Pink Floyd has earned a permanent place on rock radio, home stereos, and millions of iPods. But sometimes the same old songs end up in everyone's rotation. These ten Pink Floyd numbers rarely end up on anyone's "all-time favorite" list, but deserve more attention, airplay, and exposure.

"Candy and a Currant Bun" (1967)

It's too bad that this track, the B-side of their first single, "Arnold Layne," has been somewhat forgotten. Many casual Floyd fans don't even know it exists, and that's an injustice; edgy, rough, playful, and ecstatic, "Candy" is among the best songs to come out of the British beat/psychedelic era.

"Candy and a Currant Bun" is as adventurous and innovative as "Arnold Layne." Even more lyrically suggestive than its A-side, this stoned girl-watching reverie includes Barrett singing the phrase "walk with me" to sound like something much nastier. The guitars are twangy and rough, the keyboards cut through like scissors on silk, and Mason's insistent drumbeat emphasizes Barrett's swagger.

Just as important, this chunk of rock perfectly defines all the sub-genres it embodies in just 2:47. You want garage psychedelia? It's certainly garage psych. You want snotty white blues moves? They're here. You want punk with guitars and keyboards? This is it. You like freakbeat?

This *is* freakbeat. How about experimental sound, anarchy, British stoner humor, and even atonal noise? Dig in.

"The Scarecrow" (1967)

Syd Barrett was influenced by pastoral music and folk rock, but only on two *Piper* tracks—this and "The Gnome"—did he truly show his folk leanings, singing this childlike, agrarian-themed rhyme and utilizing a late-song burst of acoustic guitars.

The tempo of "The Scarecrow" sounds simple but is quite complex and very, very hard to follow; Mason plays his woodblocks at an odd gallop and Syd Barrett strums his electric guitar in a straight three-four time. Barrett's vocal adds yet more cross-meter, with a swooping melody and lyrics personifying the scarecrow using internal rhymes and jokes.

Spare electric organ ornamentation gives color, and once Barrett has sung his last lyrics, the instruments build up. Waters bows a bass, giving some authentic "country" frisson, and Barrett adds a beefy twelve-string acoustic guitar. The entire sonic palette is attractively understated, and

In 1967, Capitol of Canada released a 45 pairing Syd Barrett's "See Emily Play" and "Scarecrow," duplicating the British and American releases of the same two songs. Talk about a two-sided winner!

the full-band ending is among British psychedelia's most endearing moments.

Some have called this song "twee," making fun of its somewhat child-like, perhaps even feminine lyrical slant. But criticizing songs on *Piper at the Gates of Dawn* for being "twee" or not masculine only indicates a lack of understanding of British psych, which depended heavily on the introduction of feminine, earth-centered energy into the masculine world of pop groups.

"Crying Song" (1969)

Recording the *More* soundtrack gave Pink Floyd an opportunity to vary its approach, making room for jazz instruments, sound effects, and ballads, and allowing the band to stretch out in a new context that didn't depend on developing material for a stage show.

The songs on this, their third release, feature all sorts of acoustic instruments. Here, Rick Wright uses a resonant vibraphone part evoking Milt Jackson of the Modern Jazz Quartet, and Dave Gilmour plays a nylon-string guitar. The instruments establish a feel somewhat like that of a samba band in a cocktail lounge.

Roger Waters, who wrote "Crying Song," has claimed to have taken psychedelics only twice in his life, but this song—perhaps accidentally—not only sings of a trippy walk in nature, but also approximates certain parts of the psychedelic experience.

In "Crying Song" he captures some of the unexplainable mood shifts that happen under psychedelics. Moving from laughter to babbling to crying to sexual feelings to notions of death is a common occurrence, as is the cosmic understanding that "sadness passes in a while."

Gilmour's nylon-string acoustic playing is quite beautiful, and the guitar solo is a landmark. This is Gilmour's first real solo on a Pink Floyd record; here he begins to work both the sonic and the energetic parts of his playing, planting the flag of a Hendrix-influenced but very distinctive style.

Playing parts in harmony, using a slide, and taking advantage of stereo effects, he showed that he had his own melodies, mannerisms, and tricks—moving beyond simply aping Syd Barrett—and could integrate them into *this* band.

"Quicksilver" (1969)

Forty seconds into this seven-minute deep-space ambient instrumental, the listener falls into the rabbit hole, where the deeper you go, the bigger it gets.

This is one of the Floyd's most psychedelic, formless songs, creating a spectacular sense of space. While "Quicksilver" lacks the aggressive drumming of "Interstellar Overdrive" or "Saucerful of Secrets," it creates an engrossing setting with shards of melody despite not being a conventionally "musical" construction.

This track is a progression from a *Saucerful of Secrets*–type sound collage toward something even less traditionally representational. For instance, "Quicksilver" features Waters banging a gong (but not playing bass). Wright kicks in cosmic organ and vibraphone parts, Mason lays down percussion (but not drums), and Gilmour plays uncharacteristic experimental guitar runs.

Other space-rock ensembles like Can, Hawkwind, and Gong (as well as the ambient boffins of more recent times) paid close attention to what the Floyd were doing here. Appropriately, when the band used part of this song in its 1969 live show *The Man and the Journey*, it was re-titled "Sleep." This piece truly can conjure up the stuff one feels and hears in dreams.

"Love Scene (Version 4)" (1970)

This track, one of many submitted for *Zabriskie Point* but not used, stands out from its unreleased brethren. This lengthy Rick Wright solo piano piece makes clear his debt to pianists Bill Evans, Errol Garner, and Herbie Hancock and again proves that he was a lyrical player who understood jazz.

This pretty performance, romantic and languid, would have been at home on any number of 1960s soundtracks, including that of *Blow-Up*, Antonioni's previous film. Perhaps the director rejected "Love Scene" because it felt too similar to some of Hancock's work on *Blow-Up*, but there is no reason for this song to have sat unreleased for nearly thirty years.

"Love Scene," intended for the film's mystical, druggy, orgiastic desert scene, was finally released in 1997 as part of a bonus *Zabriskie Point* CD.

In addition to this version of the song, the Floyd are also represented on the bonus disc by a slinky, bluesy full-band take (Version 6) that is also a lot of fun.

"Fearless" (1971)

This symphony of guitars, football (i.e., soccer) crowd noises, and winsome vocals is a showpiece for Dave Gilmour.

Gilmour uses several interlocking guitar parts, played on six- and twelve-string electrics and acoustics, to create one of his most layered pieces. The chiming strings ring, leaving octaved notes hanging in the air. A stutter-step guitar pattern during the verse, with a gorgeous over-laid vocal, gives way to a slow, reflective chorus featuring a volume-pedal guitar run and an effectively loopy bass line from Waters.

The lyrics seem inscrutable, but the lines about magistrates and fools at least tie in to Waters' usual themes of power and sanity. The song may also have something to do with Syd Barrett, but what the "idiot" is doing on the hill is a mystery.

Mason holds the pace, rather than breaking into full-out rock, for the entire song, maintaining a tightrope-like tension through the fade-out, when Liverpool football fans sing their anthem, "You'll Never Walk Alone." The sounds of the "terrace" singers, which also appeared earlier

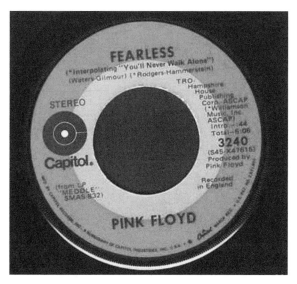

This 45 from 1971, featuring "One of These Days" on the other side, was one of several unsuccessful attempts to break Pink Floyd as a singles act in the United States.

in the song at low volume, are played backward, run through a phase-shifter, and faded up and down, again betraying the Floyd's interest in decorating their music with "atonal" elements.

As proper Englishmen, the Floyd enjoyed their football. Waters admits to having spent a lot of time in his late twenties attending games in support of his favorite club, Arsenal (based in the north of London), standing on the terrace with the other rowdies. Pink Floyd even had its own football squad for a time and planned some tours around watching local matches.

"St. Tropez" (1971)

A short acoustic Roger Waters number about vacationing in St. Tropez? No, thanks, you might say, fearing that he couldn't pull off something that simple. But if you dismiss this *Meddle* track out of hand, you're missing a good one.

This holiday reverie was loosely based on actual trips to the French Riviera. Gilmour and Barrett traveled there together in 1964, and the whole band, with wives, roadies, manager, and kids in tow, repaired to a vacation house there in 1970 when the Floyd played some gigs in the south of France. The trip apparently wasn't much fun for anyone due to tensions within the band, but Waters finds peace and small pleasures in this swinging little number.

Always proud (perhaps inordinately so) of his acoustic playing, Waters apparently insisted that he strum and sing this one himself. He does a fine job vocally and competently keeps up the syncopated rhythm, which has a bit of blues, a little Burt Bacharach, and even some Kinks lying underneath.

Wright kicks in a nice piano part, and Gilmour plays a languid, sexy electric guitar solo. Waters' lyrics are witty, using internal rhyme and a rather sweet resolution: "If you're alone, then I'll come home." The song is charming, loose, and even sexy, three qualities perhaps not present in enough of the band's work.

"When You're In" (1972)

This is among the most modern-sounding songs in the Pink Floyd catalog, forecasting "alternative" rock with its hard-rock dynamics and metal overtones, but featuring supple and creative drumming and spare production.

Pink Floyd didn't often just *get down*. This *Obscured by Clouds* instrumental features an Asian, Led Zeppelin–style riff, and the piano and organ give more sonic color than the usual early seventies hard-rock product. It's one of the group's more effective instrumentals.

The Floyd didn't play hard rock the way other bands did. Gilmour certainly understood hard-rock dynamics, and liked using them, but Wright preferred amassing classical chord clusters to fooling around with speedy, virtuosic solos. Mason didn't drum like a typical rock skin-pounder, sometimes leaving Waters to anchor the song with his bass.

The foreboding low-register bass and keyboard tones used on "When You're In" ended up gracing certain sections of *Wish You Were Here.*

"Burning Bridges" (1972)

This elegiac, organ-led waltz from *Obscured by Clouds* presages the sound of *Dark Side* with its thick keyboards, lilting Wright/Gilmour vocal, and slow Mason tempo.

The occasional writing team of Wright and Waters produced two solid efforts for *OBC*: "Burning Bridges" and "Stay." As usual, Wright and Gilmour make a terrific singing duo, although Wright's voice rarely conveys any emotion besides wistfulness.

An attractive melody, a sensitive backing, and some very interesting little touches make this underappreciated Floyd song special. Gilmour provides two terrific "I'm sure I've heard that riff before" slide guitar parts near the two- and three-minute marks, and having the singers trade sections is effective, especially when Wright's vocal heralds an unexpected key change.

A somewhat American, underproduced West Coast feel pervades this album despite the band recording *OBC* in France. Perhaps owing to how quickly PF was forced to record—and in an unfamiliar studio—everything sounds dry, i.e., without a lot of reverberation or other sonic effects, especially Gilmour's guitar work. It's an interesting, homespun, unfussy sound.

Another possible result of the hasty recording process afforded this album: an obvious and strangely amateurish tape splice at 2:16, when Gilmour and Wright begin to sing in harmony.

"The Show Must Go On" (1979)

Following "Comfortably Numb" and preceding the hard, heavy, and occasionally overcooked material on side four (on vinyl) of *The Wall*, this fairly simple exercise in harmony tends to go unnoticed.

Harmony vocals from some Beach Boys and Toni Tennille make this track feel similar to "Give Birth to a Smile," the Roger Waters song from *Music from the Body* that features an uncredited Pink Floyd providing the musical backing. Both songs feature a simple, American, country feel.

Waters' vocal is affecting as well. Pink is hoping to change and recover his soul. He knows that he's been miserable, and he wants to get off the merry-go-round, but he also knows that he can't, that it's too late.

How much of this lyric is autobiographical? If *Waters* was miserable, why didn't he just stop instead of doing something that made him unhappy? Perhaps Waters got pleasure out of making music, even though all he did was talk about how rotten his career was.

How much pressure did he feel to help bail out the band after the Norton Warburg investment fiasco? Did he stay around merely to help out his mates? And if so, did that cause resentment? (That might be understandable.) Or did Waters *enjoy* his cathartic artistic process, the one in which he constantly railed against what he had, what he'd done wrong, and what others couldn't give him?

Ten Near Misses

The "Jugband Blues" promo film (1967)
Strobe lights were a bad idea for an already flipping-out Syd Barrett.

"The Narrow Way" (1969)
Almost a good song, Gilmour's *Ummagumma* piece boasts some cool moments.

"Unknown Song (Rain in the Country)" (1969)
This interesting piece from the *Zabriskie Point* sessions, issued on the 1997 bonus disc, bogs down in the middle.

"Oenone" (1969)
This *Zabriskie Point* outtake, originally titled "Fingal's Cave," might have been a classic ambient piece if not for the ridiculous spoken parts. ("Fucking long three minutes" indeed.)

"Give Birth to a Smile" (1970)
From Waters and Ron Geesin's *Music from the Body*, this track, which features Pink Floyd, nearly gets it, falling just a bit short. The arrangement looks to the future with female backing vocalists.

"Fat Old Sun" (1970)
Perhaps if the band itself had played on it, this would have made the grade.

"Welcome to the Machine" (1975)
A lot of great craft and some interesting production ideas are used in service of an overwrought downer of a song.

"Young Lust" (1979)
It's almost rocking, but not quite. The disco beat doesn't work, and nothing about it is as strong as it could be.

"Not Now John" (1983)
This *Final Cut* single has some amusing moments, but sounds just *terrible.*

"On the Turning Away" (1986)
A nice little folk song gets the 1980s treatment, which tramples its simple charms and creates an overblown pudding.

23

I Was There— Toni Tennille

Singing for Roger and Dave, Whom Love Couldn't Keep Together

Interview by Stuart Shea

Toni Tennille was one of the most popular singers of the 1970s and early 1980s. As half of the Captain and Tennille, her musical collaboration with longtime Beach Boys auxiliary member Daryl Dragon—the two have also been married since 1975—she enjoyed seven Top 40 hits between 1974 and 1979 with an R&B-influenced MOR pop that featured careful production, stylish songwriting, and infectious enthusiasm.

Ms. Tennille's delivery of boppy, up-tempo material like "Love Will Keep Us Together," "Lonely Night (Angel Face)," and "You Never Done It Like That" and ballads such as "Muskrat Love" and "Do That to Me One More Time" doesn't seem to make her a good fit for late-period Pink Floyd, but by the time *The Wall* rolled around, Roger Waters and David Gilmour were using all sorts of session musicians and singers to get across their grand vision. And when the call went out for good singers, Ms. Tennille was first on a lot of lists.

Q: Prior to the sessions for The Wall, *had you any previous knowledge of Pink Floyd?*

TT: Not really. I had heard the name, but wasn't familiar with their music.

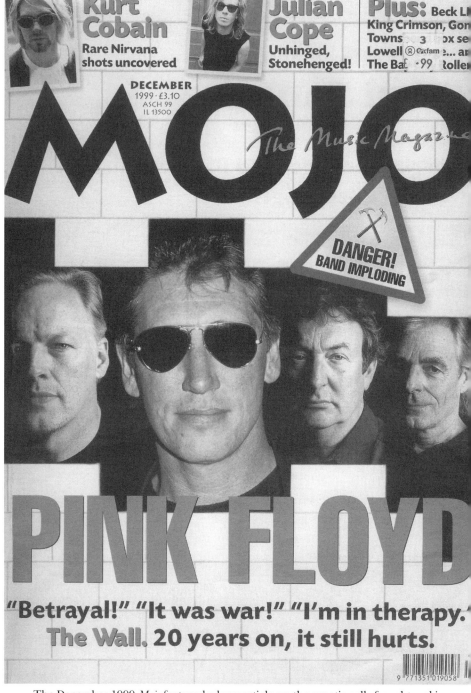

The December 1999 *Mojo* featured a long article on the emotionally fraught making of *The Wall*.

Q: What did you see as your place in the rock and roll world of the 1970s? How much community did you feel with other groups/musicians, and whose work did you listen to?

TT: Well, obviously, I was a pop singer. I was never a "rock" singer. It really wasn't my thing. Actually, my pop singing style leaned more toward R&B in many instances. I feel like the Captain and Tennille were placed in the same category as groups like the Carpenters. We were very aware that we were not considered "edgy" or "hip." However, most of our contemporaries who knew our work respected our musicianship. That was nice.

As to what artists I listened to in that time period, I loved Steely Dan (still do), Hall & Oates, Elton John, Carly Simon, Aretha Franklin, Carole King, and many more I can't think of at the moment. In addition, I was very into Frank Sinatra, Joe Williams, Ella Fitzgerald, Sarah Vaughan, Eydie Gorme, Carmen McRae, and other great singers of the forties and fifties. And since Daryl and I were both trained as classical musicians, I listened to a lot of classical music.

Q: How were you contacted to sing on The Wall?

TT: Bruce Johnston and Carl Wilson of the Beach Boys, a studio singer by the name of John Joyce [who later sang on the *Wall* tour], and I used to sing backgrounds for various artists if we all happened to be in town at the same time. We loved to do it, and we had a very nice blend. Bruce called me and asked if I was available to do a background session for *The Wall*.

Q: What, if anything, did you know concerning the album's putative content when you were hired?

TT: I didn't know a thing about the album's content. I just thought it would be very interesting to work with a rock group. I wanted to see how they conducted their sessions and how different their sessions might be from the way Daryl and I worked in the studio.

Q: There are stories that some of the Beach Boys wouldn't sing on The Wall *due to the album's subject matter. Do you know anything of that?*

TT: That's hard for me to believe. I doubt they would be that stuffy or square.

Q: How and where were your vocal parts recorded? Do you recall who worked with you on the production side?

TT: We recorded our parts on a Sunday at a studio in Hollywood called Producer's Workshop. I believe we got to the studio around noon. I don't remember who was producing, but Daryl and I were greeted at the door by Dave Gilmour, who thanked me profusely for coming, and told us that he had seen us on television that morning. He had been watching a kid's show called *Kids Are People Too* with his children, and we were the guest artists.

Q: Anything interesting about your sessions that you can recall?

TT: What I mostly recall was how absolutely professional and organized the session was. They knew exactly what they wanted from us, and were very clear in expressing it. I remember that everything was relaxed and, well, fun . . . at least for me.

Q: When the album came out, what was your reaction to the work?

TT: I thought it was absolutely brilliant, and I realized that I had been working with two incredibly fine artists and composers. I was very proud to have been a part of it.

Q: How does it feel now to have been associated with the album?

TT: I usually joke that it is my "claim to hipness," especially since people who don't know I sang on *The Wall* are so shocked and then impressed. I remember a young man, probably fifteen years old, who saw me take my seat before the performance of *The Wall* in Los Angeles. He recognized me, and said with great scorn in his voice, "What are *you* doing here?" When I told him that I was here at the invitation of Roger and Dave, and that I had sung on the album, he sneered and said, "You *didn't*." "Yes, I did," I said. "My name is on the album."

"My friend has an album. I'm going to go look," he said in disbelief, as he darted off to find his friend. A few minutes later he returned with the album in his hand and a completely different attitude. "Would you please give me your autograph?" Boy, did I love THAT!!!!

Q: Is there anything else about your experience with the Pink Floyd that you'd like to share?

TT: After the concert, Dave asked me if I would be interested in singing backgrounds for the *Wall* tour. I explained to him that Daryl and I were still touring as C&T, but thanked him for asking. It would have been a lot of fun, but I had to go back to "Love Will Keep Us Together" and the Muskrats!

24

We're Only Ordinary Men

What Cultural Celebrities Orbited Pink Floyd?

R ock groups comprise a strange fraternity. Bands with much in common musically or politically often don't get along personally—see Oasis' Gallagher brothers and Blur's Damon Albarn, or the Velvet Underground and the Mothers of Invention—while seemingly strange bedfellows can form strong friendships. For instance, Alice Cooper, Micky Dolenz, Harry Nilsson, Jesse Ed Davis, and Keith Moon were all part of John Lennon's mid-seventies retinue.

In their more than forty years in the rock underbrush, the members of the Pink Floyd encountered high and mighty, high and low, and high and sober showbiz folks with plenty of tales to tell. Here are stories of some of their encounters.

Douglas Adams

Writer, musician, philosopher, actor . . . Douglas Adams, a true Renaissance man, interacted with many of the coolest countercultural figures of the 1960s and 1970s, counting among his friends and collaborators Pink Floyd, the members of Monty Python's Flying Circus, Monkees guitarist Michael Nesmith, and singer Gary Brooker of Procol Harum.

Just trying to make his way as a writer in the early 1970s, the Cambridge-born Adams hooked up with Monty Python's Graham Chapman, wrote a few skits for the show, and even appeared in two sketches of the group's last (non–John Cleese) series.

After various careers in other fields, he found the true outlet for his writing with *The Hitchhiker's Guide to the Galaxy*, first a BBC radio series in 1978 and later a five-book series that expanded to film, comics, and even computer games. He also wrote *Doctor Who* episodes.

Adams regularly worked references to Beatles and Pink Floyd songs into his work, and counted fellow Cambridge native David Gilmour as a good friend. Adams, Gilmour, and Nick Mason shared a taste for auto racing.

As a birthday present to Adams—a left-handed guitarist who suggested *The Division Bell* as the title of the band's 1994 album—Gilmour and Mason invited him on stage to play along with the band at their London show at Earls Court on October 28, 1994.

Adams moved to California in 1999 and passed away there of a heart attack in 2001 at age forty-nine. His official biography, published in 2003, is titled *Wish You Were Here.*

The Beatles

The young members of the Pink Floyd were jazz and R&B fans first and foremost, but even they fell under the spell of the Beatles. The Merseybeat phenomenon changed the landscape and blasted open the music scene, even for converted jazzers and blues freaks trying to become proper pop groups.

Syd Barrett, more than the other Floyds, embraced both the emerging underground and the notion of pop songwriting. The rest of the band, realizing that their young leader was the only one with an idea for slicing through the pop music jungle, fell in line.

While the Beatles were already international pop stars by early 1966, they hadn't stopped checking out what was happening below sea level. Paul McCartney, in particular, was a benefactor of the London underground, lending financial support to the Indica Bookstore and the *International Times*, both of which trumpeted the Floyd's efforts. (John Lennon also, later, donated to *IT*.) These subterranean connections made the Beatles and the Pink Floyd fated to come into contact.

It's unlikely that the Beatles played any part in getting the Floyd signed to EMI subsidiary Parlophone (the Fabs' label) in 1967, but their former engineer, Norman Smith, was lobbying for bands he could produce, and had some pull.

McCartney had checked out and enjoyed the nascent Floyd at the Roundhouse ("dressed as an Arab," noted the press reports) on November 15, 1966, then again at the UFO club's premiere on Friday, December 23, 1966. A tripping Lennon visited the Fourteen-Hour Technicolor Dream on April 29, 1967. It's unlikely, however, that he stayed around long enough to hear the Floyd's set, which took place at dawn after the band arrived from another gig earlier that evening.

On March 21, 1967, ten days after "Arnold Layne" was released, Norman Smith brought Syd, Roger, Rick, and Nick into Abbey Road for a short "meeting" between his new band and the Beatles. Smith was really pulling a favor; the Beatles rarely had any visitors in the studio. On this evening, the Fabs were working on overdubs for "Lovely Rita," and as an added benefit, John Lennon was—unusually at Abbey Road—stoned out of his gourd.

While Hunter Davies in *The Beatles* characterized their meeting as a series of "half-hearted hellos," Nick Mason was a bit more loquacious on *Inside Out*: "The music sounded wonderful, and incredibly professional, but in the same way we survived the worst of our gigs, we were enthused rather than completely broken by the experience. . . . There was little if any banter with the Beatles. We sat humbly, and humbled, at the back of the control room while they worked on the mix."

Some have accused the Fabs of ripping off sounds coming from Floyd's sessions, and others believe that Barrett & Co. could have taken things they'd heard from the Beatles down the hall. Both scenarios are possible, but unlikely; there's little evidence to support either argument.

The Fabs had already experimented, by the end of 1966, with backward recording, random noise, Indian instrumentation, treated keyboards, vari-speed recording, double-tracked vocals, and sound effects, and their lyrics and melodies were the best in the field.

The Floyd were still new to the studio and in a similar position to the Beatles in 1963: recording their live set and a few new songs that rarely, if ever, were played at gigs. But PF's own musical direction was already laid out in a diametrically opposite direction from that of the Beatles. Its rock was heavier and its folk folkier, though Waters later would borrow an approach and a few ideas from John Lennon.

The two bands rarely met, although both continued to work at Abbey Road during the rest of the 1960s. The Floyd were often on tour, and often were forced to record hurriedly. Once *Piper* emerged, however, McCartney reaffirmed his interest in the group and its ability to explore avant-garde areas in which his Beatle cohorts weren't necessarily interested.

Decades later, Macca would work on multiple occasions with Barrett's replacement, Dave Gilmour, who had taken inspiration from George Harrison's guitar sounds, particularly on *Abbey Road*.

Kate Bush

British pianist and singer Kate Bush, born in 1959, was already writing songs by her early teens. Her work has always contained a variety of styles and influences, making her a progressive-rock-inspired songwriter. She incorporates elements of modern dance, spiritual seeking, humor, and classic literature into her work; few other artists could (or would) write songs about Joan of Arc, Wilhelm Reich, and Adolf Hitler.

Perhaps this far reach is part of what attracted David Gilmour to her music; he heard a demo tape she made in the early seventies and was impressed. Gilmour helped her make a more polished demo and eventually played a role in EMI's decision to sign her in 1974.

At age fifteen, she wasn't ready to record a proper album, so she spent time gigging with a hand-picked band, taking dance lessons, and writing songs. Her first album, 1978's *The Kick Inside*, produced a British number one single in "Wuthering Heights," the first-ever British number one record written and performed by the same woman.

Gilmour has retained ties with the eccentric and singular singer over the decades, singing backup on 1982's *The Dreaming* and adding guitar to *The Sensual World* in 1989. (Pink Floyd collaborators Michael Kamen and James Guthrie also worked on her 2005 *Aerial* double CD.)

The two appeared at *The Secret Policeman's Other Ball* in 1987, with Gilmour backing Bush on her 1985 monster hit "Running Up That Hill," a song that Gilmour has quoted during the occasional PF show. During a 2002 Gilmour gig in London, Bush took the stage for a version of "Comfortably Numb," singing the part created on record by Roger Waters.

Ms. Bush remains close to Gilmour and continues to publicly acknowledge him for his contributions to getting her career off the ground.

The Damned

What do Pink Floyd and a first-generation British punk band have in common? Just one album.

The Damned were the first British punk rockers to release a single, 1976's "New Rose." While they were certainly in tune with the tenor of the times, some hint of the band's 1960s sentiments emerged on the 45's flip side, a high-speed recasting of the Beatles' "Help!"

When Stiff Records considered producers for the band's second album, one name that came up was Syd Barrett, who was Damned guitarist Captain Sensible's hero. Unfortunately, Barrett wasn't available, even though the Sex Pistols, also fans, had tried to smoke him out in Cambridge.

The Damned were set to record their album, eventually titled *Music for Pleasure*, at the Floyd's Britannia Row Studios. Perversely, drummer Nick Mason ended up with the production assignment.

Nick Mason looks a tad uncomfortable with the Damned's Brian James and DJ Nicky Horne during recording sessions for the Mason-produced *Music for Pleasure*. The album was panned and James soon left the band.   *Photo by Erica Echenberg/Redferns*

Arguably the least "musical" of the Floyds and certainly the least like Barrett, the affable skinsman seemed a ridiculous choice to marshal a punk rock band into the studio (despite previous experience producing Gong and Robert Wyatt), but the band didn't have much say.

The band and Mason got on fine personally, though they had little in common. The Damned's way of working, however—quick, dirty, and few if any overdubs, amid an endless series of juvenile jokes—was in complete opposition to Mason's methods, both in the Floyd and with his outside production assignments. The group hated the album, and so did the press.

Bob Geldof, K.B.E.

Irish sextet the Boomtown Rats were perhaps the first commercial pop-punk band. Each of their first ten singles, beginning in 1977, hit the British Top 40, using a hyperactive, cartoonish style that blended punk energy with pop songwriting dynamics.

Lead singer/songwriter Bob Geldof would have seemed an odd choice to have anything to do with an old-guard band like Pink Floyd, but when *The Wall* was optioned as a film in 1981, a bankable star was needed to play the character of Pink. At that point, the Boomtown Rats were among the biggest bands in Britain, and Geldof was a pinup with charisma.

Though Geldof had never worked in film, his screen test was apparently excellent and he was game for the film's more difficult scenes. This was, however, his only feature film as an actor; he would find music (and, eventually, philanthropy) more interesting and less taxing than shaving off all his body hair, being painted with pink slime, and starring in a film featuring music by a group he couldn't stand.

Eventually Geldof became the first rock star since George Harrison to take a starring role in eradicating poverty, helping write and produce the 1984 Band Aid single "Do They Know It's Christmas?" Eventually Geldof's project became Live Aid, two rock concerts (in London and Philadelphia) held on July 13, 1985 to help raise funds to feed the hungry of the world. The Floyd weren't playing together at that time, though; having done many charity shows in the past, they regretted not being at Live Aid. Two decades later, the Floyd did help out Geldof, who by now had been knighted for his anti-poverty efforts, astonishingly reuniting for a short set at Live 8 on July 2, 2005. It was their first gig together since the four had played *The Wall* in 1981.

The quartet showed no animosities, though pushing and shoving had certainly happened behind the scenes. Galvanized to action by an uncharacteristic Waters phone call to Gilmour, Pink Floyd played five classics, three from *Dark Side* ("Speak to Me," "Breathe," "Money,") as well as "Wish You Were Here" and "Comfortably Numb," during which MTV showed its everlasting commitment to music by *cutting to a commercial* during Gilmour's guitar solo.

Geldof's response to the Pink Floyd "reunion"? "Not that I can stand you cunts, but you've made an old retro punk very happy. 'Cos I never liked the music, really."

Stephane Grappelli

Violin legend Stephane Grappelli (1908–97) was one of the greatest European jazzmen ever. A CV as varied as his—he worked with Django Reinhardt, Paul Simon, Yo-Yo Ma, bluegrass picker David Grisman, and Yehudi Menuhin, among others—would naturally have to include a Pink Floyd session.

Urbane, sophisticated, and well dressed, the string virtuoso first made his mark as the violinist with the Hot Club Quintet of France in the 1930s and 1940s, establishing unexpected musical and personal rapport with earthy, nearly illiterate gypsy guitarist Reinhardt. Despite having little in common with him, Grappelli added a solid, swinging, melodic sense to Django's fiery playing, making this odd couple of jazz one of the most charming and thrilling duos in musical history.

Following Django's death in 1953, Grappelli went his own way, collaborating with jazz giants Duke Ellington, Gary Burton, McCoy Tyner, Phil Woods, and Barney Kessel, as well as fellow violin legends Jean-Luc Ponty and L. Subramaniam.

During 1975, he and Menuhin—the finest classical violinist of his generation but also a devotee of jazz, pop, and Indian music—were at Abbey Road Studios recording a set of 1930s popular songs arranged in chamber style. Finding these two musical giants in the same studio where they were laying down *Wish You Were Here*, the Floyd thought it might be fascinating to have both of them on a track.

While Menuhin declined to participate, Grappelli (after negotiating a session fee said to be three hundred pounds) set up and began sawing away. The intention was to put his work at the end of "Wish You Were Here," and some folks swear that they can hear the fiddle. The Floyd themselves don't seem to think that Grappelli made the final mix, and didn't credit him on the album sleeve in order to avoid trivializing him.

Gilmour noted in a much-quoted interview from 1999 that part of the session with Grappelli involved "avoiding his wandering hands. Was he gay? I don't think many people would argue about that."

Grappelli, who passed away in 1997, is interred at the same Paris cemetery that holds the mortal remains of Edith Piaf and Jim Morrison.

Jimi Hendrix

The Pink Floyd and Jimi Hendrix were certainly aware of each other from their travails in the London club scene starting in 1966. The two acts didn't cross paths until 1967, though, by which time both were working on their first albums.

On May 29, the Floyd, Hendrix, and the Move all played a disastrous gig in a barn in Lincolnshire, a show "celebrated" for its horrid smell, terrible equipment, and crooked promotion. Not long afterward, Hendrix caught the Floyd at the UFO.

That summer, both bands engaged in abortive American tours. The Pink Floyd's run in the U.S. ended ignominiously when Syd Barrett flamed out in California, while Hendrix was thrown off the Monkees' tour (he'd been personally recruited by the band's drummer, Micky Dolenz) after some fans objected to his sexually suggestive stage antics.

Pink Floyd and Hendrix (and the Move) met again on a U.K. package tour that began on November 14, 1967. While the Floyd, avant-garde and somewhat arch on stage when outside of London, had already begun to lose face (and bookings) due to Syd Barrett's worsening mental state, Hendrix—the headliner, with years of experience on the R&B scene—had established the necessary chops and flair to entertain even the most provincial of fans.

Hendrix referred to the group's troubled guitarist sardonically as "laughing Syd Barrett," but apparently the rest of the band got on well with all three members of the Experience.

The next year, at the start of their second U.S. tour, the Floyd found themselves in New York without their promised stage gear. Hendrix, in Nick Mason's words, "saved us . . . he sent us down to Electric Lady, his recording studio and storage facility on West Eighth Street, and told us to help ourselves to what we needed. There are some real rock 'n' roll heroes."

Barrett's replacement, David Gilmour, was a huge Hendrix fan, right down to the Fender Stratocaster guitar, and several pre–*Dark Side* Floyd tracks (notably "Fat Old Sun" and "The Nile Song") betray a strong JHE influence.

Petit, Nureyev, and Polanski

Roland Petit, director of the Ballets de Marseille, an unlikely Pink Floyd fan, contacted the band in 1970 with the idea of a collaborative project. The Floyd, all fans of the continent, were happy to take the opportunity to go to France.

Petit came up with the idea of the band providing music for a balletic interpretation of Marcel Proust's novel *Remembrance of Things Past*. That project died, in part because none of the members of the Floyd could be bothered to finish reading the lengthy and somewhat difficult book.

Eventually the Floyd worked with the company for a week in 1972, jamming "Careful with That Axe, Eugene" and "Echoes," but not enjoying the experience very much; all four members of the band were uncomfortable with tailoring their performance to the timing of the dancers.

Some time after this gig, Rudolf Nureyev, the world's greatest and most famous dancer, organized a lavish lunch/planning session at his English home for either a filmed ballet of *Aladdin* or a ballet-cum-soft-core-porno-rock-opera *Frankenstein* (nobody was quite sure which). Waters, Mason, and manager Steve O'Rourke attended the event, along with Petit and Roman Polanski, who was slated to direct whatever project emerged from the meeting.

This evening remains legendary in Pink Floyd lore for several reasons: Nureyev's beautiful home and matchless collection of decorative arts, the lavish outlay of wine and food, a lack of planning for the proposed project, and the very *non-heterosexual* character of the evening's activities. ("Didn't you smell a rat?" Mason asked Waters later. His reply: "I smelt a few poofs.")

The whole experience, which ended just before the release of *Dark Side of the Moon*, led the group away from the higher arts.

The Soft Machine

When Peter Jenner and Andrew King got Syd Barrett into the studio to record his first solo album, *The Madcap Laughs*, they needed musicians to back him up. The full Floyd was out of the question, of course, although David Gilmour and Roger Waters tried to help out by taking over the production from Malcolm Jones halfway through the process. Eventually it was decided to bring in some members of the Soft Machine.

The Softs, like Barrett (and Dave Gilmour) hailed from Cambridge and were the second most popular psychedelic band in the late '66 and early '67 London scene. They and the Floyd were huge favorites among the London underground and at UFO. Their love of whimsy and free jazz, as well as the ability to play at hurricane-force rhythms, put them at the forefront of a progressive rock movement that seemed, at the time, limitless.

The band's early 1967 single "Love Makes Sweet Music" is among the greatest British rock songs of the era, blending the spacey rush of psychedelia with a solid rock backbeat. Despite its failure on the charts, this 45 helped establish the Softs' credentials.

Drummer Robert Wyatt was a star singer and whirlwind behind the kit; keyboardist Mike Ratledge combined jazz introspection and a sense of anarchy. Bassist Kevin Ayers and guitarist Daevid Allen were suitably gnomish characters, the former blessed with pop-star looks and a gift for melody, the latter a truly far-out character who, after leaving the group, set up the hippie collective band Gong.

By 1969 both Ayers and Allen were gone and the band, like Pink Floyd, had abandoned all pretense of pop, moving full-on into a bookish fusion of jazz and rock.

The free, rhythmically shifting Softs—perhaps the most advanced jazz-rock group in England—still had a hard time dealing with Syd Barrett in 1969–70. The group struggled just to *understand* the guitarist's directions in the studio, much less back him up competently. Eventually, David Gilmour decided to have Barrett lay down tracks and have the Soft Machine play over them later.

The Pink Floyd entertains at the *International Times* newspaper's "All Night Rave" launch party at London's Roundhouse, October 15, 1966. By this time, pop celebrities like Paul McCartney and Pete Townshend—and the cream of London's underground and "beautiful people" contingent—were picking up the nascent band's vibrations.

Photo by Adam Ritchie/Redferns

Even Kevin Ayers, the Softs' onetime guitarist (and an utterly loony psychedelic figure) couldn't clock Barrett's weirdness, although he wrote the charming fable "Clarence in Wonderland" as a tribute to Syd.

The two bands continued to interact over the years. Robert Wyatt fell from a window on July 1, 1973 and suffered a broken back. The Floyd played two benefit shows to raise money for him that November.

Mason would produce Wyatt's 1974 album *Rock Bottom* and later appear with him on *Top of the Pops*, sitting behind the drum kit for a lip-synch of Wyatt's surprise hit single "I'm a Believer." Years later, Wyatt sang on the Floyd drummer's first solo project, *Fictitious Sports*.

Wyatt has enjoyed a successful solo career, becoming almost a father figure to various contemporary folk and world artists. He curated the 2001 Meltdown music festival, and sang "Comfortably Numb" during Gilmour's performance.

Pete Townshend

By early 1966 the Who was one of the most talked-about pop groups in Britain for its auto-destructive tendencies, pop art motifs, explosive onstage energy—and for Pete Townshend's songwriting.

The Pink Floyd were nothing like the Who, but that didn't stop Townshend—in a phase during which he embraced the rock underground—from checking out the band at UFO. A tripping Townshend, viewing the elongated visage of Roger Waters, confided to a friend that he feared that the Floyd's bassist might swallow him alive.

The Who's mouthpiece was never afraid to express strong opinions about others' work to the press, famously running down the Beatles' "Strawberry Fields Forever" as well as *Piper*, which he felt was so dissimilar to the group's live show as to be bubblegum. (This from a man whose band's big 1968 single release was the trivial "Dogs.")

Both bands, or at least the *leaders* of both bands, were searching for ways out of the normal pop paradigm. While Townshend wasn't the first to do a true "rock opera"—the Pretty Things, recording with Norman Smith at Abbey Road in 1967, beat him to it with *S.F. Sorrow*—he was the first one to have a hit with the concept in 1969 with *Tommy*.

In the intervening years, the Who would engage successfully (*Quadrophenia*) and unsuccessfully (*Lifehouse*) with the dreaded "concept album," but Floyd really perfected the formula sonically and lyrically with 1973's *Dark Side of the Moon.*

While Townshend became friendly with the members of the Floyd, any hope of a long-term friendship between Roger Daltrey and the band was laid to rest when the Who's singer mistook Rick Wright for Eric Clapton at a party.

Gilmour, always more interested in working with other musicians than were the other members of the Floyd, formed a friendship with Townshend in the 1980s.

The Who's guitarist penned lyrics for two Gilmour tracks from 1984's *About Face* album ("All Lovers Are Deranged" and "Love on the Air"); the two then cowrote the anthemic "White City Fighting"—originally submitted to Gilmour but rejected because he couldn't relate to the lyric—and "Give Blood" for Townshend's 1985 *White City: A Novel.*

Gilmour also played lead guitar in Townshend's Deep End band the next year, ultimately appearing on the group's live video and CD.

When the Floyd were inducted into the U.K. Music Hall of Fame on November 16, 2005, Townshend, a peer, contemporary, and supporter, was a logical choice to introduce the band. (Only Gilmour and Mason attended, as Waters was in Rome and Wright was in the hospital having surgery.)

25

Some Rhyme, Some Ching

What Pink Floyd Songs Stick Out Like Sore Thumbs?

U nlike most rock bands of the late 1960s, the Floyd weren't concerned with love songs or taking pretty promotional pictures. Their path was odd and singular, partially because they considered themselves experimenters, partially because they couldn't really *write* pop songs.

Having failed at being a pop group, the Floyd were free to follow their experimental instincts. Light shows? Noise? Concept albums? Dogs barking? Sped-up voices? Songs using nothing but household objects? Sure, why not? The Floyd did all of those things, although not everything they recorded made it out for public consumption.

Some excellent songs, like "Embryo," "Raving and Drooling," and "What Shall We Do Now," just didn't fit in with Pink Floyd's album concept of the time, or with the type of music they were working in, or the contract they were trying to fulfill.

But some songs that they did release on high-profile albums *still* didn't slot neatly into a category. Whether bad, unusual, atypical, or simply out of time, here are ten released tracks that stick out from the remainder of the band's oeuvre.

"Bike" (1967)

The final track on *The Piper at the Gates of Dawn* is a landmark in Pink Floyd's career in that it's as close as the band came to a straight love song.

A typical Storm Thorgerson image served as the wrapping on a 2001 two-CD compilation entitled *Echoes: The Best of Pink Floyd*. Three oddities discussed in this chapter ("Bike," "Great Gig in the Sky," and "Another Brick in the Wall, Part II") were included.

Haltingly, seeming a bit lost, Syd tries to impress a girl who he believes understands him, who fits in his world.

The singer describes several of his possessions (a tricked-out bicycle, a ripped-up cape, a plate of cookies, a pet mouse) in detail. His language is twisted and somewhat confused, using terms like "I guess," "if you like," "I don't know why," and "if you think." His vocal on the chorus is heartrendingly desperate and filled with longing.

After Barrett invites his *inamorata* into a room of "musical tunes," the song grinds to a sudden halt, from which point the members of the Floyd raid the Abbey Road sound library to create a cacophony of wind-up toys, clocks, dungeon doors, whistles, and, at the end, overdubbed loops of cawing birds.

This track really represents British psychedelia: whimsical and fun, but with an ugly undercurrent of confusion, foreboding, and darkness. One wonders if Syd Barrett felt that the noise of the room mirrored the state of his brain. By the time this song was recorded, the bright-eyed young songwriter was already exhibiting some signs of incipient schizophrenia.

"See Saw" (1968)

Someone supposedly titled this song on the master tape reel, "The most boring song I've ever heard, bar two." Since the band rarely, if ever, played this live, and didn't record it for the BBC, one assumes it wasn't a favorite.

This Rick Wright waltz is, like "Remember a Day," a gauzy, misty remembrance of youth. The 4:37 track drags and nothing much "happens": i.e., "See Saw" has no great crescendo or breakthrough.

Instead, Wright's airy vocals almost float right off the record, and during the bridge sections, xylophones, free-form guitar, Mellotron, organ, and various percussion instruments pile on in a hazy, nightmarish descending line. Sounds cascade from speaker to speaker. It's as if producer Norman Smith and the group, greeted with this big mashed potato of a song, decided to ladle on the psychedelic gravy with a shovel.

It's fascinating to try and pick out what instruments are making the sounds on the track, and it's even more of a puzzle to figure out what Wright is singing . . . and, having done that, what the words actually *mean*.

It's most likely a simple series of images that evoke various parts of an idealized childhood. None of that helps explain the ridiculously high-register voices at the end, which may be the work of Norman Smith.

"A Spanish Piece" (1969)

Some music included on film soundtracks is, by definition, just filling time and space. But this track from *More* is both musically insubstantial and offensive.

Dave Gilmour's cod-flamenco guitars might have served some purpose, but it's hard to see the "lyrics" as anything but a bad joke. His unfunny portrayal of a tequila-sodden Spaniard speaking with a Castilian accent (in which "s" sounds are rendered as "th") is just *wrong*.

Most ridiculously, while flamenco music and the Castilian accent originate from Spain, tequila doesn't. It's from Mexico, from a town called Tequila, to be exact. The only connection the Spanish have to tequila is that when they invaded Mexico to steal its assets, they (along with everyone else, eventually) discovered how great the drink tastes.

"Several Species of Small Furry Animals Gathered Together in a Cave and Grooving with a Pict" (1969)

During 1969–70, Roger Waters was quite busy. Seeing his chance to establish himself as the Floyd's number one songwriter, he produced much of the music for the *More* soundtrack and contributed material to the soundtrack of *The Body*, collaborating with experimental composer Ron Geesin.

Doing his best to provide original songs for his half-side of the *Ummagumma* studio disc, he came up with this exercise in vari-speed recording and pidgin Scottish. Overdubbing several tracks of his voice sped up and slowed down, Waters created a very strange, only intermittently listenable number fully in tune with the album's experimental spirit but also suffering from its lack of melody or inspiration.

Having worked out his need to make, as Norman Smith said, "interesting noises with his mouth," Waters returned to more conventional composition in 1970.

"Seamus" (1971)

Short of material for side one of *Meddle*, the group cut this jokey track. Inspired by the baying of Steve Marriott's dog (Marriott was the guitarist and singer of the Small Faces and Humble Pie), who apparently did quite a job singing along to a wailing guitar, David Gilmour recorded a moaning dog over a blues track. The result sounded . . . like a dog moaning over a blues track.

Of course, the Floyd's penchant for using found sound and "unmusical" elements is fully evident, but "Seamus," as an attempt at humor rather than anything truly interesting or experimental, fails. It's just not funny.

Several years later, the band inserted a bit of Seamus's yowling into "Dogs," from *Animals*, indicating that the Floyd at least were on the right side of the equation regarding recycling.

Some Floyd fans feel that this is the band's worst track ever. While it's certainly bad, is this 2:09 piece really worse than the car crashes that are "Sysyphus," "A Spanish Piece," "Atom Heart Mother," or "One of My Turns"?

"When You're In" (1972)

This instrumental from *Obscured by Clouds* is ahead of its time: it sounds like 1990s Britpop. Had the group provided lyrics and a melody, this might have been one of their most impressive mid-period songs. Its modern hard rock sound, with a great riff, exotic touches, and metal-like dynamics, foretells bands such as Oasis and even Radiohead.

It's always interesting to listen to Pink Floyd just *rock*, which they did at times on this 1972 soundtrack album. Gilmour (who also provided the vocal and American-sounding guitars on the rollicking *OBC* cut "The Gold It's in the . . . ") was always happy to play fast and loud, but Wright didn't really take to this kind of music, and Waters may have found it hard to write lyrics for simple, four-on-the-floor rocking as well.

The Floyd's "rock" compels in large part because of Nick Mason, who was more influenced by Ginger Baker than by more conventional 1960s colleagues such as Charlie Watts or Ringo Starr. For the group's up-tempo material, Mason varies straight rock tempos with inside-out patterns and simple polyrhythms, sometimes playing sparely and, at times (especially live), exploding into a fury of cymbals and tom-toms.

One thing this song presages in the Floyd catalog is the use of low-register bass and keyboard tones. Such sounds graced much of *Wish You Were Here.*

"The Great Gig in the Sky" (1973)

If you're doing it "old school," then Rick Wright's "Great Gig" closes side one of *Dark Side.* This elegiac mix of classical pacing, jazz chords, and gospel feel is way out from anything the group did before or since. It begins just as Gilmour has sung about the magic spells of organized religion, and in fact the track was titled "Religion" early on in the running order.

Asked in a fan interview for his feelings on the song, Gilmour was quite frank.

Q: Be honest. When listening to "The Great Gig in the Sky," have you ever thought, "Oh put a sock in it, you silly cow?"

A: Sometimes. Sometimes no. Sometimes yes.

This worldwide hit was released with different labels in different countries, as well as being issued on white and pink vinyl. This 45 is a Peruvian issue.

"Another Brick in the Wall" Part II (1979)

Pink Floyd? Disco? A number one single? *What?*

When Roger Waters, needing collaborators, hired Bob Ezrin (and, later, engineer James Guthrie) to help construct *The Wall*, he opened himself to outside influences. The legendary "control freak" was surprisingly amenable to suggestions from both Ezrin and Guthrie.

For instance, Ezrin put forward the idea of laying a disco beat behind a few of the songs on the album. Nick Mason, who at this point was going through a playboy stage of disco dancing all night long, and Dave Gilmour, who actually went out to some dance clubs to soak in the beat (although he hated the music), helped construct the one-hundred-beats-per-minute backing track to "Another Brick in the Wall, Part II," which was more than loosely based on the same kind of Chic-inspired disco-funk that Queen would so successfully appropriate for the 1980 smash "Another One Bites the Dust."

The very idea that Pink Floyd would have a hit single—in America, no less—seems crazy. They hadn't put out a 45 in England since 1968. Sure, "Money" had made the Top 60 on the U.S. chart back in 1974, but nothing from the next two albums had made any inroads, and the Floyd were an established *album* act.

But the disco thump, an anti-establishment message, a stinging Gilmour guitar solo, and the addition of the Islington Green School choir singing the catchy and controversial "We don't need no education" verse combined to provide Columbia Records with a totally unexpected, left-field smash.

And despite all the unusual elements of the song, it still holds together as a top-notch piece of music. As Gilmour said in a 1999 *Mojo* interview, "It doesn't in the end *not* sound like Pink Floyd."

"Don't Leave Me Now" (1979)

This song is among the darkest in the Floyd catalog. Foreboding keyboards make way for a bit of delayed guitar and then Waters' desperate, at times atonal vocal. To those who are able to get through his occasional nasal screeching, it's clear that only Waters could have sung this song—the darkest and in some ways least listenable in the group's catalog—

where protagonist Pink begs the woman he's beaten up and repeatedly cheated on to stay.

Gilmour and Wright's voices were too pretty for this material, and by 1975, Waters wanted to sing his own compositions anyhow, giving vocals away only grudgingly from *Wish You Were Here* on. Knowing as he did that he wasn't a great singer, he must have found it odd, if liberating, to take on vocal duties from his two cohorts.

Then again, Waters, who in his huge vision and megalomania was rapidly becoming the D. W. Griffith of rock and roll, seemed to have no problem making music so inwardly focused, thrashing around with his personal demons and railing against the industry and fans that had afforded him a very comfortable lifestyle.

Once the music has become tuneless and intolerably bleak, the band breaks through at 3:10. Swirling organ, piano, and guitar lines underlie Pink's seemingly bottomless misery with genuine pathos and empathy.

Then Pink smashes all six of his televisions.

"The Trial" (1979)

This ridiculous centerpiece of *The Wall*'s side four sums up and ends the album's "story," as hapless rocker Pink is dragged before a judge for his "crimes," which include "showing feelings of an almost human nature." (By this point, Waters was applying the social commentary with a trowel.)

It's not clear where Roger Waters got the idea that he, or any other rock star, was being persecuted for showing his feelings, but this pseudo-opera certainly wins the derby for the most overblown piece of jetsam in the group's catalog. As a song, it's *just* bearable—which may be the point, as Waters was more interested in advancing his cranky narrative than in actually making music for something as crass as *enjoyment*—but it does give insight into the mind of a man who felt the entire world was against him and what he stood for.

This track is the only one on *The Wall* for which coproducer Bob Ezrin snagged a songwriting credit, although apparently he was very involved in the process of shaping and selecting the music.

26

The Empty Screen the Vacant Look

How Was Pink Floyd's Music Used in Films?

P ink Floyd's cinematically constructed, wide-ranging music was used in several films, either in the background or as a main component in the story. Few rock groups have been better utilized for this purpose; the Floyd were experts at crafting music that set moods and evoked feelings without words.

Not included in this list are the fifteen-minute documentary *San Francisco*, from 1968, which uses "Interstellar Overdrive," the 1970 Dutch concert film *Stamping Ground*, which includes two Floyd songs, or the more recent concert DVDs *The Delicate Sound of Thunder* and *P*U*L*S*E*. The ten choices below are more representative of the band's creative peak.

Tonite Let's All Make Love in London (1967)

Peter Whitehead's documentary of the ever-changing London scene occasioned the Floyd's first-ever proper recording session, in February 1967. The band cut an incendiary version of "Interstellar Overdrive" along with an untitled instrumental given the toss-off title of "Nick's Theme." (See "Yippee You Can't See Me.")

The film includes fascinating footage of various London music and showbiz icons, including the Small Faces, Michael Caine, Mick Jagger, Vashti Bunyan, Eric Burdon, Allan Ginsberg, and Julie Christie.

Unfortunately for the Floyd and for the film, *Tonite Let's All Make Love in London* was not released until late 1967, when most of the hype around "Swinging London" had died out to all but the most out of touch.

The Committee (1968)

This British art-house film, which was only recently released on video, starred Paul Jones, the former lead singer of Manfred Mann. The Floyd provided the score, and Arthur Brown, a fellow musician at underground clubs like UFO, performs his huge hit "Fire" in a party scene.

Jones's character, a hitchhiker, is called before the Committee, a nebulous, wealthy group representing the upholding of traditional values, to explain the gruesome killing of another man. Much of the film, which is shot in black and white, is based on psychologist R. D. Laing's observations on the individual in society.

The Floyd's contributions were taped in spring 1968, not long after Dave Gilmour joined the group. The title number, beginning with birdsong (typical for the band), is a sprightly four-four instrumental that bounces along in spite of a somewhat threatening progression.

Another version of the same song, shown later in the film, is slower, darker, and scarier, as Wright's organ drones provide the color. It's

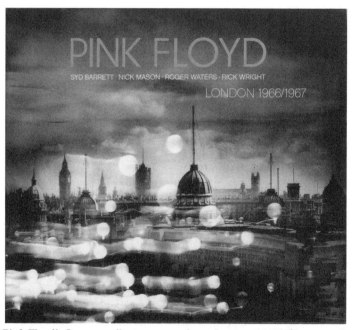

Pink Floyd's first recordings were made on January 11, 1967, as sound-track material for Peter Whitehead's film *Tonite Let's All Make Love in London.* The twenty-eight minutes of music the band laid down are collected on this 2005 CD.

really an early example of goth-rock. Forward-thinking in its approach and barely connected to anything that had come before in pop music, this is one of the group's most interesting obscure tracks.

The PF also laid down a strange, spacey instrumental that was played backward in the film. Several other tracks recorded by the Floyd were used in the background of various scenes.

More (1969)

When the Floyd took on the project of scoring Barbet Schroeder's film, they couldn't even do the recording at Abbey Road, instead being forced to work at lesser Pye Studios in London.

Perhaps the project came together too quickly to book Abbey Road, or perhaps the budget didn't allow for a top studio. Either way, this album is one of the band's "fall through the cracks" projects, despite including several excellent songs and being much more cohesive than its contemporary, *Ummagumma*.

In the film, an idealistic young German follows a glamorous American woman to Ibiza, where he falls prey to her and to heroin addiction. Ibiza was well known even at this time as a "pleasure den" for hedonistic young Europeans; all of the members of Pink Floyd journeyed there at one time or another.

The Floyd's music in the film—gauzy, psychedelic, hazy, and in some cases consciously bizarre—seems much more in the LSD/marijuana tradition than music associated with the heroin high. Some of the selections used by Schroeder differ from the versions included on the soundtrack. Two complete songs ("Seabirds" and "Hollywood") are not included on the *More* album at all.

Zabriskie Point (1970)

Following the success of 1967's *Blow-Up*—set in the very "Swinging London" in which the Pink Floyd were trying to establish themselves— legendary Italian director Michelangelo Antonioni turned his lens to America.

Zabriskie Point, the master's first film made in the U.S., was just his second in color and in English. But like his other classic films,

ZP concerned communication, or rather the lack thereof, among people who seemed to live in a perpetual fantasy world, people who rarely if ever did anything as menial as actual work.

Rather than focusing his attentions this time around on the idle rich, or on frustrated creative types, Antonioni considered the American West Coast counterculture, finding in its drug use, empty political rhetoric, and lack of direction a direct parallel to the alcohol-fueled, trivial, sex-obsessed upper-class society featured in his earlier classics *La Notte* and *L'Avventura.*

Antonioni did turn a kinder eye to the counterculture's rejection of capitalism and to its celebration of nature and free sexuality; his view of youth here is more positive than of the land-grabbing greedheads tossing up prefab houses in the pristine California desert.

Using untrained actors and a rock soundtrack, Antonioni created a film depending on and celebrating empty space: musical, physical, and emotional.

Pink Floyd, with a growing reputation as an ideal "head" band, seemed a perfect fit for the film. But the group found that working with Antonioni—whom Mason years later called a "treacherous eremite"—very difficult. Nothing seemed to please the master, and an entire album's worth of music was scrapped.

Various Rick Wright piano pieces, such as "The Violent Sequence" and various takes of "Love Scene," may have been too languid for Antonioni, and "Oenone" far too bizarre.

Eventually Antonioni used the country-sounding "Crumbling Land," the "Careful with That Axe" remake "Come In Number 51, Your Time Is Up," and "Heart Beat, Pig Meat."

Other musicians used in the film (the Rolling Stones, Jerry Garcia, John Fahey) were more "rootsy" and tied to American blues and folk traditions; the Floyd still wonder why Antonioni even bothered to hire them.

La Vallée (Obscured by Clouds) (1972)

Another exotic Barbet Schroeder outing, *La Vallée* (retitled *Obscured by Clouds* for English-speaking markets) featured Bulle Ogier as Viviane, a French politician's wife who meets a quartet of explorers in Papua New Guinea.

Instead of finding the rare birds she is seeking, however, she and the other tourists meet a tribe of "uncivilized" first-world people, the Mapuga tribe, and have to confront their own ideas of what constitutes "civilized" behavior.

With a few exceptions, Pink Floyd's music, while excellent, is not as suited to the story line as was their music for *More*. There is, however, one astonishing moment: the final track, "Absolutely Curtains," which includes a long section of tribal chants. This may be the first use of indigenous music in a rock context; such ethnic appropriation became much more common in house and techno music in the 1990s.

Pink Floyd was busy recording *Dark Side of the Moon* when these tracks were cut in France, and the contrast is quite fascinating between the fairly standard pop songs cut hastily for the soundtrack and the radio-friendly astral rock of the painstakingly constructed *Dark Side*.

Live at Pompeii (1972)

The Floyd's reach in the early 1970s is as baffling as it is brave. Their live concerts were unlike any others, and their experimentation with multisensory stimulation far more expressive than their often patchy studio albums of the time.

So the idea of recording a concert in an empty theater in Pompeii, although ridiculous in itself, wasn't that surprising in the context of Floyd's rambling, unfocused, adventurous career. So what's so odd about filming yourself playing in an ancient coliseum when you've already recorded a rock oratorio, used giant inflatable sea creatures on stage, and worked on a ballet?

To be clear, though, only three of the songs in this "concert film" were actually recorded at Pompeii (in October 1971); the others were laid down in London and stripped in behind images of the ruins, the theater, and bubbling lava.

Shots of the Floyd playing surprisingly crunchy, muscular versions of their most popular numbers are intercut with somewhat comical images of the band wandering through windstorms and around volcanic rock. One rather silly continuity problem in the film is the appearance and disappearance of Rick Wright's beard.

Following the completion of the film, director Adrian Maben found it necessary to add more shots; the band pretending to rehearse and

Pink Floyd being filmed at the ruins of Pompeii, 1971. *Photofest*

record *Dark Side of the Moon* (which at this point was already finished) found its way into the final cut. This extra footage provides an interesting document for historians but blurs the purpose of the movie.

By the time of the film's (limited) release the group had stopped performing nearly all of the music featured in it; the success of *Dark Side* had finally allowed Pink Floyd to ditch its back catalog—a millstone that Roger Waters, a man weighed down by many burdens, must have felt particularly glad to let go.

There are three different versions of this film: the 1972 release, a 1974 rerelease including the *Dark Side* footage, and a 2003 director's cut, which rearranges song order and deletes some of the 1974 version.

The Wall (1982)

Roger Waters had been thinking about his 1979 album as a film since he'd been thinking about it at all, and Gerald Scarfe, who had contributed inflatables, animation, and other ideas to previous Floyd tours, helped Waters define the possibilities of such a project.

The original concept was for Pink Floyd to use *Wall* concert footage as the basis for the film. But when director Alan Parker approached Waters with the possibility of turning the multimillion-selling album into a major film about the story of Pink, rather than just a document of the band's show, the Floyd's frontman, tired of band politics and looking for new collaborators, jumped at the chance.

Unfortunately, the partnership between Parker and Waters seemed doomed from the start. Both men are self-directed and hold to their respective visions with unshakable conviction; they clashed regularly enough that Waters was formally asked to relinquish any daily input on the project, only being allowed to make suggestions once the film was finished.

Parker, quoted in *Rolling Stone* in September 1982, said, "The difficulty came when I'd finished [the film]. I'd been shooting for sixty days, fourteen hours a day—that film had become *mine*. And then Roger came back to it, and I had to go through the very difficult reality of having it put over to me that it actually was a collaborative effort."

The finished product, starring Boomtown Rats singer and future philanthropic hero Bob Geldof as the abused, disconnected rock star Pink, was harrowing and painful to watch, but Waters later pronounced Parker's work excellent, saying it fit his original vision perfectly.

Geldof worked hard on the film, though he didn't like Pink Floyd's music. During his hotel room-trashing scene, he cut his hands badly enough that he was bleeding all over the set, but would not get medical assistance until director Parker had completed shooting.

Most of *The Wall*'s original recordings were used in the film, although many parts were changed and some songs rerecorded entirely. Geldof himself sang new vocal tracks for both "In the Flesh?" and "Stop," while he also sang on a completely rerecorded version of "In the Flesh?"

"Empty Spaces" was cut in favor of "What Shall We Do Now?" and both "Hey You" and "The Show Must Go On" were chopped entirely. Parts one and two of the explicatory "When the Tigers Broke Free" were inserted, giving more weight to the backstory of Pink's father being killed in World War II.

Waters, always comfortable as a Lone Ranger in a world full of people who didn't agree with him, felt that the film was important in that it carried forth his consistently stated message that even though you're troubled, you're not the only one. "It's bad for us when we're isolated from one another and frightened of one another," he said in a 1982 *Rolling Stone* piece. "But in the end the responsibility for what you do and how you feel about yourself is yours. You are an individual. You're alone, but that's all right."

La Carrera Panamericana (1992)

What better way to finance a trip to a Mexican cross-country road race than to make an hour-long documentary film about it?

While the race itself was nearly a disaster, as Gilmour and manager Steve O'Rourke got into a scary and nearly fatal road crash, the event did inspire Gilmour, Mason, and Wright to record some music for use in the film.

Intended mostly for racing fans, this film does have plenty of nice cars and six new, if featherweight, Floyd songs, including "Mexico '78," "Pan Am Shuffle," and "Carrera Slow Blues." Older Floyd songs are worked into the film as well. No soundtrack was ever released, but the new tunes float around on bootleg CDs.

The positive experience Wright, Mason, and Gilmour enjoyed recording this music led them to consider further projects, like 1994's *Division Bell.*

The Making of The Dark Side of the Moon (2003)

The "classic albums" series of DVDs explores some of the great pop music of our time in depth, going back to the people who made the music and delving deeper into the process of how it was produced.

Joining artists already featured in the series such as John Lennon, Frank Zappa, Nirvana, Cream, Bob Marley, the Sex Pistols, and Steely Dan, Pink Floyd got the "classic albums" treatment for its groundbreaking 1973 work.

The film features interviews with all four members of the Floyd (done in separate studios, owing Waters' disputes with both Gilmour and Wright), as well as with Alan Parsons, who provided the LP's glossy engineering, many of its production tricks, and the title of the album's overture, "Speak to Me."

In addition, album designer Storm Thorgerson (who has said he does not believe that his artwork here was especially important) is featured, along with various music industry figures.

Perhaps the most interesting moments in this DVD are those in which Gilmour and Waters sit down with acoustic guitars and play through some of the album's great moments. Waters incants his lunacy reverie "Brain Damage," while Gilmour plays "Breathe." In addition, trainspotters and bootleggers were happy to at least hear parts of an early demo version of "Time."

The Pink Floyd and Syd Barrett Story (2003)

This documentary, originally produced as a sixty-minute special for BBC television, may be the best documentary on the band and its Crazy Diamond ever to be produced.

While Barrett himself is not featured, except in old films and as a subject, nearly every other major player in the Pink Floyd story is. Waters, Wright, Gilmour, Mason, and Bob Klose are interviewed, as are former Syd flatmate Duggie Fields, album designer Aubrey "Po" Powell, producer Joe Boyd, photographer and Barrett friend Mick Rock, and Syd's post-Floyd musical collaborators Jerry Shirley (whose memories appear somewhat unreliable) and Jack Monck, among others.

The remembrances of the group's early days are sentimental, unsettling, heartbreaking, and above all reverent of Barrett's muse and of the group he played such a huge part in creating. While the original film is compelling enough, a 2006 special edition features complete, uncut interviews and is recommended for its scope.

John Edginton, who directed and produced this film, also produced a documentary on the Barrett-inspired (to be kind) British singer/songwriter Robyn Hitchcock (*Sex, Food, Death . . . and Insects*) in 2007.

Ten Vintage Pink Floyd Promotional Films

"Arnold Layne"
In which the players wander around a windy British beach with a mannequin. Ah, for simple times.

"See Emily Play"
This time, the band—in color!—tromps around a park.

"The Scarecrow"
Perhaps the most interesting Pink Floyd promotional film was shot in the countryside, in the glorious late summer/early fall of 1967. Roger Waters and Nick Mason pretend to shoot each other and fall dead in the grass.

"Jugband Blues"
Syd Barrett + blinking, flashing lights = Very Bad Idea.

"Let There Be More Light"
Filmed in color for French TV during 1968, this is a crackling live performance. Oddly enough, the band also shot a French TV "lip synch" in front of a studio audience who, ridiculously enough, *clapped along*. In the "lip synch," Gilmour strums a Gibson (!) guitar, and Rick Wright's facial hair makes a very early appearance.

"It Would Be So Nice"
An embarrassing black-and-white film in which everyone in the band appears that they'd rather be having root canal surgery.

"Corporal Clegg"
The Floyd wander through a cafeteria line in Germany, then play sitting around a huge banquet table. With shots of the band playing, war footage, David Gilmour pouring champagne all over Waters, and a final food fight, it's at least funny. (Another film for this song, a straight performance video, was shot in Belgium.)

"Paint Box" (1968, post-Barrett)
An odd choice. Gilmour mimes Barrett's part, and Rick Wright plays a Farfisa organ, which isn't present on the recording.

"Apples and Oranges" (1968, post-Barrett)
Another chance for Gilmour to "pretend" he's Barrett. His face is hidden for much of the film.

"Astronomy Domine" (1968, post-Barrett)
Apparently shot in Belgium, this clip includes a graphic that spells "Pink Floid" [*sic*].

27

Running Over the Same Old Ground

What Pink Floyd Songs Were Rewritten . . . by Pink Floyd?

From Rick Wright's "Turkish Delight" organ solos of 1967–68 and Nick Mason's often somnolent tempi to Dave Gilmour's signature Stratocaster strangling and Roger Waters' excoriations of This Miserable World, the Floyd had a bag of tricks.

As befits a quartet that created its own sound from square one, going where no rock group had dared or cared to go before, Pink Floyd hammered away at its concepts before getting them right or discarding them. As a result, the band was rarely celebrated *primarily* for its originality.

Here are ten examples of working through an idea to get at its core, sometimes getting it right with practice and sometimes beating it to death. This list doesn't count film soundtrack recasting of themes, such as "The Nile Song"/"Ibiza Bar" off *More*, or "Burning Bridges"/"Mudmen" from *Obscured by Clouds*, or "Mademoiselle Nobs," a rewrite of "Seamus," from *Live at Pompeii*.

"Let There Be More Light" as "Point Me at the Sky"

These two 1968 releases, both among Roger Waters' earliest compositions, share several elements.

Each song has a science-fiction lyrical preoccupation, and each borrows liberally from other sources. "Point Me" features a Gilmour vocal a step away from Ray Davies, while the guitarist belts out the chorus of "More Light" in a way somewhat reminiscent of Syd Barrett. Both songs also quote in different ways from "Lucy in the Sky with Diamonds" and share melodic ideas as well as their quiet-verse-to-propulsive-chorus construction.

Perhaps most obviously, Waters rewrote the chorus section of "Let There Be More Light" for the lead-up to the chorus of the more commercially aimed "Point Me at the Sky." The first attempt is built on a spaced-out middle section in which another song burst out of one speaker while the first one continued, but "Point Me" doesn't scale such heights, instead simply repeating its chorus into a psychedelic fade.

While "More Light" opened *Saucerful of Secrets*—an important achievement for Waters—"Point Me at the Sky," not surprisingly, wasn't a hit, and the song was never even put on an album.

"Careful with That Axe, Eugene" as "Come In Number 51, Your Time Is Up"

The experience of creating music to accompany *Zabriskie Point* fell far below the Floyd's expectations, despite their love of film and desire to work on soundtracks.

One track director Michelangelo Antonioni eventually used was "Come In Number 51, Your Time Is Up," a re-recording of late 1968's excellent and spooky "Careful with That Axe, Eugene."

"Axe" didn't even have a permanent title, beginning life as "Keep Smiling People," then becoming "Murderistic Women" prior to its recording for the B-side of "Point Me at the Sky." Even following its release, it was referred to in *The Man and the Journey* as "Beset by Creatures of the Deep."

So why did the group rerecord an old song and give it a "new" title? Perhaps for publishing reasons, but most likely just to save face. Since they'd already released "Axe" on a 1968 single and on the 1969 *Ummagumma* live album, it might have felt unseemly for a progressive, "noncommercial" band to release, for a third time, the exact same title.

"Atom Heart Mother" as "Echoes"/"Breathe"/ "Any Colour You Like"

The overlong title track from the Floyd's 1970 collaboration (or perhaps "collision") with avant-garde composer Ron Geesin has few riveting elements, and most of what is interesting about the entire *AHM* experience—

the genesis of the piece, the personality conflicts between Geesin and the session musicians—has little to do with the music itself. One moment of clarity in the bombast, however, does point toward the PF's future.

About ten and a half minutes into this confused piece, the Floyd—minus the choir and brass section—lay into a slow instrumental groove that leads inexorably from both psychedelia and symphonic rock and toward Pink Floyd's more singular, more lucrative future as a rock band that wasn't afraid to play spaciously or slowly, setting up tasty atmospherics and laying evocative lyrics on top.

The tempo and chord progression from this section of "Atom Heart Mother" laid the foundation for much great material to come; Mason's drumming and the general open-space approach portend the progression of both "Echoes" and *Dark Side*, while the chord progression was used later on in the breakthrough album's staples "Breathe" and "Any Colour You Like."

"One of These Days" as "Sheep"

The double bass guitar attack of 1971's "One of These Days" presaged techno music with its propulsive beat and slow build, and was among the group's most successful pre–*Dark Side* tracks on American radio.

In early 1975, while on tour, PF debuted a new song entitled "Raving and Drooling," which recast the "One of These Days" attack with an ambient sequence styled after the 1969–71 work featuring Roger Waters' screams, squalling guitar, and astral keyboards. Live recordings from the tour reveal that parts of "Raving and Drooling" echo the *Doctor Who* theme, a frequent Floyd touchstone that the band had already referenced on "One of These Days."

For some reason, however, the group never got "Raving and Drooling" into proper shape in the studio, with Waters perhaps feeling that the spacey sequence was too much of a step backward. He took the beat and the attack, attached some new lyrics about, er, sheep, and named it "Sheep." The "new" number became the climactic piece of 1977's *Animals*.

"Echoes" as "Breathe"

Meddle's centerpiece, "Echoes," sparkled with explorations into inner and outer space that PF never really revisited, focusing instead on Roger

Waters' earthbound lyrics. But the song's musical structure provided a clear starting point for the "new" post-psychedelic Floyd.

Not only did the superb Gilmour/Wright vocal harmony line on "Echoes" give the Floyd a foolproof method for delivering the medicine of Waters' harsh *Dark Side* thoughts, the lyric pattern on the verse of "Echoes" also became the pattern for the chorus of "Breathe."

"Breathe," however, had antecedents even prior to 1971. The lyrics of 1968's "Point Me at the Sky" urge listeners to "breathe in" while they still can before they are crowded out by overpopulation, and Waters' soundtrack project with Ron Geesin, *Music from the Body*, contains an anti-development tune titled "Breathe."

The 1970 composition even includes the lyric "Breathe in the air," although in a far more environmentally focused, less resigned context.

"Time" as "Have a Cigar" as "Pigs (Three Different Ones)"

The heavy guitar crunch of "Time" provided the Floyd with a new template, welding Gilmour's ever-present sense of hard-rock dynamics with a more sharpened Waters lyrical focus.

The Dylan-inspired lyrical pattern of "Time" and Gilmour's delivery of the lyrics in an almost ranting, spinning-out-of-control rhythm were central to its power. Waters, perhaps at this point realizing that lyrics, rather than innovative melodies, were his strength, rewrote the pattern and much of the melody for *Wish You Were Here*'s "Have a Cigar."

Guest vocalist Roy Harper's sarcastic delivery mixed Gilmour's singing chops effectively with Waters' bile, but the Floyd's bassist was unhappy about not singing "Cigar" himself. Certainly the end product would have felt and sounded more like Pink Floyd had Waters done so.

The band didn't work especially hard to distinguish "Cigar" from some of the harder-rocking moments on *Dark Side*. It's rather ironic that this screed against the commercialism and cynicism of the music business ended up sounding like a somewhat calculated follow-up to PF's earlier hit album.

For 1977's *Animals*, Waters claimed full writing credit for all the songs except "Dogs," but used a lot of the melodic elements from both "Time" and "Have a Cigar" for "Pigs (Three Different Ones)," his rant against greedy businessmen, Margaret Thatcher, and British bluenose/censorship advocate Mary Whitehouse.

The similarity linking the three songs even extends to the keys in which they were recorded. "Time" is in F-sharp minor, "Have a Cigar" in E minor, and "Pigs (Three Different Ones)" in F minor, lying directly between the other two.

"Wish You Were Here" as "Pigs on the Wing" Parts I and II as "Mother"

The British and American folk traditions provided Pink Floyd with the inspiration for some truly inspired acoustic pieces of its own.

Amid the machine-like synth blurbs, anti-music-biz ranting, desperate production tricks, and screaming saxophone surrounding it on the rest of *Wish You Were Here*, the album's title number stands as one of the band's most beautiful moments, its epic sweep and Waters'

This bootleg DVD, containing video rarities from the band's first several years, features color photos from 1967 (left) and 1970. Given the grammatical quality and song-title errors present, one could assume that this DVD was manufactured in a non-English-speaking country.

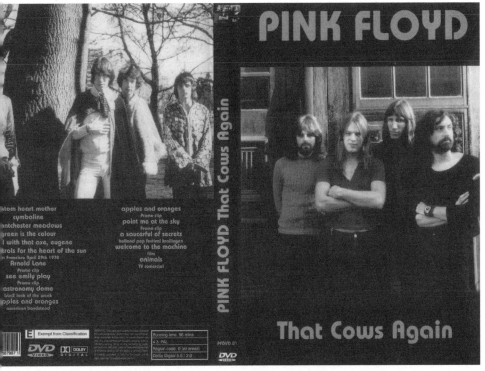

sorrowful lyrics standing tall without grandiose playing or overdone instrumentation.

Revisiting this sonic template must have tempted Waters, who by the mid-seventies was making home demos (particularly bad-sounding ones, according to Nick Mason) on his trusty acoustic guitar.

Whether he wrote the short "Pigs on the Wing" pieces on *Animals* as discrete songs chiefly to increase his songwriting royalties (as has been asserted) or if he simply wanted these pieces as separate songs to bookend the album, Waters used bits of melody and chords from "Wish You Were Here" to make short statements about his marriage or about the greater sweep of humanity. Or both.

And he did it again on the next album, recasting "Pigs on the Wing" as the mournful "Mother" on *The Wall*. While the lyrics of "Mother" don't reference his own split personality or his marriage, the Floyd's bassist does reuse the chords and folksy backing and, most obviously—and comically—revisits "Pigs" when he croaks, "Mother, do you think she's good enough . . . *for me?*"

Happily for all concerned, however, Waters avoids revisiting "Pigs on the Wing" Part II's image of burying his bone.

"Comfortably Numb" as "The Final Cut"

"Comfortably Numb," perhaps the most successful single moment on *The Wall*, was among the few songs on the epic double album that sounded like a group effort rather than a Roger Waters solo project.

Unfortunately, in the hard-to-digest *Wall* follow-up that was *The Final Cut*, Waters continued to take the best bits from successful earlier songs and weld them to new ones. The song "The Final Cut" itself simply goes on and on, and Waters just does not sing well enough to bring home words this heartfelt without wearing on the listener.

Michael Kamen, Waters' newest musical "collaborator" following the ouster of Rick Wright, the marginalizing of David Gilmour, and the firing of Bob Ezrin, adds a string arrangement and orchestral bed that sound taken directly from "Comfortably Numb."

Reusing the "Numb" arrangement makes sense given that "The Final Cut," which appears to be about the character Pink, was originally intended for *The Wall*. The use of the orchestra, and a Gilmour guitar solo

This poster advertises the Floyd's appearance at Oakland-Alameda County Coliseum on the *Animals* tour. Almost immediately, Algie the flying pig became central to the Floyd, even though punk rockers of the time thought it an unintentionally ironic comment on the band's perhaps bloated self-image.

played over major seventh chords, are reminiscent of past glories, but, stapled to an unpleasant song, they grate rather than inspire magic.

"Shine On You Crazy Diamond" Parts I and II as "Signs of Life"

The following dialogue was retrieved from an underwater bootleg cassette recording made several feet from David Gilmour's houseboat in the mid-1980s. Okay, it *wasn't*; everything written in the following three paragraphs is completely fabricated.

"Okay, lads. We need an opening for this album that reminds people of our classic material. Remember, it's our first LP without Roger, but *we're* still Pink Floyd, after all, so what can we do that really sounds like *us*?

"Hmm. Yes, well, we *could* open the first song with some ambient, fluffy synths and some sort of sound effect. We've done that before, and people will warm to it—hang on, what was I saying? The sound of the water lapping against the boat is totally distracting. . . .

"Hold on . . . back in the old days, we used accidents and odd inspirations. So can we drop in the sound of some of these waves breaking in the background, behind some of those great noodly keyboards of Rick's? Throw in some ambient glittery notes in background, I'll haul out a few mournful guitar notes, and I think we've got a winner!"

"Goodbye Blue Sky" as "Poles Apart"

Waters' pastoral music and foreboding lyrics made "Goodbye Blue Sky" one of *The Wall*'s most beguiling cuts. Since Gilmour's gorgeous vocal and some typically excellent folk-style acoustic guitar finger-picking were major elements of the song's magic, the guitarist apparently felt tempted to orbit that universe again for this 1994 recording.

The Division Bell's first-side paean to both Syd Barrett and Roger Waters, "Poles Apart," features folk picking and a pretty melody that owe much to "Blue Sky." In addition, the song—like much of the group's post-Waters work—harks back in not-too-subtle ways to the golden days.

The middle section of "Poles Apart," with its circus theme and found sound, comes directly from the Beatles-derived ethos of *Dark Side of the Moon*, while the fading guitar solo is the type of FM radio-friendly fretboard play that Gilmour perfected on *Animals*.

Ten Classic Pink Floyd Instruments

Syd Barrett's mirrored white Fender Telecaster guitar
The mirrors were just another part of the trip, sending blinding flashes of reflected light through the room.

David Gilmour's white Fender Stratocaster guitar
He used this during the late sixties, and also at times used a white Telecaster.

David Gilmour's black Fender Stratocaster guitar
His tricked-out go-to guitar for most of the 1970s, this remains one of rock's most famous axes.

David Gilmour and Roger Waters' Ovation acoustic guitars
The dense acoustic layering on *The Wall* comes from these guitars.

Roger Waters' Rickenbacker 4001S bass
He used this through 1969, eventually going over to the Fender Precision.

Roger Waters' Fender Precision bass
Waters used Fender basses throughout the 1970s.

Rick Wright's Farfisa Combo organ
Wright favored the Farfisa in 1966 and 1967, and kept it in the band's arsenal until at least 1974.

Rick Wright's Hammond C-3 organ
As the Floyd developed, Wright worked in other organ textures. This became his electric keyboard of choice by 1970.

Rick Wright's Kurzweil digital keyboard
Changing times demand new instruments, and Wright went digital in the 1980s.

Nick Mason's Premier double bass drum setup and Remo rototoms
Mason had customized drum heads with various Pink Floyd logos and designs almost from the start of the band's career. The rototoms were a 1972 addition.

28

New Car Caviar Four-Star Daydream

What Are Some of the Most Collectible Floyd Records?

P ink Floyd has become one of the most collectible pop music acts in the world. Even the latter-day albums, which sold bushels, are becoming valuable; it is hard to find a sealed original copy of *The Wall* on vinyl nowadays for less than $250.

Promotional copies of the group's singles and albums fetch a small fortune, and top condition record-company "acetate" demos of original Floyd releases—which might contain mix variations—are close to unattainable.

Bootlegs can sell for really high prices as well; a Japanese three-disc set went for more than $2,000 on eBay. But this list will focus on legitimate releases. Here are ten very valuable records that have garnered big sums in the collector's market, ranked by auction cost.

Meddle, Colombian Release, 1971

Record companies around the world come up with various schemes to draw attention to their product. Putting music on colored vinyl was an extremely popular trick in the 1970s and 1980s, especially in Europe, Asia, and, oddly enough, Colombia.

Some versions of Pink Floyd albums were issued in Colombia on translucent blue vinyl. A copy of *Dark Side of the Moon*, with only slight ring wear on the album cover, sold for $2,800 on eBay in 2007. A Colombian *Final Cut* garnered more than $1,900 at auction later that same year.

But the crowning Colombian colored vinyl sale came in early 2009, when a copy of *Meddle*—rare enough that it was not believed even to exist on blue vinyl—fetched a staggering $12,000 in an eBay auction.

"Apples and Oranges," U.K. Promotional Release, 1967

This 45, Floyd's first flop and its final single release with Syd Barrett, covers the trifecta of rarity: it didn't sell much when it was released, it's a promotional copy (not sold in stores, but only given to industry insiders) with a green label, and it even comes with a picture sleeve.

Only DJs, club owners, and publicists would have been able to snag copies of a promotional 45 from a top group back in the day. It's extremely difficult to find copies of records this old even in *good* condition, much less the nearly new version that was sold for £2,150 in 2004.

The Pink Floyd, Japanese Promotional Release, 1971

Odeon Records, an imprint label of EMI, distributed Pink Floyd records in various countries around the world. In 1971, Odeon's Japanese division produced fifty copies of a promotional sampler of PF music, one assumes for local promoters and DJs. The retrospective was packaged in an odd cover featuring a headshot of a giraffe.

The songs themselves, which cover the band's career ranging from "See Emily Play" to numbers from 1970's *Atom Heart Mother*, are not rare, but the record itself is nearly impossible to find. A near-mint copy of this *very* limited edition sold in 2005 on eBay for $4,000. Acquiring one would cost a lot more now.

The Piper at the Gates of Dawn, Acetate, 1967

Acetates are single copies of discs made for artists, producers, or record company executives to listen to, during breaks in the recording process, to judge how the new product is coming along.

These records are made in small quantities and intended to survive only a few plays. For any of them to have made it from the 1960s is a small miracle, and few of them ever get into private hands.

This 1975 Japanese 45, pairing "Have a Cigar" and "Welcome to the Machine," is not easy to find.

The versions on an acetate are almost never the final iterations of a song, so some of them have mixes that differ from the released tracks. Since they are made on lower-quality plastic, they can only be played a limited number of times before beginning to deteriorate; this makes acetates that much rarer.

This monaural acetate of the first Floyd album went for the princely sum of $3,605 in 2007. The seller noted that the tracks on the acetate were, oddly, *shorter* than the released versions.

The Piper at the Gates of Dawn, U.K. Release, 1967

Such a well-known album wouldn't seem to justify a high auction price. But this is an original 1967 "first press," meaning that the LP was among the originals copied off the album's master lacquer. This indicates that the fidelity is better than that found on later pressings. (The more albums are run from the master lacquer, the more the sound on future pressings will lose quality.)

In addition, U.K. pressings in the 1960s used a much higher-grade vinyl than they did in later years, and certainly better-quality vinyl than was used in America.

Finally, all elements of this stereo version of the original U.K. pressing—record, cover, and even EMI inner sleeve—are in mint condition. (The only real collector's value in popular old albums occurs when the vinyl is in tip-top shape.) This one went for £1,320 in 2007.

The Wall, Italian Promotional Release, 1979

Here is another special edition of a Floyd record, an Italian promotional double album issued on orange vinyl. The labels and cover of the album are the same as on the otherwise released version, but this is apparently the only pressing of *The Wall* in the world with both discs appearing on colored vinyl. A fan paid $2,550 in 2004 to own this.

Ummagumma, Japanese Promotional Release, 1969

Japanese vinyl records are among the best-sounding in the world. Few people ever played this particular one, though; it's a promotional disc of the 1969 *Ummagumma* release with the original cover, including the (later altered) photo of the *Gigi* soundtrack.

In addition to the record and cover being in top shape, the album still also has its original "obi" (a Japanese word meaning "robe"), i.e., a small paper banner wrapped around the cover containing information, in Japanese, about the record. A 2006 sale of this album netted $2,225.

The Piper at the Gates of Dawn, Japanese Release, 1967

This gorgeous red vinyl version of *Piper* sold for $2,125 in a 2005 auction. It's not clear how many copies of this album were pressed on colored vinyl, but it can't be many. And the number of them in near-mint shape, like this one, is smaller.

This record also came with a lyric sheet, even though the British and American issues of *Piper* did not (it was common for Japanese albums to have lyric sheets, perhaps to help non-English-speaking fans pick out particular words and phrases).

These lyrics were not "officially" translated but rather transcribed in English by Japanese listeners, and as a result, many are unintentionally hilarious.

Syd Barrett drew the illustration on the sleeve of the Pink Floyd's biggest hit of the 1960s. The 45's picture cover is extremely rare.

"See Emily Play," U.K. Promotional Release, 1967

Floyd's first Top 10 single (and their only one until 1979) was, like all other big-label 45s, released in a promotional version. This "Emily," with both green-label record and picture sleeve in mint condition, was preserved, apparently by a fastidious British disc jockey, from the day it was released. An Italian collector sold this pristine copy in 2005 for £1,022.

Dark Side of the Moon, Mobile Fidelity Sound Lab Release, 1970s

The high-quality vinyl industry was created for fans of albums like *Dark Side.* Well-recorded albums on better plastic sounded even more interesting than normal when played on high-end stereo systems.

Higher-quality vinyl and careful mastering made the Mobile Fidelity Sound Lab versions of 1970s and 1980s rock albums a great investment both for sound freaks and collectors.

MFSL discs, well cared for, are *far* more valuable now than they were back in the day. A pristine version of *Dark Side* went for $1,750 under the virtual gavel in 2007.

29

A Silver Spoon on a Chain

What Were the Floyd's Drugs of Choice?

T he rock world of the 1960s and 1970s offered illegal pleasures of all sorts. The Floyd had their turn taking advantage of nearly everything being offered, though their drug regimen was more conservative than that of many other musicians. Some of the drugs they used were simply social conventions, while others were used in an attempt to unlock greater mysteries.

Cigarettes

Everyone in Britain smoked during the late 1950s and early 1960s, and the members of the Pink Floyd, growing up upper-middle-class, and with the money to afford decent cigarettes rather than the cotton-wool cheapies others had to settle for, were no exception. Both Waters and Wright, according to Nick Mason, smoked on stage, and all the members of the band were avid devotees of the more than occasional fag.

Rock and roll, like other businesses, used to be carried on in smoke-filled rooms, as cigarette users generally weren't aware of the true dangers of the habit. Now, much of the world has "seen the light," and people simply don't smoke as much. Ciggies are now banned in many pubs, airplanes, restaurants, and concert halls. The world, and singers, are healthier for it.

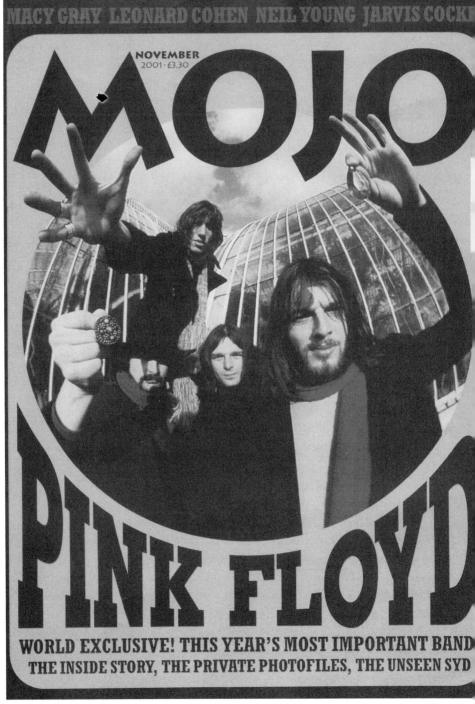

Pink Floyd's visual images, as shot by Storm Thorgerson, were often as hypnotic and psychedelic as their music.

Uppers

Speed, whether in inhalant or pill form, was the "do-it" drug for many musicians in the 1950s and 1960s. Playing long sets and traveling around the country in broken-down vans necessitated staying awake and alert for long periods of time.

It's not clear whether anyone in the Floyd took amphetamines; nobody's ever fessed up, although every big band of the time seems to have gulped pills just to keep rocking. Think of April 29, 1967, when the Floyd played at dawn at the Fourteen-Hour Technicolor Dream . . . after having pulled into the Alexandra Palace parking lot from another gig earlier that night . . . *in the Netherlands!*

And what drug is Pink given in "Comfortably Numb"? If it isn't speed, it's something close. The amphetamine rush gives instant energy but leads to jumpy nerves and violent thoughts and keeps people up for hours and hours. The 1960s mods took speed to dance all night; all sorts of entertainers, from Elvis Presley and the Beatles on down, have depended on speed to get them on the stage. Modern screwups take crystal meth, an even more powerful and destructive form of speed that leads to increasingly violent behavior.

Marijuana

Pot was a godsend to young beatniks in postwar Britain. Adding some sunshine to the gray 1950s and early 1960s, marijuana helped expand the horizons of creative types, and inevitably led to the exploration of art, music, and literature from different cultures (in particular, for British youth, of Marrakesh, India, and Ibiza).

Half the original Floyd were pot smokers. While Roger Waters demurred for years, and Nick Mason took nothing illegal until the late seventies, Syd Barrett and Rick Wright were enthusiastic late 1960s users, though Wright years later admitted to *Uncut* magazine that he'd "had some terrible times on pot," only enjoying it when he had literally *nothing* to do.

Dave Gilmour, too, was a fan of the demon weed, enjoying it as part of his regular routine, though being quite circumspect about it, as is the usual English way. "It's nice to listen to [*Dark Side*] that way. It's an accidental by-product, really," he told Carol Clerk of *Uncut.* Discussing the band's habits, he noted that "Roger and Nick were the drinkers, and Rick I would have a puff on a reefer."

Oddly enough, Gilmour and Barrett, from bucolic Cambridge north of London, were the swinging stoners, while the more urban, London-based architectural students, Mason and Waters, were the "squares." Waters eventually joined in, but gave up smoking dope, as he recalls, in the mid-1970s.

By the time of *Animals*, in fact, he was ripping his own audience—drinking, screaming, and stoned—as a bunch of sheep spending valuable time smoking grass while the wild dogs of corporations and religion took advantage of them.

Hashish

Hashish, as has often been written, was much easier to get in the U.K. in the late 1960s than was marijuana. When visitors to the old UFO and Roundhouse gigs of 1966–67 discuss the old times, they're usually not recalling the distinct whiff of pot smoke, but rather the heady mix of incense and hashish.

Syd Barrett certainly smoked plenty of hash as well as pot, writing the joyous "Let's Roll Another One" about his drug experiences.

The effects of hash are much stronger and more opiate-like than the effects of pot, and Waters years later claimed to have spent much of the early 1970s completely stoned on hashish joints in an attempt to wean himself from cigarettes—which he quit by 1975.

LSD

Barrett is said to have first taken liquid LSD, spread on a sugar cube, in summer 1965. The psychedelic experience touched a nerve in this uncannily creative young man, who in his reverie began to jump up and down in his friends' communal bathtub and scream, "No rules! No rules!"

Like John Lennon, Barrett was "thinking psychedelically" before drugs, if his own artwork and writing (as well as his study of literature, art, and music from different cultures) are any guide.

Unfortunately, once Barrett moved into the London underground scene, where the impetus was "go forward" no matter the cost, he began to overindulge in LSD. This may have helped him unlock some creative doors but was no help to his permanent mental makeup. Not only was Barrett taking a lot of the drug on his own—apparently going on a six-day bender at one point—but he also was supposedly being dosed by some of his roommates.

No wonder the poor boy was impossible to work with: he was completely fried. Psychedelics can force a person to notice his own world and experiences in such detail that they can affect the ability to consider others. Barrett appeared unaware of the effect of his destructive acts on his bandmates.

Gilmour claimed to have used acid fairly often in the 1960s, and never ran himself down for it publicly. Waters admits to having taken acid twice, claiming the first time was great and the second time was torture. He got the point, then, of the psychedelic experience: it's not candy and balloons.

Mushrooms

One of the more popular YouTube videos concerning Pink Floyd is a nine-minute feature, filmed in 1966 by Nigel Lesmoir-Gordon, entitled "Syd Barrett's First Trip."

While not an account of Barrett's *first* trip, it apparently shows his first experience ingesting psychedelic mushrooms. The border-dissolving power of the plant is evident in the film, which in its first half shows a short-haired Barrett looning in nature, running up and down hills (which could have been quite dangerous), examining plants closely, and appearing completely caned by the sight of his own hands, writhing in the curious and unexplainable mix of psychedelic agony and ecstasy.

Roger Waters and Rick Wright are shown along with Barrett in London during this film, but this "band" footage dates from a later time.

It is impossible to know, of course, how Syd's psychedelic experiences changed him. The idea of an "acid casualty" did not exist in 1967; no studies had been made of psychedelics to help anyone determine how much was too much. But Barrett clearly overindulged, and his prodigious intake could not have helped an already unsteady mental state.

Cocaine

The great rock-and-roll drug of the 1970s was cocaine. By decade's end it had infested boardrooms as well as bedrooms and assumed its position as legal tender in the music industry. Some people still feel that coke runs the business.

It can be argued, in fact, that the sixties really *ended* at the 1967 Monterey Pop festival, when Brian Jones introduced the American music underground to the "pleasures" of this addictive narcotic.

While Pink Floyd have always been circumspect about the use of hard drugs, both for legal reasons and because they didn't want to bring up the suffering Syd Barrett experienced in his worst periods, it's accepted that Rick Wright lost a lot of time and money in the 1970s and early 1980s to a destructive cocaine habit, and that he didn't really get himself together for several years. Waters likely based lyrics of *The Wall*'s "Nobody Home" on the errant keyboardist. Gilmour is said to have been a casualty of the cocaine wars as well.

It is inconceivable that coke, by the late 1970s already bound at the waist to rock and roll, *wouldn't* have been around during the *Animals/Wall/Final Cut* era—at least at meeting rooms, on the town, and backstage. Wright told Sylvie Simmons of *Mojo* in 1999 that "[cocaine] was taken without a doubt by [Waters], me, Dave, Nick, Bob Ezrin, but purely socially, it wasn't lying around at the studio."

Downers

It's not clear why Syd Barrett began taking the barbiturate Mandrax, but take it he did, and the depressive effects of these pills (which 10cc later discussed in their single "I'm Mandy Fly Me") added to the singer's instability during his dark night with the Floyd.

Perhaps Barrett turned to Mandrax to help him calm down and deal with the crazy pace of his life with the band; perhaps he just liked the physical effect of relaxation and occasional euphoria. Or maybe he was just incredibly confused. Certainly in 1969 and 1970, he took a lot of downers.

A legendary event in Pink Floyd lore has Barrett crushing several yellow Mandrax pills and rubbing them into his gel-filled hair just before taking the stage. The resulting spectacle had Barrett's permed coiffure dripping brightly-colored liquid, making his face appear to melt under the hot stage lights. Everywhere you look in Syd Barrett's life, you see a metaphor.

Alcohol

Nick Mason described his recreational drug intake around the time of *Dark Side* as "a bit of rum and blackcurrant." Floyd's drummer preferred the traditional English method of getting out of one's head: drinking oneself silly. But then, sitting around the pub was something everyone did when they came of age in England. Rick Wright even wrote "Paint Box" about it.

Much of the players' alcohol education came on their first trip to America, where, while doing several shows in San Francisco, they were, er,

Following the band's show in Hamburg, Germany on November 14, 1970, Rick Wright, David Gilmour, and Nick Mason took part in an interview. Wine was a common backstage presence. *Photo by K&K/Redferns*

fortunate enough to run into Janis Joplin. The talented, troubled American songstress, an unwilling participant in psychedelia, is said to have turned the Floyd's rhythm section on to the particular joys of Southern Comfort.

Mason and Waters, close friends for decades despite their more than occasional differences, are both lovers of fine bottled goods. One memorable episode during the 1969 *Zabriskie Point* soundtrack sessions saw the two musicians order an increasingly pricey series of wines to use up their per diems while temporarily employed by Michelangelo Antonioni.

In 1984, David Gilmour told journalist Parke Puterbaugh, "I didn't drink before I joined this band, but I soon saw the error of my ways." All members of the band came to enjoy a good tipple. While the band opened plenty of Dom Perignon bottles backstage in the early 1970s, the Floyd were never associated with the "drink until you puke" partying habits of many other rock stars of the day.

Heroin

Syd Barrett is said to have tried heroin, drug of choice for bummed-out musicians, before joining the Pink Floyd. His heroin habits, however, don't appear to have ever gotten out of control.

What is clear, though, is that his post-Floyd look, from 1968 through 1970 or so, was an early example of heroin chic. Barrett was sloppy and dirty, dressed in fine but wrinkled clothes, and sported wild hair that looked as though it hadn't been washed for days. That's the kind of "rock and roll" look that, these days, says *I am on very bad drugs.*

None of the other members of the Floyd are thought to have gotten *near* heroin; each one of these well-raised young men would have likely been horrified by the very notion. Perhaps that's why the music recorded for the soundtrack of *More*, a heroin film, sounds like acid music.

30

Pile On Many More Layers

Any Interesting Pink Floyd Sidelights to Share?

S ome of the most interesting things about Pink Floyd don't fit in a category or a chapter. Here are ten essays intended to rise above the level of trivia and actually get to a deeper understanding of the band's lives and career.

Stranded in the Tower

Tower Records, a subsidiary of Capitol Records and the Pink Floyd's first label in America (but no relation to the record store chain), was where the odd acts went. The Capitol empire had acquired some great but weird bands such as the Chocolate Watch Band, the Standells, Davie Allan & the Arrows, and Them. These groups, with aggro energy and/ or druggy ambience, all seemed to end up on Tower.

The label tried to use the "Beatle formula" for the Pink Floyd, adding the U.K. hit single "See Emily Play" to the original British version of *Piper* while deleting "Astronomy Domine," "Flaming," and "Bike" from the running order and rearranging the songs that remained. (Tower execs also misspelled "Pow R. Toc H." and "Take Up Thy Stethoscope and Walk.")

After the band's abortive fall 1967 American tour and the failure of the excellent-but-probably-too-progressive-for-America singles "Emily" and "Flaming," the Pink Floyd was stillborn in North America.

Therefore, the band's sophomore album, *A Saucerful of Secrets*, didn't receive an overabundance of attention from the label. Although this

Pink Floyd's first American record label, Tower, released many exotic offerings, such as "Kites," a trippy, Asian-inspired 1967 British hit single by Simon Dupree & the Big Sound, who usually played R&B.

time Tower didn't fool around with the songs or their running order, album details still fell by the wayside. Side two's title track was mislabeled "A Saucerful of Secrets Suite," and to make matters worse, the Floyd's new guitarist was referred to as "Dave Gilmore" on the sleeve and record label—though to be fair, this error was introduced by the band's U.K. label, EMI.

(This wasn't the last indignity Gilmour would suffer on a record sleeve. On the front cover of the 1974 European compilation *Masters of Rock*, which used a hand-colored, smaller-scale version of the image inside the *Meddle* album, Gilmour's head is cropped from the group shot and replaced with a shot of a mad, curly-haired Syd Barrett.)

Following the band's third album, the summer 1969 soundtrack from *More*, PF was removed from Tower and placed on the parent Capitol label. But the Floyd never forgot how they felt at the hands of their original U.S. label, departing for Columbia as soon as they got the chance (following the release of *Dark Side of the Moon*).

Must Youth Have Its Day?

Many issues drove wedges between the various members of Pink Floyd, primarily the competitive Roger Waters and guitarists Syd Barrett and David Gilmour. One reason for their fights could be the (relative) youth of the two six-string men.

Longtime friends Barrett and Gilmour had dissimilar personalities. Barrett, exuberant and impulsive, was a songwriter of amazing talent. Gilmour, less a songsmith than an arranger, guitarist, and producer, didn't provide the kind of ground-level direction that Barrett had, but was more ambitious and stable in his personal habits.

When Barrett emerged as a star in the young Pink Floyd, the other, older members of the band hitched their multicolored wagon to his talent. And when Barrett—still referred to decades later by the older Mason as "the psychedelic kid"—began to lose control, the anger and resentment among the remainder of the band was palpable, especially for Waters, who turned his frustration into extra effort to compose once the band was minus its only real songwriter.

Gilmour was asked to join Pink Floyd because the band—art students, not natural musicians, and having few friends in any music community— didn't know a lot of guitar players. Desperate and under the gun, the band had few options. More conventional in his tastes, and younger than the rest of his new colleagues, Gilmour did not share the experimental obsessions of the other members of the band, always pulling in a more commercial and sonically pleasant direction (to the ultimate disgust of Roger Waters).

It's not clear that the youth alone of both Barrett and Gilmour caused problems with the rest of the band, but in the late 1960s, the members of the Floyd were still very young men, and most twenty-one-year-olds view nineteen-year-olds with some condescension.

The Mono Mixes

Before the late 1960s, most listening to recorded music—pop, jazz, even classical—was done in monaural rather than stereo.

Yes, in those dark days, all sound was filtered through just one speaker. There were no wild sonic effects going from left ear to right ear, no separation of instruments by channel. While all of the Beatles' albums, for instance, were *recorded* in stereo, far more were sold in mono format than in stereo format because most home listeners had inexpensive stereo systems, often with just one speaker.

The notion of the "audiophile" barely existed, and was certainly not a factor in rock and roll, much of which was created to be listened to through cheap transistor radios. (Pink Floyd, of course, was among the bands that sought to make rock music a valid concert experience in the late 1960s and early 1970s.)

Rock albums were still released in both stereo and mono through 1968. This means that separate "mixes" were made for *Piper at the Gates of Dawn* and *A Saucerful of Secrets*. The original monaural versions of the first two Pink Floyd albums were quickly deleted by their American and U.K. labels, and as a result most of the group's 1970s-vintage fans heard only the stereo versions, which were used on *A Nice Pair*.

Unfortunately, since the discontinuance of mono, record companies have been inadvertently cheating fans of sixties-era rock. Prior to mid-1968, engineers and producers spent far *more* time making monaural mixes, since a greater number of people would hear them than would hear stereo recordings.

For instance, the mono versions of classic 1966–67 Beatles LPs *Revolver* and *Sgt. Pepper*, the Stones' *Aftermath* and *Between the Buttons*, or Love's *Da Capo* and *Forever Changes* are what the bands, and their technicians, intended to be heard by the majority of listeners.

Soon word got out among rock fans that the rare old mono mixes were definitely worth the trouble of finding on vinyl. Certainly this is true for *Piper*; it's literally a different record, with effects, instruments, and entire sections varying from the more well-known stereo mix. The same can be said for *Saucerful*.

After years of having to trawl secondhand stores or eBay to find originals, fans can now hear the original mono mixes on special-edition LPs or, in the case of *Piper*, on the fortieth-anniversary edition CD set.

If you enjoy these albums at all, listening to them in mono provides new joys; you will hear things you never heard before: different sound effects swirling through "Interstellar Overdrive" and "Flaming," different guitar and vocal parts on several songs, various drum fills, and the odd production trick.

The Floyd's early singles were released in mono; 45 rpm records were not, as a rule, issued in stereo until the late 1960s and early 1970s. (Even "Hey Jude" first came out in mono.) So what of "Arnold Layne," "Candy and a Currant Bun," "See Emily Play," "Paint Box," "Apples and Oranges," "It Would Be So Nice," "Julia Dream," "Point Me at the Sky," and "Careful with That Axe, Eugene"?

Several of those early tracks, initially available only on singles, were issued in stereo on 1970s compilation albums such as *Relics* and *Masters of Rock*. (In fact, only "Point Me at the Sky" has *never* been set free in stereo.) Finding the mono versions of those early singles isn't easy; the first five are on the Piper fortieth-anniversary three-CD box, and the others are not currently available.

The Cult of Barrett

Some Syd Barrett fans are as sick as the man himself was at his worst. Despite the voluminous evidence of his excessive drug use, physical assaults on girlfriends and business associates, disastrous attempts at recording and gigging, and largely incoherent interviews from his post-Floyd period in the late 1960s and early 1970s, there are those who wish to romanticize his illness as a willful subversion of pop stardom.

It was nothing of the kind, regardless of the words of such admirers as Jim Reid of the Jesus and Mary Chain, who told *Mojo* following Barrett's passing that "he got a bit frazzled by taking the wrong drugs in the sixties but came through them and just didn't want to be involved."

Such muddy thinking reflects a misplaced romanticism; Reid, and others who think identically, didn't have to live with Barrett like the other Floyds, or his managerial team, or even old friends such as Storm Thorgerson did. All the firsthand observers agree that Barrett was sick, not in control, and certainly not involved in some art project to screw up his career.

And then you have the likes of former Humble Pie drummer Jerry Shirley, who essentially accused the Floyd's former front man (in a TV

This Dutch compilation album from the early 1970s collected several early Floyd rarities, but featured a truly hideous cover in which the *Meddle* inner sleeve photo was altered and colored, with David Gilmour's head removed and replaced with Syd Barrett's.

special) of faking his mental illness. That simply shows a lack of understanding of schizophrenia, which can allow the sufferer to seem and feel quite close to "normal" at many times only to spin out of control without a warning.

Even in hindsight, that kind of misunderstanding of a very real human tragedy is dangerous, not only to Barrett's legacy but also to those who care about the human equation of rock and roll. What Syd Barrett went through—the cannon-fire of fame at an impressionable age, surrounded on one side by older, far straighter band members who couldn't communicate with him and on the other by hard-partying fellow-travelers—might have destroyed anyone, and an incipient schizophrenic taking a ridiculous diet of drugs was no match.

Devices

Any careful listener will eventually hear similar themes in Pink Floyd's lyrics and sounds. These oft-used lyrical and sonic devices are a form of shorthand for communicating the band's baseline thoughts.

Beginning with the sounds of geese used on *Piper*'s "Bike," Pink Floyd's incorporation of bird calls set them apart from other bands that only occasionally utilized found noises or sound effects. Seagulls on

"A Saucerful of Secrets" and country songbirds on "Cirrus Minor" and "Grantchester Meadows," for instance, take us through 1969. The following year, Waters' "Seashell and Stone" from *Music from the Body* contained the unmistakable call of gulls, as did 1970's beautiful "Embryo."

The following year's "Echoes" featured squalling seabirds, with the song more than any other Floyd number invoking the image of a deserted beach and the life above and below the water's surface. "Sheep" also ends with the peaceful sound of birds. Many years later, after abandoning the natural world for the inner reaches of the mind, the Waters-less Floyd again invoked their classic sound with birdsong on *The Division Bell*'s "Marooned" and "High Hopes."

While birdsong reminds us of the unspoiled, natural world, the use of children's voices evokes innocence. The Floyd used kids' cries and yells at various points on *The Wall*, during live performances of "Embryo," on "The Final Cut," and on *Division Bell*'s "Take It Back."

Another one of the group's devices is Roger Waters' use of the stone, in his lyrics, as a metaphor for the various weights and tribulations of life. He used this image several times, including in "Crying Song," "Dogs," "Hey You," and "Wot's . . . uh the Deal." On "Sea Shell and Stone," Waters also refers to a "lady of stone," although the protagonist in the song was surely not attempting to carry her.

Green Is the Colour

Several members of the Pink Floyd grew up in the British countryside. Roger Waters, Dave Gilmour, and Syd Barrett interpreted their sometimes idyllic pastoral upbringings in songs that didn't necessarily hew to folk-rock or country-rock conventions, but got rid of drums altogether if they weren't necessary.

Barrett's "The Scarecrow," lyrically inventive and evocative of green fields and harvest time, is a very *English* folk-rock tune, making room for an unusual meter (try to tap your feet) played on woodblocks, tinny organ, and bowed bass. During the fade, Barrett adds a rich swath of acoustic twelve-string guitar. Rural, old-fashioned English images also came into play in Barrett's "The Gnome" and some of his solo songs.

As a less-than-enthusiastic rock and roller, Rick Wright rarely composed specifically for electric guitar (the calculated "It Would Be So Nice" notwithstanding); as a classicist and jazzman, Wright wasn't inclined to write pieces for guitar in general, and being a city boy, he lacked a pastoral focus.

But Waters, originally a guitarist before Bob Klose and Syd Barrett teamed up on axes (thus moving Waters to bass), was an enthusiastic finger-picker, applying his skills on acoustic guitar to several excellent Floyd ballads. "Grantchester Meadows" (1969), arguably the only salvageable song on the *Ummagumma* studio album, describes the memory of an ideal day in the countryside.

Other Floyd songs such as "If," "Wish You Were Here," "Green Is the Colour," "Cymbaline," "Wot's . . . uh the Deal," and "A Pillow of Winds" continued the band's occasional and effective forays into folk-inspired acoustic balladry.

As Waters' introspection turned to bitterness and anger, the use of acoustic guitar and folky backings seemed to ebb from the Floyd's oeuvre, though one of his most beautiful melodies and lyrics, "Goodbye Blue Sky," turned up amid the ugliness and misery of *The Wall*.

The Division Bell's finale—the last recording Pink Floyd has produced—is "High Hopes," a rumination on Gilmour's (as well as Waters' and Barrett's) childhood in Cambridge. "The grass was greener, The light was brighter," Gilmour sings, thinking of a time before he and his old friends were "encumbered forever by desire and ambition." Church bells end the song, as they did back on Gilmour's 1970 *Atom Heart Mother* piece "Fat Old Sun."

Nightmares

Like other British psychedelic songwriters, Syd Barrett found joy in the unexpected, mysterious visions he garnered during trips to the lysergic state. "See Emily Play," "Flaming," and "Apples and Oranges" seem to have emerged from the world of dreams fully formed.

Roger Waters' dreams, on the other hand, generally were not candy-colored. In fact, from the evidence of some of his songs, just closing his eyes was an act of sheer bravery that could lead to misery and darkness.

"Set the Controls for the Heart of the Sun," with lyrics cribbed from Chinese poetry, described the dream state, with night turning into morning, leaves trembling, trees providing strength, and love—not often a subject in Waters' lyrics—serving as a critical part of evolution. For Waters, this kind of predawn reflection was relatively optimistic.

"Julia Dream" (1968), among the first Waters songs that Pink Floyd released, featured Mellotron, acoustic guitar, and a supple David Gilmour vocal, but the lyrics were anything but feathery. The song's abject terror is quite a striking contrast to Gilmour's delivery; the words describe being chased, wrapped in the arms of trees, trapped between knowing and not knowing, and beset by worries that one is dying.

The following year, on the soundtrack of *More*, Waters implores "Cymbaline" to wake him from his nightmares of walking a tightrope-thin path far above the earth, pecked at by ravens and surrounded by broken-winged butterflies. (It is difficult to tell who or what Cymbaline is; while an ancient Scottish king and a Shakespeare play share the name *Cymbeline*, the alternate spelling is a dry well.)

Meddle (1971) includes with "A Pillow of Winds," a gorgeous number that is foreboding despite Waters' lovely lyrics about lying down with

David Gilmour had been in Pink Floyd for just a month when the band traveled to Belgium in mid-February 1968 to shoot some promotional videos. These films showed PF as a four-piece, without Syd Barrett, but the troubled guitarist was still officially a member of the group until March 2.

one's love at the end of the day. As the music of this acoustic ballad darkens, Gilmour sings, "Behold a dream . . . the dream is gone." With his images of daybreak eclipsing the moon, and rain falling amid sun, Waters effectively balances night and day, joy and terror, and life and death.

(Later on the same album, in "St. Tropez," Waters, alone, dreams of his ladylove calling him home. In "Echoes," "a million bright ambassadors of morning" wake the singer from his sleep, inciting him to call across the sky to the albatross who has risen above the corporeal world.)

When it comes to terror, though, no Waters lyric can match "The Gunner's Dream" from *The Final Cut.* Every night, the song's central character has nightmares of those who died in World War II and returns to the frustrated dream of a peaceful world—the one that wars were supposed to bring about—that has not yet come true.

But is a nightmare better or worse than insomnia? The turgid "One Slip" from *Momentary Lapse of Reason* describes a man torn apart by his own passion (and possibly infidelity), unable even to relax into the temporary respite of sleep.

New Machines

Rich rock stars need new playthings and passions. All five members of the Floyd found various ways to indulge their interests and their need for creative outlets.

Following his increasingly disastrous attempts at pop stardom, Syd Barrett settled into some form of normalcy back in Cambridge. Interacting with few people and eschewing his time as a pop star, Barrett returned to painting, which many maintained was his first real love.

Although Barrett never made a name for himself as a painter, because he destroyed nearly everything he produced, he was apparently able to hold himself together enough to live a relatively peaceful, if austere, life, as long as nobody reminded him of his days in Pink Floyd. After his death in 2006, his sister Rosemary Breen told *Mojo*'s Danny Eccleston, "He was very mad."

Not so mad was Nick Mason, who developed a serious interest in road racing in the 1970s. In 1979, during sessions for *The Wall,* he went with Floyd manager Steve O'Rourke to drive at Le Mans, a French race that allows "amateur" drivers to compete with seasoned professionals. (Other celebs, including George Harrison and Paul Newman, became interested in motor sports around this time.)

The Floyd's drummer enjoyed the experience enough that he went in deep, buying expensive, high-performance cars and visiting whatever races he could. He returned to Le Mans in 1982 and drove at the 1984 World Endurance Championship Race in Canada, where he was filmed for the documentary *Life Could Be a Dream.*

Around this time, Mason and Rick Fenn (formerly of 10cc) recorded an album together entitled *Profiles* and set up a company to provide incidental music for movies and advertisers. The company brokered a deal by which Mason was able to drive in the 1984 Le Mans race.

One of Mason's great regrets, noted in his biography *Inside Out*, was a painful decision to sell his 1962 GTO Ferrari—for more than £600,000—in order to help finance the band's 1986 *Momentary Lapse of Reason* tour.

But don't cry; Mason has plenty of other vintage cars, and in fact wrote a book about them, 1998's *Into the Red*. He also founded a company, Ten Tenths, that rents vintage vehicles (cars, motorbikes, and planes) for film, television, music videos, and photo sessions.

In 1988, Mason and O'Rourke drove in the revived La Carrera Panamericana, a Mexican road race first held in the 1950s. Three years later, the two, joined by Gilmour, went to Mexico again, intending not only to ride in the race but also to make a film about it (which would also include a soundtrack).

The three Floyds and a friend drove two Jaguars, but tragedy nearly struck on the third day. Gilmour and O'Rourke's car went over a cliff, with the manager suffering the worst of it with a broken leg; the car was a loss. As a consequence, the film was less climactic than the band had hoped, but the three-man Floyd did record some music for it.

In an attempt to deal with the fear of flying all four members suffered from during the 1970s, Mason, Gilmour, and O'Rourke all chose to take piloting lessons. All three enjoyed the experience. In 1990, Gilmour founded Intrepid Aviation, a clearinghouse for rental planes, but eventually sold it, keeping just one old biplane to fly. Mason also remains a registered pilot, but his vehicle of choice is a helicopter.

The time the two Floyds spent in planes inspired much of the stage design for the *Momentary Lapse* tour, as well as the album's first single, "Learning to Fly."

Rick Wright went in a different direction: he took up yachting. Perhaps needing a break from the insanity of rock and roll, the keyboardist moved to Greece and went the slow route, engaging in solitary pursuits that took him far from his time with the world's biggest bands.

Meanwhile, Roger Waters, often in the gum-booted company of Steve Winwood and Eric Clapton, went in for fishing and fox-hunting. Waters, who has called himself a "hunter" rather than a gatherer, views fox-hunting as a classic British tradition. Even though he writes anti-violence lyrics and has an almost pacifist political stance, Waters has no problem with the shedding of blood for sport.

Many of Waters' post-Floyd accomplishments have fallen on relatively deaf ears, while his old group has, on its occasional sorties, done much better business. For such a competitive person as Waters, losing in the marketplace to his old band mates may have been a real crusher. But that alone doesn't explain his shift from a left-winger, who gave away much of his money to community causes, to a traditionalist/royalist who left England for America in 2005 simply because his homeland banned fox-hunting.

The Pink Pythons

Monty Python's Flying Circus, perhaps Britain's finest-ever comedy troupe, symbolized the 1970s phenomenon in which comedians became rock stars. The adoration afforded to the Pythons made it perfectly sensible for them to inhabit the same social circles as musicians such as Keith Moon, George Harrison, Led Zeppelin, and Pink Floyd.

By the early 1970s, rock and roll had become a large enough industry that artists had to find ways to invest money to avoid Britain's punitive tax rates. Film was a logical investment, and it took just a short step to involve rock stars in a Monty Python film, since musicians liked the show anyway. Like most smart young lefty Brits of the time, the Floyd were huge fans of Python's BBC-TV series, which aired from 1969 through 1973.

But how did the band become *officially* involved with Python? The foursome was asked to help produce the 1974 feature-length *Monty Python and the Holy Grail*. This, the first of three films of original Python material, cost around £230,000, and by this time, the reception of *Dark Side of the Moon* had given the Floyd the money to invest.

Scottish-born, Sorbonne-educated Michael White was the film's producer. *Holy Grail* was just the second film project for the thirty-eight-year-old, who'd cut his teeth in the movies with 1972's *Oh! Calcutta!* He had spent most of the 1960s as a theatrical producer in London and knew how to raise money.

He also had a yen for avant-garde and eccentric work, which led him into popular music. He produced Yoko Ono's 1966 London show *Music of the Mind*, worked on rock musicals *Joseph and the Amazing Technicolor Dreamcoat* and *The Rocky Horror Show*, and with former Brian Epstein associate Robert Stigwood, manager of the Bee Gees, on a pair of shows in 1970–71.

Kim "Howard" Johnson, Monty Python expert/chronicler/comrade/sometime extra, informed the author that according to both Eric Idle and *Holy Grail* coproducer John Goldstone, it was Tony Stratton-Smith, whose Charisma label released Monty Python's records (as well as those by Floyd contemporaries Genesis, the Nice, Atomic Rooster, and the Bonzo Dog Band) in the U.K., who reached out to the Floyd.

Both Stratton-Smith and White had met an increasing number of both rock-and-roll and movie industry people, and so Stratton-Smith worked aggressively with the management of PF, Led Zeppelin, and others to help meet the film's budget. A longtime London rock manager, football fan, and visionary, he also financed former Bonzo Dog band singer/trumpeter Vivian Stanshall's film *Sir Henry at Rawlinson End.*

Graham Chapman of Monty Python appeared at the 1975 Knebworth Festival on the same bill as Pink Floyd, doing skits and routines with a pickup group of comic actors.

The Dark Side of Oz and Echoes 2001

The rise of home video has created some strange bedfellows. While one can understand linking the music of Pink Floyd with the work of legendary director Stanley Kubrick, it's slightly more difficult to see what the band has to do with Ray Bolger and a band of Munchkins.

Apparently, no one knows who came up with the idea to synchronize *Dark Side of the Moon* to a video of *The Wizard of Oz*, but it's just the kind of thing that stoned (or even sober) obsessive fans of a band do when they've got little else going on. The members of the Floyd have responded dismissively to the notion that playing the album while watching the film leads to amazing synchrony. "That's fuckin' ridiculous," Waters said in a 2005 Belgian interview.

One would assume that *any* pairing of music and film can bring about "realizations" owing more to coincidence than anything else. Years after the "Dark Side of Oz" invention, rumors began to swirl that similar "revelations" came from pairing *Meddle*'s epic "Echoes" with a section of Kubrick's *2001*.

While the band has some connection to Kubrick's film—having turned down a request to provide music for it, leading to one of Waters' great regrets—the notion of synchronicity is just as insane as that linking Judy Garland's fantasy epic to Pink Floyd's 1973 blockbuster. But that won't stop such rumors from spreading, and doesn't hurt the video rental industry!

Ten Great Officially Unreleased Pink Floyd Recordings

- "Lucy Leave," demo, 1965
- "Scream Thy Last Scream," studio recording, 1967
- "Vegetable Man," studio recording, 1967
- "Flaming," BBC "Top Gear" recording, September 30, 1967
- "Pow R. Toc H.," BBC "Top Gear" recording, December 19, 1967
- "Let There Be More Light," BBC "Top Gear" recording, June 25, 1968
- "Julia Dream," BBC "Top Gear" recording, June 25, 1968
- "A Saucerful of Secrets," 1972 (live at Pompeii)
- "Raving and Drooling," live recording, 1974
- "You Gotta Be Crazy," live recording, 1974

Afterword by Ginger Gilmour

I met David Gilmour in Ann Arbor, Michigan in October 1971.

Every year the University of Michigan held a four-day rock and roll festival, and Pink Floyd was one of the headline acts. My partner Roger Pothus and I had three boutiques in Ann Arbor and were regularly given backstage passes. It happened that one of my closest friends, Morpheus, had just returned from England during which time he had befriended Chris Adamson, one of the Floyd's roadies. He had tickets and encouraged us to come with him to experience their music. It turned out that evening was to open the doorway to some of my dreams.

As I stood speaking to one of my customers backstage, David approached and said, "Hi. I am David." I looked at him but before I could respond both my boyfriend and Morpheus joined us. Being a shy person in these circumstances at the time, I introduced myself and everyone else and then left them chatting. The next three days were spent taking the band and roadies to various events until they had to leave Ann Arbor to continue their American tour. Our time together—that is, David's and mine—has become a mythological story of romance . . . a story that may, one day, be told.

Our last moments were spent having lunch in my favourite Chinese restaurant before he was to leave. David's departing words were that if I ever chose to leave my relationship, then to please call him.

Over the previous years I had wanted to leave my relationship and move to New York, but hadn't. This experience put me into a deep review. Two days later, I decided to go into my future, to follow my dream, whether it was to be with David or not. I called him; we met at the airport and from thenceforth we didn't leave each other's side, except when he was on stage.

At the time I had no idea of what led me from one moment to the next except to trust a feeling deep within. Now at sixty years of age, on reflection of my life, it seems that a guiding force has always placed me within environments and experiences of beauty and creativity.

It was so when I met David and continues to be so now. At that time, not only was I involved with fashion and modeling but I was also about to embark on a career as an actress in an *Easy Rider*–style movie as the lead female.

In my decision to go to New York, I left that all behind me as I stepped onto the plane and entered the world of Pink Floyd. For me, the beauty they created became my safety net within the storm as well as an inspiration. In addition, the love that David and I shared was a dream come true, the depth of which is something we all, as human beings, have in common, once our power to dream is activated.

During the course of the band's last few weeks in America, David asked if I would like to come to England. As a teenager cruising on the weekends at Arby's, I used to put on what I thought was an English accent. I dreamed of Merseyside and the Beatles. I have often wondered if this was a premonition . . . or did I manifest David into my life with the wish?

I cannot say, but this was a very special moment of change—to live in England and be with my Prince Charming—though a rock-and-roll life was not what I had expected. Fortunately, the Floyd had a philosophy that valued what was private, special, and human.

Our life at home was normal, i.e., caring for each other, our friends, and our family, as well as being creative. David's family became *my* family away from home, and over time I grew very close with the other wives, especially Juliette Wright. Everything was a big learning curve; this was my first time in a different culture, different bacteria, a different sense of humour—really a different language—but what an exciting adventure! My only real hardship, as I can recall, was the size of the fridges; they were the size of an American dishwasher. There never seemed to be enough room for all the groceries.

Four years passed. Then, on July 7, 1975, we married. It was a rather spontaneous affair with a few friends as witnesses in the Epping registry office. Equally, our reception was short and sweet at our local pub, for David had to be at Abbey Road Studios; the Floyd were working on *Wish You Were Here.*

The whole day was magical. We had each other and our marriage was a symbolic gesture of our commitment and celebration of heart. This quality between two individuals is what continues to matter to me more than what any of us might have or might "do."

Upon entering the studio, Roger approached David silently and asked him to look at the person sitting on the couch in front of the mixing desk. It was Syd, pear-shaped and hairless. Apparently, the drugs he was on within the clinic induce this type of behaviour, that is, to shave all facial and body hair, including the eyebrows, head, arms, etc. It was this that inspired some of the imagery for the *The Wall.*

As I look back upon this phase of my life I most remember magical concerts, and moments of the sound of David's guitar drifting through the air, rather than their albums. Having said that, I most often still listen to *Meddle* (especially "Echoes"), *Wish You Were Here*, and "Comfortably Numb."

One of the group's most memorable concerts was in Cincinnati. As the sun set into a swirl of pink, lavender, and deep blue, from far behind the stage and above the large Marlboro and Winston billboards, our tour airplane, with lights flashing, came toward us!

The sound of the low-flying plane over an unsuspecting audience created such a burst of emotion of release that we were all taken within a bubble of great stillness and calm. As the soft notes of "Sheep" began, individual puffs of smoke filled the air, deepening the colours of the approaching night. As the mist drifted across the air, large parachute shapes of sheep descended, floating into the audience.

For me, this is just one moment of many which the Floyd created for us all to share. It is said that when beauty marries with stillness and all become one, in our unique difference true magic appears. In this instance, it appeared through the art of creativity within those concerts and our lives. I feel honoured to have been a participant in the magic of Pink Floyd. Needless to say, we did have many challenges within the rock-and-roll life, but the beauty always won.

I feel this is very important to emphasize when telling the band's story, for it is a microcosmic part of the bigger story of us all. Dr. Werner Engel, president of the Jungian Society in New York, came to one of the concerts. His comment to me was, "Ginger, I do not know whether you would agree with me, but what we seek through meditation, your husband's music achieves through transforming chaos into harmony though beauty."

This I now understand as the basic key to harmony in a world of chaos. I do not know whether the Floyd would agree, but I do know that it happened that way for many of us. This is what their music offers, in my opinion, and is why it speaks to so many over so many years. Their music carries an archetypal message of transcendence.

Through the last forty years I have been graced to meet many great philosophers and teachers who have opened the doorways to my own conscious creativity. My time within the Pink Floyd afforded me many examples of creativity inducing an experience of unity and beauty among many. It touched the very nature of my soul, which probably allowed me to survive in what sometimes were very harsh conditions.

Now through my teachers I have been inspired to become and create beauty through my own innate talent as an artist. I was never without a creative energy—it was often expressed through the care of my children and home—but it was my destiny to awakened, to be more than I WAS. Thus I have come to realize that we are all creators of our stories . . . and another chapter is just beginning for me through the art of creating beauty.

I ask,
WE ALL KNOW THE IMPORTANCE OF FOOD AND WATER TO SUSTAINING LIFE, BUT DO WE KNOW THE IMPORTANCE OF BEAUTY?

Ginger Gilmour was born with the "soul of an artist."
For the first half of her life she expressed her nature
Through her family, marriage, and the caring of her children,
While quietly, silently, the "soul of the artist"
Took in colour, shapes, movement, music, and the beauty of Life.
Now within her newly created Artistic Center in England
She gives herself the freedom to be . . .
"The soul of the artist."
www.gingerart.net

Selected Bibliography

Pink Floyd has inspired many books, some glossy and jammed with photos, others crammed with gig information or intense philosophical and/or psychological analysis of the band.

Here are a few books on the Floyd that the author recommends. (All publishers are of U.S. editions unless otherwise noted, and the editions are the latest for which we have record.)

Boyd, Joe. *White Bicycles: Making Music in the 1960s.* London: Serpent's Tail, 2006.

Boyd, the Floyd's first producer, talks not only about Syd and the band but also about his experiences in London's psychedelic underground. His experiences with the Floyd do not constitute the entire book, but the overall story is fascinating.

Cavanagh, John. *The Piper at the Gates of Dawn.* New York: Continuum Publishing Group, 2007.

From the popular 33 1/3 series, which examines great albums in depth, comes this fine, compact exploration of Pink Floyd's first.

Fitch, Vernon. *The Pink Floyd Encyclopedia.* Burlington, ON: Collector's Guide Publishing, 2005.

This publisher, which puts out books on music, collecting, and space travel, found a band that can fit the trifecta.

Manning, Toby. *Pink Floyd: The Rough Guide.* London: Rough Guides, 2006.

The Pink Floyd book to have if you're choosing just one . . . besides this one, of course.

Mason, Nick. *Inside Out: A Personal History of Pink Floyd.* San Francisco: Chronicle Books, 2005.

In this, the closest thing to a full inside story, Mason—as usual—sits on the fence about his bandmates, but does so in a charming and entertaining way. Great photos.

Miles, Barry, and Andy Mabbett, *Pink Floyd: The Visual Documentary.* London: Omnibus Press, 1994.

This volume, initially published in the early 1980s, is the first book that most Pink Floyd fans saw about the band. Necessary for its firsthand stories of the early days, it's been through several reprints.

Nicholas Schaffner's *Saucerful of Secrets*, a delightful narrative history of the Pink Floyd's first twenty years.

Palacios, Julian. *Lost in the Woods: Syd Barrett and the Pink Floyd*. London: Boxtree Publishing, 2001.

Controversial for its intimations of Barrett's thoughts, this is a thoughtful examination of the causes of his breakdown.

Povey, Glenn, and Ian Russell, *Pink Floyd in the Flesh: The Complete Performance History*. New York: St. Martin's Griffin, 1998.

If you care at all about the band's live history, this is the next book you should find.

Reisch, George. *Careful with That Axiom, Eugene! Pink Floyd and Philosophy*. Chicago: Open Court Publishing, 2008.

This philosophy publisher has collected works from sixteen writers on the subtext and deeper meanings of Floyd songs.

Schaffner, Nicholas. *Saucerful of Secrets: The Pink Floyd Odyssey*. New York: Dell Publishing, 1991.

An excellent telling of the band's story by a musician and writer who had the pleasure of following the Floyd from the late 1960s until his premature death shortly after this book was published.

Taylor, Phil. *The Black Strat: A History of David Gilmour's Black Fender Stratocaster*. New York: Hal Leonard Corporation, 2008.

Gilmour's guitar tech tells all. Rich in photos and guitar-geek details.

Thorgerson, Storm. *Walk Away René: The Work of Hipgnosis*. New York: A&W Visual Library, 1978.

Thorgerson and Po Powell's Hipgnosis design studio grew up with Pink Floyd, and several stories about the band are included in this very hard-to-find trade paperback.

———, and Peter Curzon. *Mind over Matter: The Images of Pink Floyd*. London: Sanctuary Publishing, 2003.

Stories of Thorgerson's work on most of the Floyd's albums. As you would guess, it's fascinating to look at, too.

Watkinson, Mike, and Pete Anderson, *Syd Barrett, Crazy Diamond: The Dawn of Pink Floyd*. London: Omnibus Press, 2007.

This is generally viewed as the best bio of Barrett.